THE TRINITY IN CONTEMPORARY THEOLOGY

CLAUDE WELCH

SCM PRESS LTD
56 BLOOMSBURY STREET
LONDON

First British Edition 1953

Printed in Great Britain by
Fletcher & Son Ltd Norwich

To my Father

VIRGIL CLEON WELCH

Preface

The doctrine of the Trinity has long occupied a critical place in the history of Christian thought. At least until modern times, so far as the main stream of Christian theology was concerned, the central Christian doctrine of God was affirmed to be the doctrine of the Trinity. By the time of Tertullian, in the third century, this conception was specifically denoted the prime distinction between Christianity and Judaism (and by implication all other monotheistic religions). And in the writings of Athanasius and Augustine the Trinity became truly a Christian *arché*, a fundamental point of conflict with classical culture. Once the doctrine was firmly established in the fourth century, it was the subject of continuous and vigorous discussion in Scholasticism, in the Reformation period, and in the controversies of the sixteenth, seventeenth and eighteenth centuries.

But after about the first quarter of the nineteenth century, or roughly since the second edition of Friedrich Schleiermacher's *The Christian Faith* (1831) and the comprehensive historical study by F. C. Baur, *Ueber die Christliche Lehre von der Dreieinigkeit und der Menschwerdung* (1841 ff.), the doctrine of the Trinity abruptly disappeared from the forefront of Protestant theological discussion. In the dominant systems of theology in the nineteenth and early twentieth centuries, the trinitarian conception was either ignored or relegated to a relatively unimportant place in the theological structure. There were exceptions to this trend, particularly in the continuing lines of conservative thought and in the temporary alliance of theology with Hegelian philosophy, but these were subordinate to the prevailing directions of thought.

The general attitude of distrust and indifference which developed had, of course, roots which reach deep into Christian history. From the first there were charges that the trinitarian notion was unscriptural and irrational. The Reformation saw not only a new outbreak of conscious anti-trinitarianism, but also a failure of the Reformers to relate the doctrine effectively to the fundamental principles of the Reformation. And in the eighteenth century the tendency of rationalism to reduce the gospel portrait of Jesus to that of a teacher of moral excellence and to purge Christianity of all distinctive characteristics left little room for a unique doctrine of God which claimed to rest upon a particular historical revelation. Moreover, the predominant concern with natural religion, the empirical attitude stemming from Locke, the scientific disclosure of unity in the material world and the philosophical emphasis on "clear and distinct ideas," all tended to focus interest on the unity of God rather than on any notions of inner distinctions.

Yet there was a notable change in the nature of thought about the doctrine of the Trinity after the close of the eighteenth century. With the rise of biblical criticism and the revolution of theological method inaugurated by Schleiermacher, the bases of theological construction were radically altered and theology entered on a new phase, the implications of which have by no means yet been fully worked out. These factors, much more than such developments as the impact of natural science on theology and the preoccupation with "philosophy of religion," lay behind the signal shifts in thought about the Trinity—though such other influences were important in determining the directions of theological endeavor.

Contemporary theological developments, however, point to a reversal of the nineteenth-century trend and to a renewed and growing interest in the trinitarian conception. This is to be seen not only in the appearance of major constructive works on the doctrine and of numerous less extensive but important statements, but also as a corollary of recent concern with the problems of revelation and of Christology. Both the basis of the trinitarian affirmation and the content of the doctrine have been re-examined.

This book has grown out of the belief that what now most needs to be done is to bring together in a single focus the widely divergent lines of thought represented in the contemporary theological scene, ranging from complete indifference or outright opposition to the notion of the Trinity, to explicit efforts to restore this doctrine to the central place in the theological scheme. I am convinced that this is indispensable for a clear understanding of the possibilities and problems of the further development of Christian trinitarianism.

The period with which I am primarily concerned may be said to begin, roughly, with the close of the first World War and the publication of Karl Barth's *Römerbrief*. However, because of the persistence of nineteenth-century modes of thought in the present scene, and because our own concern with the doctrine of the Trinity must start in part with presuppositions given us by the last century, I have begun with a sketch of nineteenth-century theology as it bears on the Trinity and as it provides a key to the understanding of the role of the doctrine in contemporary theology.

In the analysis of contemporary patterns of thought, which comprises Parts II and III of this book, I have had always in mind four main problems. First, the distinguishing of the principal types of attitudes toward the doctrine of the Trinity. Second, the theological "interest" or "motivation" of these attitudes. This brings into sharp focus the crucial question of the *basis* of the trinitarian affirmation, and also provides what is to my mind the most useful and illuminating method for understanding the range and variety of recent thought about the Trinity. Third, the relation of the various restatements to "classical" Christian views. For obvious reasons, I have nowhere set forth a systematic statement of traditional interpretations of the doctrine, but enough is said in the course of the argument to give even the reader who is unfamiliar with the history of Christian theology a reasonably full picture of the central elements in the classical formulations and of the historical development of the doctrine. Fourth, the value and viability of the recent interpretations in terms of their relevance and meaning for contemporary religious problems and thought.

My own constructive suggestions regarding the basis and significance of the trinitarian conception, and the systematic reform-

ulation of the doctrine, are drawn together in Part IV. I should
like to say, however, that these final chapters should be read in
the light of all the previous discussion. The work is conceived
as a whole, and the full meaning of the positive construction will
be seen only in the perspective of the development of the entire
work.

I am deeply grateful to the many friends, colleagues and
teachers who have given me counsel and criticism during the
various stages of the writing of this book. The work was begun as
a dissertation presented for the degree of Doctor of Philosophy in
Yale University, 1950; it has since been thoroughly rewritten and
recast. Special thanks are due to Professors Paul Ramsey and
George F. Thomas, with whom I served in the Department of
Religion at Princeton University during the period when most of
the writing was done and who were unfailingly encouraging and
helpful in their criticism; to Professor Paul L. Lehmann of Princeton Theological Seminary, who read the entire manuscript and
made many valuable suggestions for the final revision; to Professors Julian N. Hartt and H. Richard Niebuhr of Yale and
Professor Albert C. Outler of Perkins School of Theology, who
have helped in every way through all the course of the writing;
and to Mr. Gordon Kaufman of Yale, who has given most com-
petent assistance in correcting the proofs.

CLAUDE WELCH

Sterling Divinity Quadrangle
September, 1952

Table of Contents

PART I

BACKGROUND

CHAPTER I

The Doctrine of the Trinity
in the Nineteenth Century

1. *The Reduction of the Trinity to a Doctrine of the Second Rank*

The two factors which in early nineteenth-century theology were most directly responsible for subsequent questioning of the importance and validity of the doctrine of the Trinity were the development and growing acceptance of the methods of biblical criticism and the writings of Friedrich Schleiermacher. 1) Historical analysis of the Bible did not originate in the nineteenth century, but the period with which we are concerned marked the transfer of theological leadership to the German universities, and in this freer atmosphere the method of "objective" historical research was widely accepted for the first time. This fact is of vital importance for nineteenth-century theology. It was the successful application of literary criticism to the gospel texts, more than the attacks of the rationalists or even the work of Schleiermacher, which breached the walls of the traditional concepts of revelation. It was the abandonment of the literal and final authority of the scriptures which made plausible the effort of the Hegelian theologians to establish doctrine on another basis, which opened the door to the liberal picture of Jesus of the Ritschlians and the *religiongeschichtliche Schule*, and which is at the root of contemporary concern with the nature of revelation. Conversely, the popularity of the new methods of Schleiermacher and the Hegelians made the "higher criticism" appear less offensive by minimizing its effect on the essentials of faith.

The first major blow to the doctrine of the Trinity was the elimination of the Fourth Gospel as a primitive historical source. Johann G. Herder had seen as early as 1796 that the gospel of John cannot be reconciled as an historical source with the synoptics, and that it was, at least partly, a theological work. But not until Strauss was the question decided and the true character of the gospel widely recognized.[1] In every case of comparison of the synoptics with John, Strauss's decisions were unfavorable to the latter, and through F. C. Baur's work, the general position of the historical superiority of the synoptics was firmly established. The inevitable effect of this upon the doctrine of the Trinity is readily apparent, for John's gospel had been from the beginning the happy-hunting ground for those who sought trinitarian proof-texts. When doubt was cast upon the authenticity of Jesus' utterances concerning himself in the Fourth Gospel, serious question was raised about a fundamental root of the doctrine of the Trinity.

The effect of biblical criticism with respect to the Johannine roots of trinitarian theology was, of course, only a particularly striking example of its consequence for the authority of the New Testament generally. Not only was there uncertainty regarding Jesus' claims for himself, but the deepening understanding of the process of development of the New Testament dealt a fatal blow to the notion of the literal revelation of the scriptures. The whole New Testament witness to Christ and the revelation of God in him was brought within the framework of human history, therefore within the limits of fallibility, and upon that witness rested the doctrine of the Trinity.

2) Friedrich Schleiermacher's attitude toward the doctrine of the Trinity is suggested by his relegation of the dogma to an appendix at the conclusion of *The Christian Faith*. There are at least two considerations involved in this classification. The traditional scheme of dogmatics (e.g. Calvin, Thomas Aquinas) treated of the Trinity in conjunction with the general discussion of the being and attributes of God. This is quite improper, thinks

---

[1] D. F. Strauss, *Leben Jesu* (1835).

Schleiermacher, for the doctrine cannot be intelligibly viewed until after account has been taken of Jesus Christ and the Holy Spirit. But this fact alone would not justify reducing the dogma to an appendix. The controlling motive in Schleiermacher's judgment of the Trinity is his conviction that the doctrine in itself is an unnecessary and unwarranted addition to the faith. It means well, one might say, but is misleading and over-reaches the mark.

There is a genuinely essential element expressed in the dogma, viz., "The doctrine of the union of the Divine essence with human nature, both in the personality of Christ and in the common Spirit of the Church," [2] for the idea of redemption in Christ and of the Church as the bearer of redemption requires such a union. That it was truly the divine essence which was so united is the element that the doctrine was established to defend.

But the ecclesiastial dogma, which alone justifies the use of the term Trinity, goes far beyond this, tracing the union with Christ and the union with the Church back to eternal distinctions in God, posited independently of such unions. It is not, therefore, "*an immediate utterance concerning the Christian self-consciousness but only a combination of several such utterances.*" [3] Since Christian theology consists in the explication of the contents of the Christian self-consciousness, the doctrine of the Trinity can be assigned no important place. Schleiermacher is willing to go all the way here, asserting that even if the fully developed doctrine arose definitely out of the teachings of Jesus and the apostles, it would still not properly be a doctrine of faith. We should have to accept it on the basis of the testimonies about "supersensible fact," but our fellowship with God would be *no different* from what it would be without such knowledge. The essentials of the Christian faith are thus altogether independent of this doctrine.

We may identify several facets of Schleiermacher's thought which lie behind his insistence that the doctrine of eternal distinctions in the divine nature can neither be read off directly from the contents of Christian self-consciousness nor be shown to be in essential relation thereto. One is the pervasive subjectivism which

[2] *The Christian Faith*, § 170, 1.   [3] Ibid.

haunts his theological method. Schleiermacher may indeed have meant to include apprehension as an important component of the feeling of absolute dependence, so that the feeling involves a direct grasp of God as its Cause, a genuine laying hold of the Objective Reality on which we are dependent. Yet Schleiermacher is forever compromising this, in his view of doctrines generally as statements simply about religious affections,[4] and particularly in his view of the doctrine of God. In speaking of the divine attributes, he insists that

all attributes which we ascribe to God are to be taken as denoting not something special in God, but only something special in the manner in which the feeling of absolute dependence is to be related to Him.[5]

Referring to the doctrine of the Trinity, he writes in similar vein:

We have only to do with the God-consciousness given in our self-consciousness along with our consciousness of the world; hence we have no formula for the being of God in Himself as distinct from the being of God in the world, and should have to borrow such a formula from speculation, and so prove ourselves disloyal to the character of the discipline with which we are working.[6]

But there is nothing in Schleiermacher's account of "the origin of dogmatic propositions, as having arisen solely out of logically ordered reflection upon the immediate utterances of the religious self-consciousness," [7] which gives us a principle for deciding what *are immediate utterances*. Schleiermacher clearly approaches the doctrine of God with an *a priori* limitation of the knowledge which man may have of God in himself—a limitation derived in part from Kant and in part from a pietistic conception of theological method.

Closely related to this is another reason for Schleiermacher's refusal to admit that the phenomena of Christian experience imply significant distinctions in God: he does not see any real distinc-

---

[4] See *The Christian Faith*, § 15.   [6] Ibid., § 172, 1.
[5] Ibid., § 50.   [7] Ibid., § 16.

tion between the presence of God in Christ and God in the Church. For him, there is no difference which is significant for the nature of God, between the *forms* of union. The presence of God in Christ, i.e. his God-consciousness, is not essentially different from the presence of God in the Christian. For Schleiermacher, both the being of God in Christ as an individual and in the Church as a whole are only parts of "the omnipotent presence of God in the world in general," and any attempt to draw distinctions would inevitably lead to anthropomorphism.[8]

This suggests the hidden domination of Schleiermacher's thought by rationalist principles. He eschews speculation, but God is always for him the absolute unity. "God is the unconditioned and the absolutely simple." [9] In him there can be no distinctions or difference. Thus Schleiermacher contends that the divine attributes refer only to states of consciousness:

if as such they [the attributes] present a knowledge of the divine being, each one of them must express something in God not expressed by the others; and if the knowledge is appropriate to the object, then, as the knowledge is composite, the object too must be composite. Indeed, even if these attributes only asserted relations of the Divine to the world, God Himself, like the finite life, could only be understood in a multiplicity of functions; and as these are distinct one from another, and relatively opposed one to another, God likewise would be placed in the sphere of contradiction. *This does not fulfill the requirements of the speculative reason* . . .[10]

The view of the Trinity follows accordingly. If from the standpoint of the feeling of dependence all ideas of divine attributes represent nothing objective in the self-identical Original Being, and, on the other side, God as the causal nexus of nature is absolutely simple being, what place can there be for the doctrine of the Trinity?

In *The Christian Faith* Schleiermacher says little about the *content* of trinitarian doctrine. Commenting briefly on some of

[8] Ibid., § 172, 1. [10] Ibid., § 50. (Italics mine.)
[9] Ibid., § 96. See also §§ 56; 167.

the difficulties in the traditional view, he concludes that it is untenable but declares himself favorably disposed toward the "Sabellian" interpretation of the doctrine. According to Sabellius, as Schleiermacher interprets him in a lengthy essay,[11] the three "persons" develop successively in the relation of the Divine Unity to the world: the Son is the development in redemption; the Spirit is the union of God with the Church. There is then a real and continuing distinction between Father, Son and Spirit, but only in terms of God's relations to the world. The Trinity can be consistently held to exist only in respect of the various methods and spheres of divine operation. This interpretation of the doctrine was very influential in nineteenth-century America in the thought of Moses Stuart and Horace Bushnell, and it appears again in the contemporary period.

But Schleiermacher's most important influence came from his estimate of the role and importance of the doctrine of the Trinity. This was the more true because of his revision of theological method. In response to the attacks of rationalism upon Christianity, Schleiermacher forced consideration as to whether religion was not *sui generis*. He insisted on the distinctive nature of Christianity as an historical positive religion, hence free from subjection to philosophy and speculative reason. He abandoned the method of deducing doctrine from propositions of scripture or reason and sought to establish theology as a strictly empirical discipline.

Thus Schleiermacher opened a method of approach to Christianity which did not presuppose the concept of an infallible revelation in scripture. And in so doing, he did not see how the new method left any place for the doctrine of the Trinity. Succeeding theologians, who accepted in principle the abandonment of the old concept of revelation and the revision of methodology,

---

[11] "Ueber den Gegensatz zwischen der Sabellianischen und der Athanasianischen Vorstellung von der Trinität," *Sämmtliche Werke*, 1:2, 485–574. This essay was translated, with extensive notes, by Moses Stuart, under the title "On the Discrepancy between the Sabellian and Athanasian Method of Representing the Doctrine of the Trinity," *The Biblical Repository and Quarterly Observer*, VI, 19 (July, 1835), Andover, 1–116.

tended also to accept Schleiermacher's judgment that upon such a basis it was impossible to defend the notion of Trinity in any sense which justified the use of the term.

Added force was given to Schleiermacher's dictum by his insistence on the organic character of the theological enterprise. Prior to Schleiermacher the custom was to justify each doctrine on largely independent grounds. Because of the atomistic use of scripture fostered by the theory of verbal inspiration, any dogma could be attacked or defended pretty much in isolation. But *The Christian Faith* is all of one piece, an organic whole, centering in a specific organizing principle. After Schleiermacher and the changes in the concept of revelation required by biblical criticism, the method of Peter Lombard's *Sentences* or the *Loci* was no longer possible. Every doctrine had to be justified in relation to every other and to the central principle of the system. The argument was the more damning because the central principle of Christianity, according to Schleiermacher, was the redemption accomplished by Jesus of Nazareth. From the consciousness of redemption, affirmations might properly be made about the person of Christ and a doctrine of Incarnation formulated, but nothing was to be asserted about the being of God. Once again, the argument made it appear that the doctrine of the Trinity could not be defended in connection with the fundamental basis of Christian doctrine.

In sum, then, Schleiermacher's reduction of the Trinity to a doctrine of the second rank was especially important because it was so closely associated with certain far-reaching (and fundamentally valid) *formal* revisions of theological method: the abandonment of piecemeal deduction from verbally inspired scripture, and the organization of doctrine about a single principle— Jesus Christ. His attitude toward the Trinity was not, as we have seen, determined by these principles, but by other and extraneous considerations. Yet for a long time, those who accepted the principle of his methodological approach (especially Ritschl and Liberalism generally) accepted also Schleiermacher's dicta about the Trinity.

2. *Trinitarianism Transplanted to Hegelian Soil*

The philosophy of religion of Georg Wilhelm Friedrich Hegel offered an attractive possibility for surmounting some of the problems raised by the older rationalists, by Schleiermacher and by the biblical critics. Their combined result with respect to the doctrine of the Trinity had been to deprive that doctrine of its traditional historical basis. Hegel's program seemed to provide a means for preserving many of the basic concepts of the Trinity and of the Incarnation. If the metaphysical aspects of theology could not be supported according to the principles of Schleiermacher, they became central in Hegel's interpretation of religion.

1) The doctrinal formulations of theology are, for Hegel, symbolic and pictorial representations of the highest truths. Philosophy enables faith to understand itself for the first time. This does not mean that the religious symbols are untrue; on the contrary, Hegel asserts, "In faith, the true content is certainly already found . . ." [1] Piety of the naïve kind needs no other justification: it receives the truth as authority and experiences satisfaction and reconciliation by means of this truth. Philosophy, therefore, does not actually set itself above the truth of religion; philosophy may even serve to restore importance to dogmas toward which the contemporary religious world is quite indifferent. The trinitarian symbols of religion are far more truthful than the categories of the "understanding," which by virtue of their terms of externality fail to comprehend the true nature of God. The Christian doctrine of the Trinity expresses the true thought that God is not the abstract unity, the barren identity without difference conceived by rationalism or by Judaism, but a richer concrete entity composed of inner movement and process. [2]

The doctrine of the Trinity is the ultimate truth; the proof of this is the whole of philosophy, which shows the essential nature of every definite conception or notion. But it must always be un-

---

[1] *Lectures on the Philosophy of Religion*, III, 148.
[2] Cf. ibid., I, 19 ff.; III, 12 ff.

derstood that the categories of theology are only pictorial. The relation of Father, Son and Spirit is "a childish natural form"; Spirit does not, of course, actually enter into such a relation. The content of faith is true, but the form of faith is inferior to the form of thought. Philosophy does set itself above the *form* of faith. In this assertion we see the other, and perhaps the fundamental, side of Hegel's attitude toward religion. In the same passage in which he insists on the truth of the content of faith, he asserts that "thought is the absolute judge before which the content must verify and attest its claims." [3] Religion gets its ultimate justification, not from itself, but from philosophy. Philosophy is the final court of appeal. Faith and doctrine are strictly subject to its jurisdiction. Feuerbach rightly remarks, "speculation only lets religion say what speculation itself has thought and said much better; it determines religion without being itself determined by religion." [4]

The clear implication of this relation between philosophy and theology is that Hegel's doctrine of the Trinity is a philosophical truth, resting entirely on general philosophical premises. The truth of that doctrine can be established and elaborated in complete independence of religion. Indeed, it can be understood and *known* to be true *only* by the speculative reason through the analysis of the nature of logic and concrete actuality. "God" means Absolute Spirit, which posits itself in three forms, according to Hegel. Spirit is the eternal process of self-differentiation and resumption, of "diremption" and reconciliation. God is the activity of pure thought, and knowledge implies the existence of an object or Other. But God has not gone outside himself in being in the other; what is distinguished is identical with that from which it is distinguished—this is the form of love, such that the identity is posited or brought forward into actuality. These three moments in the life of Spirit are what is figuratively represented by the religious terms Father, Son, and Holy Spirit. They suggest

[3] Ibid., III, 148.
[4] Quoted in H. R. Mackintosh, *Types of Modern Theology*, 107.

the inner movement or dialectic of Absolute Spirit, by which process Spirit determines itself, and the Universal as totality is Spirit.

The question may be raised whether this conception of the nature of Absolute Spirit corresponds essentially to the doctrine of the Trinity. This question must be answered in the negative. Hegel undoubtedly felt that his teaching secured the essential Christian truth the more firmly. Certainly the distinctions which he sees in God are immanent in his Being, and some of Hegel's terminology is reminiscent of the traditional *psychological* analogy [5] and of classical discussions of the generation of the Son and the unity of Father and Son in the Spirit. But at least two crucial differences must be noted.

First, Hegel apparently means to equate the second person of his trinity with finite existence. The Son is identified with the force of particularization, and the kingdom of the Son, the Otherness or other-Being, is physical nature and finite Spirit.[6] God's self-knowledge, whereby he is God, "is His self-consciousness in man, is the knowledge man has of God, which advances to man's self-knowledge *in* God." [7] A more orthodox interpretation might be drawn from some portions of Hegel's argument,[8] and Hegel is notoriously open to diverse interpretation, but the prevailing immanentism and monism of this thought suggests that for him the generation of the Son and the "creation" of the world are not essentially distinct. The processes of nature and history are at least "organic to the dialectical process in which the Divine self-consciousness is itself constituted and eternally realized." [9]

Second, the conception of an "economic" Trinity—i.e. the

[5] That is, the interpretation of the Trinity by analogy from a threefoldness of finite personality. This was first given elaborate expression by St. Augustine in books IX-XV of *de Trinitate*, in terms of memory, understanding and will.

[6] See Ibid., III, 2; and part C., § II: Creation.

[7] *Encyclopaedie*, § 564.

[8] Cf. his discussion of God in His Eternal Idea in-and-for self (*Phil. of Rel.*, III, 7 ff.).

[9] C. W. Lowry, art. "Trinity" in *Encyclopedia of Religion*, Vergilius Ferm, ed. (1945), 795.

Trinity of operation, or the divine threefoldness as it relates to the work of God in history—has been abandoned or altered beyond recognition.[10] The divine *oikonomia* for Hegel has relation not to the revelation and redemption in Christ and the inspiration of the Holy Spirit, but only the general world-historical process. From the point of view of the traditional interpretation of the doctrine, this is a denial of its theological (i.e. historical) foundation. Hegel does attach considerable significance to the rise of the idea at the time of Christ, who perceived the unity of God and man. The idea of God-man necessarily arises at a point in history, and this point is the appearance of Christianity. But he also asserts categorically that "it is in the first instance a matter of no importance whence that doctrine [of the Trinity] may have come: the only question is, whether it be essentially, inherently true." [11] Since all history is the basis of the God-man of the divine self-manifestation, no single point in it can be final and the connection with Jesus is little (if any) more than accidental.

2) Hegel believed sincerely that the religious doctrine of the Trinity, starting from the Jesus Christ of the gospels, was at least analogous to the doctrine now established by philosophy. But in the left and right wing schools of his disciples, theology and philosophy came to be sharply disjoined. Both David Friedrich Strauss and Alois Biedermann tried to show that the whole notion of the dialectic of Spirit and its eternal incarnation gains in consistency when it is not bound to a single figure in the historical process. At the very least, they succeeded in dispelling the notion that Hegelianism and Christian belief were two expressions of the same truth. At the most, they may have shown the essential incompatibility of Christian belief with consistent Hegelianism.

Strauss's early criticism of the historicity of the gospels in his *Life of Jesus* (1835) was ostensibly not intended to harm the essence of the Christian faith. That essence, he held, lies in the idea of the God-man and its corollaries, now understood fully by

[10] For a discussion of the terms "economic" Trinity and "immanent" Trinity, cf. Appendix A.
[11] *Phil. of Rel.*, I, 39. Cf. III, 29 ff.

"science" and speculative theology. But the identification of those doctrines with a particular historical individual is a mistake, for it cannot be defended by philosophy. Philosophy can deal only with what must happen and can therefore show the necessity of the dialectic of Spirit and the union of God and man, but from the general system of Hegelian philosophy, it does not necessarily follow that the ideal of God-man should ever have been realized in an historical individual—on the contrary, Strauss writes, "Is not the Idea of the unity of the divine and human natures a real one in a far higher sense, when I regard the whole race of mankind as its realization, than when I single out one man as such a realization?" [12] In *Die Christliche Glaubenslehre* (1840), Strauss goes further and tries to show irreconcilable conflicts between the doctrines of Christianity and the truths of speculative reason. Strauss himself here develops an idealistic pantheism, and the way is prepared for Feuerbach to invert the Hegelian scheme into a dialectical humanism, according to which God is the finite self projected and the Trinity only an hypostatization of the social impulse. The real being of God is in man alone: the actual movement is not from "Father" to "Son," but vice-versa—"in the consciousness which man has of God first arises the self-consciousness of God." [13]

Biedermann, though commonly classified in the opposite wing of the Hegelians, also draws a sharp line between speculative views of the Trinity and the ecclesiastical doctrine. The dogmatic question of the religious principle of Christianity, the principle of the God-man, is not to be confused with the ethical or practical question of the meaning of the person of Jesus Christ for Christianity. True Dogmatics, seeking the rational kernel of doctrine, can be concerned only with the principle, not with the historical accidents. The ecclesiastical doctrine of the Trinity developed out of the identification of the divine principle of Christ with the ego of Christ himself. When this error is avoided

[12] *Life of Jesus*, 895. Cf. 894–897.
[13] Ludwig Feuerbach, *The Essence of Christianity* (1840), 230.

(by the dissolution of the traditional forms of the doctrine), it appears that the true content of the doctrine consists simply in this: that the principle of God-manhood finds expression as the essential moment of the notion of God itself.[14]

The doctrine of the Trinity is not, then, as Hegel would have it, truly a figurative representation of a philosophical truth. Biedermann finds that to reduce the affirmations of faith to strictly philosophical (hence permanently valuable) terms requires a very considerable alteration of orthodox theology, including the elimination of the notions of the personality of God, and the uniqueness of the event of the Incarnation, as well as the doctrine of the Trinity as traditionally understood.

3) In contrast to the men we have been considering, there were many among the German theologians of the nineteenth century who thought it possible to effect a lasting alliance between theology and the regnant speculative philosophy. They were not so naïve as to suppose that Hegelianism and Christian doctrine were the same thing, but they were confident that the two could be reconciled in such fashion that the philosophy would support and help to interpret the doctrines of faith. I. A. Dorner is probably the most important of these thinkers.[15]

For Dorner, as for many members of this group, the doctrine of the Trinity is the distinctive feature of the Christian understanding of God. Together with the Incarnation, it constitutes the highest insight of the faith. Dorner is much concerned to trace the biblical basis of the doctrine and emphasizes its relation to genuine religious interests and its origin from practical religious roots. The doctrine of the Trinity follows directly from the evangelical principle of faith, so much so that the latter is impossible without the former. Faith itself includes traces of divine "triality," and in the "economic" Trinity is to be found the

[14] Biedermann, A. E., *Christliche Dogmatik*, II, §§ 814–819, 839–842 (2te aufl., Berlin, 1885).
[15] Esp. his *System of Christian Doctrine* (Eng. tr., Edinburgh, 1880, 4 v.). Others of a similar attitude are Hans Martensen, C. A. Liebner, C. H. Weisse, and R. Rothe.

legitimate road to the immanent Trinity, i.e. to the eternal and internal threefoldness of the divine essence.[16] Thus it appears that Dorner's notion of the root of the doctrine is quite different from the thought of Hegel. And he criticizes sharply Hegel's view of the world as the Son of God, and of the Spirit as God returning to himself or becoming conscious of himself in man.

But when Dorner begins his positive exposition, it appears that the justification and significance of the doctrine are largely speculative. It is the means of synthesizing God's transcendence, or his self-maintenance, with his immanence, or his self-impartation to the world—thus guarding against abstract monotheism, heathen polytheism and pantheism. The doctrine provides a necessary basis for the divine attributes and is a guarantee of the absolute Personality of God. Most important to Dorner is the "ethical" derivation of the Trinity, from the nature of God as love: the Father is holy, righteous being, i.e. the existence of the ethically necessary in God himself; the Son is a "second mode of divine Being in relation to the ethical," viz. freedom; but freedom strives to return to the necessary and condition itself thereby, just as the necessary rejoices in the free, hence the two are united by the Holy Spirit, the truth of which is love.

This process is that by which God is "eternally absolute Personality," the "*eternally present* result in the trinitarian process of the Life and Spirit of God." [17] Note that here God is specifically designated as *one* Personality. Father, Son and Spirit participate in the Divine Personality, not as themselves persons or personal, but as modes of divine existence which in combination are personality, though God "exists as a person and not merely as a power" in each of them. The process is eternally self-renewing, such that the Divine Personality depends always upon the modes and each of them on it and on each other.

This view, as Dorner presents it, establishes an indissoluble bond between the notions of God's personality and his triune nature, and avoids the Hegelian confusion of the Son with the world. But Dorner does not fully escape from the other, greater

[16] Cf. Appendix A.   [17] Op. cit., I, 447.

difficulty which seems to haunt the efforts of all the speculative theologians, viz. the establishing of a progression from the economic to the immanent Trinity, the relating of the abstract form of the absolute essentially to the concrete facts of the historical Christian revelation. Dorner has a deep interest in the moral revelation in Christ, in the biblical basis of the doctrine of the Trinity and its relation to "religious" interests, yet of his positive derivations of the doctrine, only one could possibly be said to move from an economic to an immanent Trinity—and this proceeds from the revelation of God's essence as love to his personality and *then* to his triune nature, so that the argument is essentially a defense of God's personality. The doctrine of the Trinity becomes mainly instrumental to the justification and understanding of divine personality. When he comes to treat of the economic Trinity, Dorner has nothing to say about God's presence in Christ and the Holy Spirit.[18]

The question remains, then, whether the alliance with speculative rationalism did not actually mean the abandonment of the distinctively Christian basis of the doctrine of the Trinity. And if so, was this any longer the Christian doctrine? In other words, could the speculative Trinity be *essentially* and *directly* related to the economic Trinity, and if not, then was it of real value as a buttress for Christian faith? This is the question raised vigorously by Albrecht Ritschl and his followers, though the Hegelian pattern of thought continued strongly in British idealism, where the doctrine of the Trinity came to be interpreted as an affirmation not only of God's personality but especially of the immanence of God (e.g. in Edward Caird, Andrew Seth Pringle-Pattison, and W. H. Moberly). The sway of idealism in Britain was also to result in the development of a new pattern of Trinitarian thinking, the explicit description of God as a divine society (see below, section 4).

[18] Cf. Ibid., II, 9-20.

3. *The Ritschlian Influence*

1) By the end of the third quarter of the nineteenth century, the influence of Hegelianism was definitely on the decline in Germany. Into the position of preëminence left by the speculative and mediating schools, and contributing much to their downfall, stepped the theology of Albrecht Ritschl, which was to dominate the scene for over a generation. In opposition to the "pernicious" subsumption of theology under metaphysics by the speculative theology, he insists upon the independence of religion. Every part of the system of doctrine is to be viewed and judged, not according to the general principles of philosophy or natural knowledge, but "from the standpoint of the redeemed community of Christ." [1] Theology must be guided at every point solely by the revelation in Christ. But Ritschl is also opposed to all attempts to formulate Christian doctrines out of the contents of the existing religious consciousness (e.g. Schleiermacher, F. H. R. Frank). The norm of theology is rather "the gospel" given in Christ—thus in the New Testament, and not only in Jesus' words about himself, but also in the apostolic religious consciousness.

A part of Ritschl's opposition to speculative theology is unquestionably derived from his Kantian epistemology and the resultant metaphysical agnosticism. We must distinguish, he holds, between theoretical cognition and religious knowledge. The latter consists exclusively of the independent value-judgments of faith. "We know the nature of God and Christ only in their worth for us." [2] The possibility of a "disinterested" knowledge of God is to be excluded absolutely. Religion is essentially a practical matter, and metaphysical theory is of no importance for value-judgments. Ritschl does not mean to deny the objectivity of what is valued—this is presupposed—but he does wish to expel from theology all assertions (e.g. about God or the person of Christ) which might be termed speculative or metaphysical.

The consequences of this methodology for the doctrine of the

---

[1] Ritschl, *Justification and Reconciliation*, III, 5. Cf. 202.
[2] Ibid., 212. Cf. §§ 28 f.

Trinity are not hard to see. That doctrine had been hailed as a supreme truth of speculative thought, and Ritschl seems inclined to accept this denomination, for the Trinity nowhere appears as a part of his system. It is denied (by implication) even such relation to essential elements of the faith as Schleiermacher had seen. The fundamental element of the Christian conception of God is held to be his personality. "Personality is the form in which the idea of God is given through Revelation. As theology has to do with the God revealed in Christ, this is justified scientifically as the only practicable form of the conception of God." [3]

The full description of the biblical revelation of God is given in the name "God and Father of our Lord Jesus Christ." Nothing further is intended when the terms Father, Son and Holy Spirit, are used of God, "for the name denotes God insofar as He reveals Himself, while the Holy Spirit is the power of God which enables the community to appropriate His self-revelation through His Son." [4] Nothing can be said about God "in himself" or even about distinctions in God's nature as revealed to us. Ritschl cites with approval Luther's comment that the doctrines of the Trinity and the Person of Christ are incomprehensible to the understanding and that "the more we speculate about them the darker and less intelligible do they become." The judgment that Christ, in his personal character, is the bearer of the revelation of God, is a value-judgment of the most direct kind. But the Christological formulae (e.g. Chalcedonian) belong to the sphere of disinterested scientific knowledge. So also the doctrine of the Trinity is largely irrelevant to the main business of theology, as Ritschl conceives that business; if the Trinity is not purely a speculative elaboration of theoretical cognition, it is at least so involved in speculation as to be indefensible from the standpoint of value-judgments.

2) Ritschl himself does not discuss the doctrine of the Trinity in systematic fashion, and we are left to piece together his few references as best we can. In his disciples, however, we can see clearly what are the consequences of this mode of thought. Harnack, at the extreme "left," develops in radical fashion the

[3] Ibid., 237.   [4] Ibid., 273.

anti-metaphysical bias and the limitation of the revelation of God to his Fatherhood. Jesus, he asserts, "desired no other belief in his person and no other attachment to it than is contained in the keeping of his commandments." [5] He associated himself with other men in relation to God, his Father, his God; God is his Father in the same way that he is the Father of all men, though Jesus knew him in a new way and sought to communicate this. Thus, *"the Gospel, as Jesus proclaimed it, has to do with the Father only and not with the Son."* [6] Accompanying this "liberal" understanding of Jesus and his message, is Harnack's distrust of all Trinitarian and Christological doctrinal formulations as a perversion of the majesty and simplicity of the gospel, since they tend to assume the position of chief importance and thus to displace the fundamental religious interest.

Other leading followers of Ritschl (the "right" wing—notably Wilhelm Herrmann, Theodore Häring, and Julius Kaftan) were more tolerant of doctrinal formulations as such. Herrmann, for example, is willing to draw a much sharper distinction between Christ's relation to the Father and others' relation to the Father than Ritschl allowed, and consequently makes more far-reaching assertions about the Person of Christ. Christ's relation to God is different from that of any other man, a relation capable of expression only by the biblical phrase "Son of God." His divinity means that he gives us what only God can give and "is to us what only God himself can be." [7] The doctrine of the Trinity (discussed briefly in the last section of Herrmann's *Systematic*) arises from the necessity of beginning with God's revelation of his one nature in a three-fold way and shows that we can properly picture the God who redeems us only in the three aspects of loving Father, Jesus' power working on us, and spirit overcoming nature in ourselves. Furthermore, the Church was right in going on to say that this three-fold revelation must be essentially involved in God's nature. But any attempt to comprehend this necessity only

[5] Adolph Harnack, *What is Christianity?*, 135.
[6] Ibid., 154.
[7] W. Herrmann, *Systematic Theology*, 138.

obscures the thought, for while faith grasps the three-foldness, it also sees "that God remains unsearchable to us—an eternal mystery." [8]

A similar sort of agnosticism is expressed in Häring's discussion of the place of the Trinity in dogmatics. He treats it as the last item, under the heading of eschatology—not because the doctrine is only an appendix to theology, but to avoid burdening the clear and firmly founded true Christian faith with obscure speculations, and to indicate that part of our hope is the removal of the limitations of our knowledge of God. There is, to be sure, no question that our faith "is faith in God as Father, in Jesus Christ, and in the Holy Spirit of God and Christ." [9] But there is serious question whether the idea of the triune God expresses this faith accurately and unobjectionably, and it is not for us to pry into the inner life of the deity or speak of eternal distinctions therein. The only permanent value of the doctrine is its assurance that the revelation in Christ is actually the full self-revelation of the God of holy love and that through Christ we actually have personal communion with him. The doctrine of the Trinity is in this sense a buttress of monotheism, but we ought not to detract from the dignity of the faith in one God the Father Almighty "by the use of pretentious language on the matter of the One and the Three." [10]

3) Herrmann and Häring are manifestly embarrassed by the doctrine of the Trinity. They do not wish to abandon it altogether yet are hard pressed to find any place for the doctrine within the legitimate bounds of their systems. It is apparent that they have not moved very far from Ritschl's deep agnosticism with respect to the doctrine of the Trinity. The same cannot be said of Julius Kaftan. To be sure, his indebtedness to Ritschl in terms of methodology is obvious. [11] But Kaftan thinks it possible to move from those premises to the content of the confessions of

---

[8] Ibid., 151 f.
[9] T. Häring, *The Christian Faith*, II, 915.
[10] Ibid., 922.
[11] J. Kaftan, *Dogmatik*, cf. 10, 15 f., 28 f. References are to the 7te u. 8te aufl. (Tübingen, 1920). (1te aufl., 1897.)

the evangelical (Lutheran) Church. He is insistent that religious knowledge, while different from "objective" knowledge, is nevertheless knowledge in the proper sense, knowledge *that* God is and *what* he is. In short, Kaftan wants to abandon the total exclusion of metaphysics from theology, and rejects only "disinterested" theoretical knowledge, as exemplified by the Hegelian schools.

Indicative of Kaftan's real divergences from the other members of the Ritschlian school is the restoration of the doctrine of the Trinity to a central place in the doctrine of God. "The specifically Christian . . . concept of God is that of the triune God. Apart from the doctrine of the Trinity there is properly no doctrine of God to be called Church doctrine in a definite sense." [12] The problem is to place the concept in vital relation to evangelical faith, for when the new understanding of salvation prevailed in the Reformation Churches, the doctrine lost its immediate significance for piety and became only a speculative presupposition of faith. Hence Kaftan sets himself the task of shaping the doctrine in conformity with the evangelical understanding of salvation and therewith placing it in living connection with evangelical faith.

The ground of the Christian knowledge of the triune God is to be found in a "self-revelation of God in the historical life of the person Jesus Christ and a self-communication of God to Christian believers through the Holy Spirit, which is the Spirit of God and Jesus Christ," as declared in the New Testament.[13] It is not, therefore, an item of general knowledge, nor to be identified with the so-called trinities of other religions. This knowledge is bound entirely to the revelation in Christ. Kaftan believes that the doctrine of a Trinity of essence may rightfully be affirmed. The revelation of God in history does reveal God as triune in his eternal essence, for it would contradict the faith to say that in faith we do not know the eternal God himself. The doctrines of the oneness of essence and co-eternity of Father, Son and Spirit are to be maintained.

[12] Ibid., 153. Cf. 231 ff.   [13] Ibid., 209. Cf. 232.

But we may not properly proceed to the ecclesiastical doctrine of inner relations in God (the generation of the Son and the procession of the Spirit), for this involves drawing inferences from the knowledge of faith and to that extent remains a speculative *theologoumenon* and a pushing aside of faith-knowledge. At this point Kaftan's Ritschlianism begins to manifest itself. The caution with which he phrases all statements about the essential nature of God, and the careful avoidance of "inferences," suggest that the Kantian epistemological premises are by no means abandoned. Nevertheless, Kaftan represents a marked departure from the timidity of the other Ritschlians, and because of this, he moves definitely along the road toward a constructive doctrine of the Trinity. His argument reveals that in the Ritschlian methodology the factors which obstructed trinitarian thought were an overly simple and soon outmoded reading of the New Testament witness to the revelation in Christ, and an *a priori* epistemology.

Kaftan, however, is an exception. The main impetus of Ritschlianism is in quite another direction, tending to deny the relevance of the doctrine of the Trinity to the heart of the evangelical faith and, by surrounding it with the cloak of mystery, to remove it from the proper area of theological investigation.

4. New Directions of British and American Thought

A. LIBERAL AND UNITARIAN TENDENCIES

The transmission of Ritschlianism to the English-speaking countries in the late nineteenth century served strongly to reinforce a negative attitude toward the doctrine of the Trinity which had been developing throughout the century, partly as a result of a revival of Unitarianism but more especially as a consequence of the broader movement toward theological liberalism.

The original protest of the Unitarians was not simply against trinitarianism but was part of a general revulsion against current interpretations of the doctrines of total depravity, eternal punishment, election, atonement and what the Unitarians thought to be the consequent immoral character of God. This protest was vigorously anti-trinitarian because, in relation to the doctrines of sin and redemption, the popular concept of the Trinity often pictured the Father and the Son as contracting agents bargaining for the salvation of men. The Father is portrayed, says Channing, as "the depository of the justice, the vindicator of the rights, the avenger of the laws of the Divinity. On the other hand, the Son, the brightness of the divine mercy, stands between the incensed Deity and guilty humanity, exposes his meek head to the storms, and his compassionate breast to the sword of the divine justice, bears our whole load of punishment, and purchases with his blood every blessing which decends from heaven." [1] Channing sees that this sort of thought is incompatible with the unity of God, for it presupposes that there are in God three distinct persons, each with "his own particular consciousness, will, and perception," who converse with each other and who "perform different parts in man's redemption, each having his appropriate office and neither doing the work of the other." [2] How more explicitly, asks Channing, could we conceive three Gods?

The English Unitarian leader, Martineau, though probably not typical, is able later to assert that the *chief* characteristic of the group is not necessarily its anti-trinitarianism, but rather its liberalism and open-mindedness—i.e. its protest against all exclusiveness and closed theology, whether trinitarian or unitarian. Martineau himself accepts the unitarian position, but rejects its claim to be the only true line of spiritual descent and sees a material decline in the relative importance of the controversy—this being due to better insight into the origin and meaning of trinitarianism and its terms, and the now general divorce of the Trinity from the objectionable ideas of "original sin, satisfaction, election, [and] eternal punishment." [3]

[1] W. E. Channing, "Unitarian Christianity," discourse at Baltimore, 1819; in *Works* (Boston, 1877), 373.

[2] Ibid., 371.

[3] James Martineau, letter of Aug. 6, 1859, to S. F. MacDonald on "The Unitarian Position," *Essays, Reviews and Addresses*, II, 371–380. See his "A Way Out of the Trinitarian Controversy" (*Christian Reformer*, 1886), *Essays*, II, 525–538.

The first major response of New England "orthodoxy" to Channing was Moses Stuart's publication of a translation of Schleiermacher's essay on the Trinity, together with extensive comments.[4] Stuart agrees with most of Schleiermacher's argument. But he does not think it necessary to take the line of Sabellius and Schleiermacher in making the Trinity entirely a development dependent on the manifestations with respect to redemption. No doubt God has so manifested himself, but it does not follow that the trinitarian distinction "has commenced altogether in time, and has no foundation in the *Monas* itself of the divine being." This would be an effect without a cause. Consequently, there must be in God, antecedent to creation and redemption, "something which was the foundation of all the developments made in the same," and which was *"manifested or developed to creatures in time."* [5]

Stuart affirms that we have no data for comprehending the precise nature of the modification or property or distinction as originally existent in the Godhead. He definitely rejects the notion of three divine persons in the modern sense (of three consciousnesses, wills, affections, etc.) because this makes theoretical tritheism inevitable. But he feels that the term person cannot *now* be dismissed from the Church's vocabulary. We need only to remember that the term is not to be taken literally. And we must avoid the license involved in representing the persons as a mutual society, conversing with one another, etc. The latter error is based on a misinterpretation of passages which really refer to the logos *incarnate*, the "theanthropic" person of the Son. Moreover, the trinitarian *names* do not so much characterize the *original* distinctions in the Godhead, as those by which God is revealed to us in redemption. The terms Father, Son and Spirit arise from and are specially characteristic of redemption, and may be compared with the words creator, lord and governor, which can be applied only in anticipation before the actual creation of the world. Stuart feels that all the difficulties and errors of trinitarian orthodoxy stem from trying to read the fully developed distinc-

---

[4] In the *Biblical Repository* (1835). Cf. above, p. 8, n. 11.
[5] Op. cit., 94 ff.

tions of Father, Son and Spirit, back into the *original* state of Godhead itself. Sabellius and Schleiermacher were right in seeing that the developed distinctions cannot be so read back into the original unity, but wrong in failing to see that such distinctions have to be *grounded* in the eternal nature of God.

Stuart's view is reflected in the highly influential work of Horace Bushnell, who probably more than any other man marks the beginning of the "liberalizing" of American orthodoxy. In *God in Christ* (1849) Bushnell contends that the Trinity is instrumental or modal, a method of revelation: Father, Son and Spirit are "incidental to revelation," though they "may be and probably are from eternity to eternity," since God may have revealed himself from eternity.[6] We can speak of three modes of personal action through which God discloses himself, but never of three persons in God, for God's personality is really incomprehensible to us. In *Christ in Theology* (1851) Bushnell expresses himself as more favorably disposed to what he takes to be the meaning of the Nicene definitions and admits a certain confidence in ascending from the "trinity generated in time" to "the conviction that the conditions and grounds out of which it is generated in time are eternal, and that so it is itself eternal," but he still insists that Trinity is "predicable only of God as in act" or economy, not in essence.[7] In a later article, "The Christian Trinity as a Practical Truth," Bushnell moves somewhat further toward the Nicene theology, speaking of God as "datelessly and eternally becoming three, or by a certain inward necessity being accommodated in his action to the categories of finite apprehension."[8] It is apparent that Bushnell here intends a certain real immanence in God's Being of the threeness, yet at least a potential relation to the finite as its ground.

The modalism of Bushnell is carried on and developed in the New England school by Joseph Cook, Lyman Abbott, and A. H. Bradford. Cook, in his three lectures on the Trinity (1877), offers

[6] *God in Christ*, 112 f.
[7] *Christ in Theology*, 177ff., 184.
[8] In the *New Englander* (Nov., 1854), p. 502.

the analogy of the sunlight, rainbow, and heat in one solar radiance, and speaks of God as "one person in the strict sense." Abbott considers the terms Father, Son and Holy Spirit as different names for one person; and Bradford prefers to speak of three distinctions in one person.

W. Newton Clarke's view of the Trinity represents a logical outcome of the "liberal" development we have been describing.[9] Though he offers some very sympathetic comments on the origin and intent of the doctrine of the Trinity, Clarke suggests that it is essentially unrelated to large areas of Christian thought and that today we can dispense with the traditional forms of the doctrine. Modern theistic thought and Christianity agree that God is "a single mind, with one all-embracing consciousness and a single will. For this we argue in our Apologetics, and to this we must be faithful in our doctrine." Moreover, "without the necessity of differentiations in his Being, the one divine Mind and Will is capable of doing all that has been accounted for by the doctrine of the Trinity." [10] The modern conception of immanence absorbs the older conceptions of Incarnation and of the outpouring of the Spirit.

The influence of Ritschl can already be seen in Clarke, but comes to special prominence in the thought of William Adams Brown, probably the foremost American "neo-Ritschlian." Brown distinguishes two sources of the doctrine, the "experimental" and the philosophical. The experimental roots are the historic revelation in Christ, and the religious life through which God was known as an indwelling presence. The philosophical source is the logos doctrine, through which a basis was sought for the revelation in the being of God. Brown, unlike the so-called left-wing Ritschlians, does not wish to reject the metaphysical interest here evinced, for the development of the doctrine of the Trinity was a part of the process by which Christianity made itself at home in the prevailing intellectual environment.[11] In the type of interpre-

[9] *Outline of Christian Theology* (1898) and *The Christian Doctrine of God* (1909).
[10] *The Christian Doctrine of God*, 237 ff.
[11] *Christian Theology in Outline*, 140 ff.

tation represented by the Athanasian creed, however, particularly in the doctrine of *perichoresis*, or mutual indwelling of Father, Son and Holy Spirit, he thinks that the "last reminiscence of the original source of the doctrine in the historic revelation that came through Jesus" disappears.[12]

The Trinity can best be understood as a summary of the ways in which one may know God in experience—viz. as the Absolute, as self-revealing, and as self-imparting. From this point it is necessary to go on to the metaphysical aspects. We ought not, however, to try to define inner relations in God or to describe the nature of God in himself apart from our experience. In the past, Trinitarians have been unwilling to stop with the Trinity of manifestation, because that seemed to resolve the doctrine only into an analysis of human experience. But now we seek God *within* rather than without the world, and believe that the only way to know him in himself is to unfold the meaning of his revelation. Therefore, "the antithesis between the Trinity of essence and that of manifestation disappears. The self-revealing God is the real God,—the only God we either can or need to know." [13]

With Clarke and Brown we come to the beginning of the contemporary period. In their thought we find expressed the basic motifs of "liberal" thought with respect to the doctrine of the Trinity. Though favorable judgment is often passed on the "experiential" sources or aspects of the doctrine, the trinitarian conception as such plays a definitely subordinate role in liberalism's understanding of God. There is general suspicion of the classical formulae, rejection of the doctrines of internal relations and *perichoresis*, and acceptance of the principle that the modern notion of divine immanence solves many of the problems posed by the ancient formulations. The influence of Ritschl is everywhere

---

[12] Ibid., 149.
[13] Ibid., 161. Cf. 156 ff. Comparable to Brown's view is that of the prominent British Ritschlian, A. E. Garvie. Cf. *The Christian Doctrine of the Godhead* (1925), and *Revelation Through History and Experience* (1934). Cf. also the view of H. F. Rall, the latest spokesman of American "neo-Ritschlianism," Ch. II, below.

observable, though in varying degrees and forms. We shall see in the next chapter how this liberal tradition continues to make itself felt in contemporary theological discussion.

B. "SOCIAL" THEORIES OF THE GODHEAD

It was suggested earlier that by the last quarter of the nineteenth century, Great Britain had become the center of the influence of Hegelian idealism. An indirect consequence of British idealism was a truly novel and fairly widespread development in the interpretation of the doctrine of the Trinity: the deliberate equation of Father, Son and Spirit with selves or egos, i.e. *persons* in the modern sense, and the description of God as a divine society.

In its early stages (Green and Caird) British idealism was willing to take personality as the ultimate, but the further elaborations of Bradley and Bosanquet (and Pringle-Pattison's criticism of Green in *Hegelianism and Personality*) confirmed the suspicions of those who thought that absolute idealism made of God not a person, but only the universal rational element. Thus an opposing school of personal idealists arose, and (more important for our study) several theologians—notably W. Richmond, J. R. Illingworth and R. C. Moberly—worked out a theory which recognized with the idealists that personality could not exist in mere isolation, yet insisted that spiritual life is ultimate. To assert the unipersonality of God seemed, on the absolute idealist analysis, to lead to the dependence of God on the world for his personality, but a doctrine of divine tripersonality avoided this defect. Further, since the notion of the necessarily social nature of personality seemed to imply a radically permeable character of personal existence, it appeared feasible to speak of God's tripersonal being without compromise of his unity. The general tenor of the argument is summarized in the following passages from W. Richmond (to whom most of the writers of this group refer):

It is the individuality of personal life which marks the characteristically modern idea of a person, as, e.g., when we speak of personal sympathy, of personal antipathy, of personal affection, of personal religion. All these emotions are eminently personal in the sense that they are eminently individual. They intensify the sense of individual life. . . . But on a moment's consideration it is plain that in such cases as these, what evokes and intensifies the personal life of the individual person is some relation to a person other than himself. Personal religion is perhaps the most suggestive instance. . . . Religion is here conceived as a relation between the personal being of God and the personal being of man; . . . The closer consideration, indeed, of this and similar uses of the word would suggest the hypothesis that the word 'personal' is only rightly applied to any feeling of the individual, when the feeling is a consciousness of relation to another person.

[Thus] when Christian theology conceives God as a personal being, it does not conceive God as *a* person. Personality attaches to God not as one Person, but as Three. God is One, individual, in the sense that He is whole, complete in Himself, but . . . His unity is a unity of Persons, and it is as a unity of Persons, and as a unity of Persons only, that Personality is conceived to be the supreme Reality. Personality in the form in which it is supposed to be most intensely and unmistakably real, is a communion, a fellowship of Persons, a communion of will and character, a communion of intelligence and mind, a communion of love, implying that each Person is, in these various phases or aspects of personal life, capable of complete communion with others. . . . God *is* a fellowship, a communion of Persons.[14]

J. R. Illingworth comes to this "social" conception of the Trinity from a previous inclination toward the Augustinian type of analogy, expressed in *Personality, Human and Divine* (1894). There he had spoken of the individual finite personality as essentially triune, though dependent on society for its actualization. In perfect Personality (of whom finite persons are only pale copies), that triunity is eternally realized from within. But in *The Doctrine of the Trinity* (1907) he definitely passes from the psychological to a social analogy for the Trinity, speaking there of God as a "society" or, "what is perhaps safer language, as existing in a mode of which the family, the unity of human society, is the created and faint reflection." [15] This concept, he holds, answers to the

[14] W. Richmond, *An Essay on Personality* (1900), Edwin Arnold, England, II, 18, 17.
[15] *The Doctrine of the Trinity*, 143.

metaphysical and moral difficulties in conceiving of the absoluteness of God; it indicates an adequate object of his experience
(knowledge) and love within his being.

Illingworth takes for granted that what we mean by person is
what the ecclesiastical definitions intended by the Latin *persona*
and the Greek *hypostasis*. Charles F. D'Arcy is more careful in
his interpretation of the Fathers. He notes that they had no clearly
defined concept of personality, that *persona* meant more for
Augustine than for Tertullian, and more for us than for Augustine. Nevertheless, he insists that the Church Fathers were tending
in the direction of the modern notion of personality in their use
of *persona*. "It is much better," he says, "to interpret the Trinitarian doctrine with the help of the modern conception of personality than by means of the Latin word *persona*; for if the connotation of the word has altered, its denotation is, in this case, the
same, and the change of meaning was simply the inevitable
development." [16] Therefore, "when we speak of Divine Persons,
we use the term person in the sense in which it is used of human
beings. . . . The man is a person, because he is the self-conscious
subject of an experience, because he refers to himself as 'I'. And
it is in this sense that personality is predicated of each of the
Divine Three." [17] What, then, of the unity of God? D'Arcy
abandons the attempt to find a *personal* unity in God. Personality,
he suggests, is the highest category, but "not the ultimate form of
being. The unity of God is a higher unity: He is personal and
more, 'super-personal.' " [18]

---

[16] Art. "Trinity," in *Dictionary of Christ and the Gospels*, ed. J. Hastings,
1908, II, 762. See *Idealism and Theology* (1899), 213f.

[17] *Idealism and Theology*, 215f.

[18] *DCG*, op. cit., 766. Cf. *Idealism and Theology*, 95: "If the conception
of personality is not adequate as a final description of Deity, then we must
believe in God as ultimately superpersonal unity." D'Arcy is atypical at this
point, going much further with the absolute idealists than most of the others
of this school would allow. The transcendent unity of the divine persons is
for him the all-inclusive Universal, the concrete totality, which is also the
unity of all persons. "The Divine subject *includes* all other subjects. The
human *excludes*." (*Idealism and Theology*, 92. Cf. 230 and Lecture VI, "The
Ultimate Unity," *passim*.)

D'Arcy's description of the nature of this unity is worth quoting at length
here since it anticipates so vividly the view which we shall later find in

R. C. Moberly carries on the attempt to reconceive personality as essentially permeable. He feels that the word person is by far the best as a description of the divine distinctions, and in any case the only one available for us, being a real advance on *hypostasis* by the addition of personal associations. But we must get rid of our common concept of personality as primarily distinctness; applied to God it means mutual inclusiveness, not exclusiveness. Admittedly, analogies do not carry us far here, and this is to be expected, since tripersonality cannot be made intelligible, as from within, to a unipersonal consciousness.[19]

In the United States, the foremost representative of the social analogy was Francis J. Hall. Hall does not come to the notion of social Godhead from the standpoint of the requirements of per-

---

Leonard Hodgson's work on the Trinity. "The final superpersonal unity is, therefore, the most intimate of all unities. It is the perfect, the absolute, unity. It is a unity to which the unity of the ego bears no comparison, and for that very reason it is by us inconceivable. For us, there is no thinking on any other basis than that of the self-conscious subject or ego. When we essay to think the final unity we do so in terms of the unity which we ourselves possess. Our self-consciousness stands as the symbol of something far more concrete, more intense in its unifying virtue, than itself.

"Here then is the complete answer to the charge of tritheism. Instead of regarding the Divine Three as a group of persons, bound together merely by corresponding emotions or similarity of purpose, our view regards the ultimate unity in which they coexist as so intimate, so intense, that even the unity of personality can yield no conception of it." (*Idealism and Theology*, 232.)

In attempting to describe the characteristic distinction of that unity, "all we can do is to take the relation in which the self as unifying principle stands to elements lower than itself in the scale of reality and make this relation a symbolical representation of the relation (let the term be used with the necessary reservation) which the final unity bears to the self." Therefore we speak of the divine unity as super-personal, without denying the reality of finite selves. We attribute to God, "not a mere numerical unity, nor yet the abstract unity of an all pervading principle . . . He is the concrete, Universal One, Who, though all-inclusive, yet secures to each finite person the full possession of his individuality." (234, 235.)

It is hardly necessary to point out that this view rests specifically on the premises of absolute idealism. The fact should be remembered when we come to the discussion of Hodgson.

[19] *Atonement and Personality*, 156–60, 170ff. Other expressions of the notion of the Trinity as a "divine society," though not always as explicit, may be found in Andrew Fairbairn's *Place of Christ in Modern Theology*, James Orr's *Christian View of God and the World*, and Charles Gore's *Incarnation of the Son of God*, and *Belief in Christ*.

sonality but from the terminology of scripture. The reciprocal use of pronouns in the scriptures as between Father, Son and Spirit, suggests directly the term persons. Positively, this means distinct "selfs" or "egos"; negatively, it does not mean separate individuals. Hall notes that Descartes was the first to attend to the fact that *ego* or *self* constitutes the basic reality in personality, yet holds that this was clearly implied in the terminology of the fathers—in the selection of *hypostasis* to stress "real and distinct Selfs," and of *persona*, which even in its forensic sense implies self. Modern thought has created a difficulty, however, by using "person" to mean all that goes to make up "an individual, self-conscious, and rational being." [20] We must explain, then, that in the trinitarian terminology, "person" means what moderns mean by "self" or "ego." Precisely what the distinction is between the self or person, and an individual, self-conscious and rational being, Hall does not inform us. The fundamental problem, how three personal egos can exist in and possess one indivisible essence and being, does not admit of solution by finite minds, but this is no more insoluble than the problem of our own personality and is not (formally) self-contradictory—furthermore, this is "an incidental problem, the answer to which is no part of the doctrine." [21]

George A. Gordon also appears among the defenders of the social theory, but upon a radically immanentist basis. He is not interested in the origin of the doctrine but only in its meaning, which is simply "the essentially social nature of God; the faith that he is in his innermost being an eternal family." The only question is whether God is social or unitary, and the decision must be made on the basis of which conception best corresponds to the pattern of humanity: "The contest today is between God as an eternal egoist and God as an eternal socialist. If God is an eternal egoist, he is the contradiction of humanity; . . . If God is an eternal socialist, he is in himself the ground and hope of humanity." In sum, "the consistent use of man as a guide to God necessitates a God with society in himself. . . . Further, no other God is worth anything as cause and fountain of mankind. . . . If,

[20] *The Trinity*, 187, 191f.   [21] Ibid., 162.

therefore, the cause must equal the effect, the social man can be accounted for only by the social God." [22]

5. *Continuing Conservative Modes of Thought*

While the new and vital forces of nineteenth-century theology found expression mainly in the various movements we have been describing in their relation to trinitarian doctrine, nevertheless there was a strong undercurrent of conservative Protestant thought (both on the Continent and in Britain and the United States) which served as a protest against the subjectivist, speculative and agnostic tendencies in the other movements' attitudes toward the Trinity. Though in the main these conservative theologians move within the framework of traditional trinitarian thought, and may therefore be mentioned briefly as representing a common interest, nevertheless they served throughout the century as a reminder of the importance of the doctrine of the Trinity in "orthodox" Christianity and in some respects provided a point of contact for the reconsideration and reconstruction of the doctrine in contemporary theology.

Among the most conservative Germans, we may note briefly such men as Hengstenberg, Philippi and Luthardt, who were willing to stand simply on the authority of the historic confessions, urging a return from the subjectivism of the newer Protestantism to objective authority, as represented by the infallible Bible and the theology of scholastic (Lutheran) Protestantism. Standing in close relation to this school are the Biblicists, represented, for example, by Johann Tobias Beck. Christian doctrinal science is for him neither speculative *gnosis* nor a phenomenology of consciousness, but is the reproduction of something given, namely, the biblical revelation of truth. He speaks of the organic unity and completedness of the Revelation in the gospels in which God is known as Father, Son and Spirit, therefore eternally and in himself triune.[1]

[22] G. A. Gordon, *Ultimate Conceptions of Faith*, 364, 374, 382f.
[1] J. T. Beck, *Die christliche Lehr-Wissenschaft, nach den biblischen Urkunden* (2te aufl., 1875), 114. See 79-119.

More important for us are a group of confessional theologians, mainly in the "Erlangen school," who were willing to take a conciliatory attitude toward the newer movements in theology yet insisted on the primacy and authority of the historical revelation, and all of whom would retain the doctrine of the Trinity in its traditional place in the scheme of theology. Whereas the first impulse of reaction to Schleiermacher had been a fairly blunt appeal to authority, this group felt that a way could be found from the new emphasis on religious experience to the objective confessions of the sixteenth century.

For Gottfried Thomasius, founder of the Erlangen school, the doctrine of the Trinity is based on and centers solely in the historical actuality of Jesus Christ. We know God as Father and ourselves as the object of his grace only in Christ and stand in this relation to him only through Christ, who is thus a living, personal, connection between us and God, and is called Son by the scriptures. Our community with God also involves an immanence of God in us, God as the giver of our faith and our whole Christian life. This we call the Holy Spirit, a personal subject differentiated from the Father and the Son—the bond of our fellowship with Father and Son. Yet our faith no less essentially joins these in *one*, for there is but one community with God, one gracious will and love. The three subjects of these works are the common (*gemeinsam*) object of our faith; we have them only in and with one another. Thus our actual relation to God leads us to the necessity of saying "that Father, Son and Spirit on the one hand differ personally from one another, on the other are essentially one with each other" [2]—this is the economic Trinity in that it manifests itself in the saving act of God for us and in us and is reflected in our saving relation to him.

To the question whether these definitions reach objective reality, we must reply that the community we have with God through faith in Christ presupposes the objective permanence of

[2] G. Thomasius, *Christi Person und Werk, Darstellung der evangelisch-lutherischen Dogmatik.* Bd. I: *Die Voraussetzungen der Christologie* (1853). 48ff.

those relations in God so essentially that we could surrender none of these moments without abandoning the faith itself. The difference and unity must be immanent in God, else the historical actuality of our salvation is lost. This doctrine is clearly to be distinguished from all formulae of speculation: it is the result simply of reflection on the Divine Word, on the experience of salvation and on Church tradition. Yet Thomasius is willing to relate the results of his trinitarian discussion to the modern notion of the personality of God. The hypostases are God's threefold self-definition, not mere modes but "distinct, self-dependent persons in One absolute personality, immanent definitions which God gives himself through the eternal fact of his will."[3] Absolute personality is not the result of the process, but its presupposition. Thus there exists within the divine unity a relation of origination, by virtue of which the first person is the ground of the others, and sets and has himself as object in the second, and in the third the first and second come to objective unity—though in all it is the *one* absolute personality which defines itself in a threefold manner.

In A. F. C. Vilmar, as in Thomasius, we find the insistence that the economic Trinity, though not in its full form, is revealed in the scriptures, especially in Jesus' assertions about himself as recorded by John.[4] This doctrine is not simply a matter of thought, though the understanding of God's triunity is a necessity for an adequate grasp of salvation and creation; the content of this doctrine is actually "the content of the Christian life," *the* life of love being possible only through the redemption in Christ, and the presence of the Holy Spirit. Furthermore, from the fact that from the first, Father, Son and Holy Spirit were the objects of Christian worship, we see that in each case, the worshipper must stand over against a worshipped Person. Father, Son and Spirit are not just attributes or powers, but such distinctions in the divine essence that each expresses the whole essence.[5]

[3] Ibid., 91f.
[4] A. F. C. Vilmar, *Dogmatik* (1874), I, 267ff.
[5] Cf. also Carl F. A. Kahnis, *Die lutherische Dogmatik historisch-genetisch dargestellt* (2te aufl., 1874-5). F. H. R. Frank also stands with the con-

At the close of the period with which we are now concerned the "conservative" line of development is carried on in Germany most notably by Martin Kähler and Reinhold Seeberg. In *Der sogenannte historische Jesus und der geschichtliche, biblische Christus*, Kähler argues (against the regnant biblical criticism) that it is impossible to reach the "Jesus of history" and that therefore we must start from the biblical ecclesiastical witness to Christ. We may thus retain the full content of the Bible (without the dead weight of verbalistic and legalistic Biblicism) as the authentic record of the primitive Christian confession and the charter for the Church's proclamation. Theology must center in Jesus as the biblical Christ, in his traditional character as the revelation of God. In *Die Wissenschaft der christlichen Lehre*, Kähler applies this principle briefly to the doctrine of the Trinity: "The knowledge of God as the Trinity proceeds exclusively from the saving revelation, and its systematic exposition must be contained strictly in this connection. Consequently only from the actuality and the form of the divinity of Christ does one know the Trinity of communication or the essential revelation, and from this in turn the Trinity of the personal life which is properly God." [6]

The development of the dogma is thus based on the biblical witness to the so-called economic Trinity, i.e. on the fulness of the revelation of God in Christ. For Christ not only brought but *is* the revelation of God, and his continued relation to the world proceeds from his eternal connection with the Father. Therefore the basic demand of the Christian confession requires us to speak of the one divine essence of his life in three hypostases by means of threefold personal relations. Beyond this point Kähler is reluctant to go. He feels that "further expositions" serve only the

---

servatives in insisting on the objectivity of Christian knowledge (against Ritschl and to some extent Schleiermacher), though he differs sharply in the less biblical nature of his thought. Beginning with the Christian condition of "subjective assuredness," he develops the ecclesiastical doctrine of the immanent Trinity as a necessary assertion of faith. Cf. the *System of Christian Certainty* (Eng. tr., 2nd ed., 1886) and esp. the *System der christlichen Wahrheit* (3te aufl., 1894), I.

[6] Op. cit. (2te aufl., 1893), 312f.

rejection of confusing ideas. For the latter purpose "the theologumenon of the Trinity is necessary to the exposition of the Church's teaching; however, for the appropriation in faith of salvation it has only a qualified value." [7]

Reinhold Seeberg strikes out in a significantly different direction in his view of the Trinity. The doctrine is for him based in the threefold revelation of God—in the natural connections of events in the world, in the historical life of the Church whose head is Christ, and in the individual Christians. The Trinity, therefore, refers to *differentiations in the divine universal activity*, to the "threefold will of God in relation to nature, history and personality": as Father, God is lord of nature (the entire created world); as Son, he is lord of history (and Church); as Holy Spirit, he becomes effective in and through individuals.[8]

Seeberg is well aware that this way of putting the doctrine represents a departure from the tradition, though, of course, Origen can be cited as a parallel for the sort of distinctions Seeberg has in mind.[9] He defends this view against the charge of modalism by affirming the eternal nature of the distinctions. God is simultaneously and equally Father, Son and Spirit. This is an eternal threefold self-determination of God which, if we wish, we may designate as the "immanent" Trinity, Seeberg says, though in doing so we acquire no new knowledge of God. Seeberg's own construction is consciously in the area of the economic Trinity, and he is sharply critical of traditional theories of the immanent Trinity. As a summary of his concept of the unity of the divine will and the threefoldness of the divine willing and working, Seeberg suggests the formula *una persona, tres personæ*—which means that God's "self-determination as a per-

---

[7] Ibid., 316. Cf. 318. Kähler does not say so specifically, but the aspects of the doctrine which he has in mind here are probably the concepts of internal relations.

[8] *Christliche Dogmatik*, I, 379ff.

[9] Specifically, Origen's notion of the "economy" of the Godhead, in which the Father is seen as the author of existence, the Son as the source of rational nature, and the Spirit as the giver of holiness. Cf. *de Principiis*, I, iii, 8.

son is at the same time an eternal self-determination in a threefold personality." [10]

With Kähler and Seeberg, we come to the threshold of contemporary continental thought. While in both men we can see a liberalization of confessional theology, and in Seeberg a reformulation of the trinitarian concept in terms reminiscent of Schleiermacher as well as Origen, nevertheless these men stand in a tradition of conservative thought which was neither absorbed by the Hegelian religious philosophy nor reduced to the "liberalism" of Ritschlianism. This tradition was, as we have suggested, overshadowed in the nineteenth century, but it persisted and became, if not a basis, at least a point of contact for contemporary continental theology.

The moderate conservatism of Kähler and Seeberg is reflected in English-speaking countries by theologians like P. T. Forsyth. Forsyth is a vigorous opponent of the dominant evolutionary (and idealistic) concept of religion in Britain, as well as the theological liberalism of Ritschl and the *religiongeschichtliche Schule*. The center of Christianity for him is not evolution, but revelation; there is an essential conflict between *a* revelation in Christ and *the* revelation in him. Christianity is not a matter of believing *with* Christ but *in* Christ, and particularly in the work of Christ—in his power of salvation, the cross and the atonement, which constitute our Christian experience. Christ gives us new creation, eternal life, forgiveness, and "for this creative work no mere man is sufficient"; we are driven to assert the existence of an eternal Son, equally real with the Father.[11]

Forsyth shows much sensitivity to continental theological devel-

---

[10] Ibid., 391. By way of contrast to Seeberg's *una persona*, we may refer briefly to Richard Grützmacher, *Der dreieinige Gott–unser Gott*, (1910). Grützmacher goes to the opposite extreme, asserting that Father, Son and Spirit are distinct I-centers, with special consciousnesses and wills. God is thus a society of persons, operating side by side and bound together in a common nature of love and holiness. Grützmacher stands pretty much alone in German thought (except for the Catholic theologian, Anton Günther). It is in Britain and the United States that the notion of the Trinity as a divine society becomes important.

[11] *Person and Place of Jesus Christ* (1909), 281ff. See also 88; ch. X *passim*.

opments. Most conservative British and American theologians, however, seem largely content to restate the traditional defense and forms of the doctrine of the Trinity—for example, Robert L. Ottley and T. B. Strong among the Anglicans; W. P. Pope and John Miley representing a Wesleyan point of view; Charles Hodge, the chief advocate of the Princeton school; and W. G. T. Shedd and A. H. Strong.[12] A favorite theme among these writers is the essentially mysterious and incomprehensible (though not contradictory) nature of the doctrine of the Trinity. This is especially true of Pope and Miley, but also of Hodge and A. H. Strong. Thus for Hodge the doctrine must be accepted because it is clearly revealed in the infallible scriptures, and while incomprehensible it is no more so than any other great truth and cannot be said to be impossible. To expect that we can explain the mysteries of the Godhead—*perichoresis*, generation, procession—is altogether unreasonable; we must believe though we cannot understand. Nor do philosophical forms of the doctrine serve in any way "to make the inconceivable intelligible." [13]

The problem of the use of the word person for Father, Son and Spirit is generally recognized, but dealt with hesitantly. Miley and Ottley see that the term in its ecclesiastical usage does not correspond to the modern sense of the word, and are content to state only that as applied to God it means something between mere manifestation and independent, exclusive individuality. Hodge insists that the Father, Son and Spirit are properly called three persons and that "the idea expressed by the word in its application to the distinctions in the Godhead, is just as clear and definite as in its application to men," but does not enlighten us further.[14] Shedd tries to utilize both the psychological approach and the social approach, suggesting that in God there are "three hypostatical

---

[12] Ottley, *The Doctrine of the Incarnation*, II, part X. T. B. Strong, *Manual of Theology* (2nd ed. 1903), 134-190. Pope, *A Compendium of Christian Theology* (2nd ed. 1877ff), I, 255-287. Miley, *Systematic Theology* (1892), I, 223-275. Hodge, *Systematic Theology* (1874), I, 442-482. Shedd, *Dogmatic Theology* (1888) I, 249-333. A. H. Strong, *Systematic Theology* (rev. ed. 1907), I, 304-352.

[13] Hodge, op. cit., I, 478.

[14] Ibid., 459.

consciousnesses but only one self-consciousness." He would speak of the "*personality* of the essence" of God, i.e. of "three persons and one personal Being." [15] Both A. H. Strong and T. B. Strong find value in the notion of intercommunion and permeability of personality and the possible overcoming of the exclusiveness of finite personality in the infinite personality of God, though A. H. Strong is much more cautious in his use of the analogy.

In general and in contrast to the German conservatives, the tradition represented by these theologians cannot be said to do much, either positively or negatively, with the concept of the Trinity. In opposition to liberalism, American conservative Protestantism (or at least the vocal sector thereof) tends to fall into Fundamentalism, and while the Trinity is maintained as a necessary part of the faith, it is mostly accepted on authority and left aside as largely irrelevant to life. In the series of tracts called *The Fundamentals* (1912), for example, the Trinity does not rate a separate essay. And the doctrine is not mentioned in B. W. Warfield's essay on the "Deity of Christ," G. Campbell Morgan's essay on "The Purpose of the Incarnation," or Robert E. Speer's discussion of "God in Christ the only Revelation of the Fatherhood of God," and only by implication in Torrey's defense of "The Personality and Deity of the Holy Spirit." The trinitarian understanding of God is doubtless in the background in all of these, but it is obvious that the interest of this line of conservative thought is centered elsewhere.

[15] Shedd, op. cit., 283, 194.

PART II

THE PERSISTENCE OF NINETEENTH-CENTURY
PATTERNS IN CONTEMPORARY ATTITUDES
TOWARD THE DOCTRINE OF THE TRINITY

CHAPTER II

The Trinity as Second-Rank Doctrine

The contemporary revival of theology, which may be said to begin about the time of the publication of Karl Barth's *Römerbrief* (1918), is analogous to the movement begun by Schleiermacher in at least one major respect: it also represents an attempt at a major re-orientation of theology, and a (partial) rebellion against immediate theological predecessors. Contemporary theology is widely characterized by protests against the immanentistic tendencies of nineteenth-century thought, against excessive optimism about human nature and its potentialities, against "Kulturprotestantismus," against "liberalism," against the tendency to reduce theology to philosophy of religion, and against the more radical departures of the last century from classical Christian affirmations. At the same time, it is obvious that the newer movements in theology are by no means simply reactions to "liberalism." The nineteenth century marked a growing freedom from the bonds of rigid orthodoxy, a sincere effort to get back to the central elements of Christian faith and to orient all of theology about those elements, and a recognition of the need to restate the principles of Christian authority in a manner consonant with the discoveries of biblical criticism. However sharp the conflict of the newer theology with "liberalism," the theological reconstruction of the present day presupposes these gains of the last century.

In respect both of its continuity and its discontinuity with the preceding theological era, contemporary theology comes inevitably to the question of the doctrine of the Trinity. There are, furthermore, at least two special characteristics of recent theology which particularly require examination of the problem of the Trinity. First, the revival of the category of revelation as the foundation of Christian affirmation opens the way to reconsideration of the classical Christian view of the revealed nature of God. Second, the general pattern of theological discussion since World War I may be said to be moving in the direction of the doctrine of God. One of the first interests of the new theology was a reassessment of the nature of man. This has resulted in a widespread and quite conclusive repudiation of the optimism of the late nineteenth century and a renewed appreciation of the tragic aspects of human existence, of the precariousness of man's achievements, and of the depth of sin. It having been generally concluded that men are in need of something more than their own apparent capacities if their problems are to be resolved, the trend of interest is naturally toward the question of deliverance or redemption, i.e. soteriology. Among Christians this means the question of the work and person of Jesus Christ, and we can detect now the logical development of this pattern in a growing interest in Christology. With the focusing of attention on soteriology and Christology, contemporary theology is being confronted increasingly with the problem of the nature of God.

It is apparent from these factors that the crucial question about the doctrine of the Trinity is still the question of its role in the theological system. *Is* the doctrine truly important and integral to the faith? If so, *how* is it integral? What is its relation to other central themes of theology? Is the doctrine of primary or only secondary importance? These questions are all comprised in the general query as to the theological "place" of the doctrine of the Trinity. This general question therefore provides a useful and illuminating typological principle for the understanding of contemporary thought on the Trinity.

Of the several views of the role and significance of the doctrine which find expression in contemporary theology, three fundamental attitudes may be said essentially to represent continuations of one or another of the patterns which we have identified as important in the nineteenth century. 1) After the manner of

Schleiermacher and Ritschl there are those theologians, generally but not always in the "liberal" tradition, who continue to deny that the doctrine of the Trinity is essential to the expression of the Christian faith, though some would hold it useful. They therefore reject the concept or relegate it to a definitely subordinate role in the theological schema. The doctrine is for them not indispensable. 2) Corresponding roughly to the Hegelian adoption of theology into philosophy is the interpretation of the doctrine as equivalent to the expression of a philosophical or metaphysical truth which can be established more or less independently of the Christian revelation. An essential element of this view is the attempt to justify and defend the doctrine on the grounds of its philosophical usefulness. 3) Finally there are those, probably representing the numerical majority of Christians, who accept the doctrine of the Trinity because it is held to be a direct and unmistakable deliverance of an authoritative scripture or of a tradition rooted in scripture and interpreted by an infallible Church. The first of these three views we shall discuss in its various forms in this chapter. The second and third views will be treated in Chapters III and IV.

In those areas of contemporary theology where there appears a significant *renewal* of interest in the doctrine of the Trinity, we may discern two contrasting types of approach to the problem. 1) Probably the majority of those contemporary theologians who wish to restore the doctrine to a central place in the structure of theology consider it as a necessary "synthesis" of the several fundamental elements of Christian revelation and experience, e.g. the monotheism which Christianity inherited from its Jewish parent, the Incarnation or the new experience of God in Christ, and the new experience of the work of the Holy Spirit in the Christian community. The doctrine of the Trinity is thus interpreted as the completion of the doctrinal system, as the keystone which brings together in a unity the various aspects of the faith and which is therefore of great importance as the ultimate and necessary safeguard of the doctrinal system. The Trinity is the final, the ultimate doctrine of faith. 2) It is possible, however, to conceive the doctrine of the Trinity not as the last but as a first item of Christian theology, and we shall have to consider the view that the concept of the Trinity is an immediate implication of the revelation, i.e. that it is essentially identical with the content of revelation. It therefore does not arise from a theoretical interest in the completion of doctrine but is an ἀρχή, a *first* principle, of all Christian thought and life. These two approaches to the doctrine of the Trinity we shall consider at length in Chapters V and VI.

1. *Explicit Rejection of the Doctrine*

The pervasive tendency in the nineteenth century to consider the trinitarian conception of God as of only secondary importance is continued in the contemporary period in a wide variety of ways. Conceptions here range from those which judge the doctrine of the Trinity to be wholly irrelevant and superfluous, to those which consider it of real importance for certain limited theological purposes. But these represent differences only of degree in the qualification which is placed on the usefulness and necessity of the doctrine in the structure of Christian faith.

At the one extreme are those who take an almost wholly negative attitude toward the trinitarian conception. In *The Place of Jesus Christ in Modern Christianity*, John Baillie pays his respects to the Trinity in a concluding chapter entitled "Some Final Clarifications." He there labels the assertion that the Trinity is the distinctively Christian idea of God as "seriously misleading." "What is true is that from the third century onwards the distinctively Christian idea of God began to fit itself into a trinitarian mould." [1] This mould was adopted and adapted from Hellenistic philosophy and was used to express the distinctively Christian idea of God as redemptive love. It is the ethical character of the Christian Trinity which distinguishes this from the triads of other religions. Baillie is willing to speak of a threefoldness of Christian experience: God in his transcendent being, God as manifest in

[1] Op. cit., 185.

Christ, and God as present in the heart and spirit. These elements account for the traditional trinitarian terminology, but there is no doctrine of the Trinity in the New Testament and we need no such doctrine. The New Testament references to God the Father, to Jesus Christ, and to God's Spirit in our hearts are clear and simple enough, and all we need for faith and practice. Baillie would allow a certain manifoldness in God's nature, but does not see that the number three has any ontological significance and would not distinguish so formally between God the Father and God the Spirit, or between God's presence in Christ and in us. He does not blame the theologians of the third and fourth centuries, who did the best they could with the materials they had, but would censure those who now "lazily perpetuate their mistakes." [2]

A similar judgment upon the doctrine appears in A. C. McGiffert's *History of Christian Thought*. McGiffert does see a genuine religious as well as philosophical element in the doctrine—the religious interest, firmly rooted in Christian faith, being "to find God in Christ." He recognizes that the opponents of Arianism were interested in affirming the deity of Christ in order to guarantee the uniting of man to God, but thinks that it was only the prevailing Platonic philosophy which made it necessary to maintain the deity of Christ via the theory of pre-existence and the logos doctrine. "If the Stoic metaphysics had been dominant . . . and the immanence of God, or the oneness of divine and human nature, had been recognized by the Nicene theologians, the doctrine of the Trinity would have been unnecessary; the religious interest—to find God in Christ—could then have been conserved, as it was by the modalists, without distinguishing the pre-existent Son of God from the Father." Therefore, the distinction of the Son from the Father is a philosophical element, "the product of

---

[2] Ibid., 185-193. This book should not be taken as representative of John Baillie's present view, which is very close to that of D. M. Baillie (cf. below, esp. 208ff.). *The Place of Jesus Christ in Modern Christianity* was a very early work, which Dr. Baillie subsequently refused to have reprinted. The book is important, however, in that it did speak for a widely held "modern theology," and presents a view still current in some quarters.

metaphysics," without which the religious element in Christian
faith can maintain itself very well.[3] Both the Christological and
trinitarian problems are therefore consigned to the limbo of the
purely "ontological," the "metaphysical and speculative." Their
metaphysical subtleties do not really matter either ethically or
religiously.

In the view of D. C. Macintosh, the doctrine of the Trinity
is perhaps even less essential to Christian faith. For from the
standpoint of his religious empiricism neither Christology nor certainty of the historicity of Jesus is *logically* necessary to "an
essentially Christian faith in God and an essentially Christian
experience of moral salvation through the right religious adjustment." [4] Macintosh gladly affirms, however, that Christology is
psychologically necessary to Christianity and adds indefinitely to
its richness of content, and defends the reasonableness both of the
historic Jesus and of Christology. He is therefore ready to affirm
that "Jesus may be said to have been *divine in the quality or value
of his personality*," and that "*God must have been in Christ*," who
represents the acme of divine immanence.[5] From this viewpoint,
Macintosh believes it possible to accept the "vital religious essence"
of the doctrine of the Trinity, which is simply that

'God the Father,' the God of moral optimism, is not a different
God from 'God the Holy Spirit,' the God of the religious experience of moral salvation . . . [and] that it is this one God, the
Father or Holy Spirit, who indwelt in such fulness the life of the
historic Jesus and gave him so divine a value and function in
human history and experience . . . [These are] one and the same
Being . . . viewed under different aspects corresponding to his
different revelations to men.[6]

But this is all that theology ought properly to say.

What goes beyond this in the traditional doctrine of the Trinity
(by which we mean the doctrine of three eternal Persons who are

[3] *History of Christian Thought*, I, 275.
[4] *Reasonableness of Christianity*, 137. Cf. 138, 155.
[5] Ibid., 150, 152. Cf. 153 f.   [6] Ibid., 154.

nevertheless but one divine Being), is the product of a Greek speculative philosophy of the early centuries of the Christian era—a philosophy which can hardly be said to be the philosophy of the modern mind. Modern theologians and philosophers have sought in various ways to galvanize it into a semblance of life, but with very doubtful success. What we have set forth here as the vital essence of the Trinitarian thought is all we need to be concerned to defend as reasonable and true.[7]

In the three views just cited, particularly those of Baillie and McGiffert, it is not difficult to perceive the continuing influence of that suspicion of "metaphysical" doctrines which we have seen to be associated with Ritschlianism. There is the characteristic sharp distinction between the "religious essence" or "value" of the doctrine and the speculative or philosophical encrustations. Modern theology is supposed to strip off these husks in order that the kernel of truth may not be smothered by ancient and fruitless speculations. In the case of McGiffert and Macintosh, this hostility to speculation is qualified by a willingness to substitute for the old philosophy a new one which makes the doctrine of the Trinity unnecessary.

From a quite different sector of "liberal" and "empirical" theology we find F. R. Tennant objecting to the classical doctrine as irrational and religiously valueless.[8] Tennant is struck by the disparity between the traditional Christological aspects of the conception, which seem to him inevitably to imply a plurality of subjects, hence tritheism, and the formulations of the trinitarian dogma itself, which he holds to have been always "rigidly monotheistic, or monarchian and consequently modalistic." To be sure, the academic expositions did not intend the latter result; they sought to conceive a sort of reality intermediate between the

[7] Ibid., 155. Macintosh would not only say that the Trinity is not the essential Christian idea of God, but apparently means that faith in Christ does not involve any fundamental modification in the conception of God. He declares: "It goes without saying that the belief in the historicity of Jesus is logically indispensable to Christian faith in *Jesus Christ*: but what we are dealing with is Christian faith in God." (Ibid., 140. Italics mine.)
[8] Cf. his art. "The Present Position of the Doctrine of the Trinity," *Congregational Quarterly*, January, 1925, pp. 8–16, and *Philosophical Theology*, II, 168 ff., and 267 ff.

substantival and the adjectival, a "substantival adjective" or an "adjectival substantive," but this is impossible. "Such a concept is a monstrosity, ruled out by grammar and logic," and whenever the theologians were not simply vague, they always were monarchian.[9]

Thus interpreted, however, trinitarian doctrine has nothing new to contribute to theism. "It possesses no unique philosophical import, and it can scarcely have any religious or devotional significance. This it only acquires when it is subconsciously interpreted . . . tritheistically. If God is triune only in a sense in which any human being can be called a trinity, the fact seems insignificant both for theology and for practical religion."[10] Similarly, the current sort of argument that God cannot exist as personal in solitariness, and that a plurality of Persons is a condition of attributing eternal and perfect love to the Godhead, cannot be used to support anything less than tritheism.

Tennant does believe that the concept of a plural or social Godhead, understood for what it is, has a philosophical value which merits consideration. In such terms, he would speak of God as consisting of several individuals in a society, with equality of nature, *homoousia* (sameness of essence, not *monoousia*, or oneness of essence, as really intended in the Nicene doctrine) and harmony of will. The concept of *perichoresis* could be taken . literally as meaning an interpenetration of selves to a far greater extent than is possible under human limitations. The unity of God would be a "unity of concurrent wills, of joint purposes, of moral harmonies, and of co-operant agencies."[11] In such an interpretation the number of the persons could, of course, not be fixed. Tennant does not urge this view, for he does not see that philosophical theology has any real ground for preferring one divine being or a divine society. But in any case, it is all up for traditional trinitarianism: "we cannot stop short of tritheism at

[9] *Cong. Quart.*, 9 ff. Cf. *Philos. Theol.*, II, 267 f.
[10] *Philos. Theol.*, II, 268.
[11] Ibid., 172. Cf. 170 ff, *Cong. Quart.*, 13 ff.

all . . . unless we refrain from advancing a step from modalism: it is verily a case of all the way or none." [12]

From a viewpoint far more sympathetic to neo-Reformation theology, we may note an equally vigorous and explicit repudiation of classical trinitarianism. Wilhelm Pauck, commenting on the first edition of Barth's *Christliche Dogmatik*, is furious because Barth seriously means to accept and defend the doctrine of the Trinity. It is incredible to him that Barth believes the doctrine to be an important expression of revelation. Pauck is favorably impressed with Barth's theological principle, as that is expressed in the *Römerbrief*, but will have nothing to do with abortive attempts to revitalize the ancient theologies:

As if it were really a matter of life and death, that as members of the church of the Twentieth Century—we should accept the dogma of the Trinity! Professional theologians may think that it is absolutely necessary for us to be concerned with the theological thought-forms of the past, but—God be thanked!—the common Christian layman is no professional theologian, and he may be a better Christian just for that reason. . . . What [the preacher] needs to know is who God is and how man can be put in relation with him into the abundant, full, rich, meaningful life.[13]

Pauck confesses that Barth intends the latter goal, but asserts that he falls far short precisely because he goes in for theological hair-splitting. As for Barth's use of the doctrine of the Trinity as a means of maintaining the idea of the subjectivity of God—"This is an intolerable and provoking speculation. The air of significance with which Barth presents it cannot compel any one to consider it important." [14] Aside from this passionate impatience with theological niceties and a general repudiation of all supernaturalistic metaphysics, precise reasons for Pauck's vehement opposition to the doctrine are not forthcoming.

[12] *Cong. Quart.*, 12.
[13] W. Pauck, *Karl Barth*, Harper and Brothers, New York (1931), 189f.
[14] Ibid., 193f.

2. *The Trinity as a Dramatic Symbol*

Not many contemporary theologians have been as explicit in their rejection of trinitarian doctrine as the foregoing. Most contemporary "liberals" seek to maintain a more positive relationship to the classical Christian formulations. This is clearly illustrated in A. C. Knudson's *Doctrine of God*, in which the discussion of the Trinity opens with the assertion that this "is the specific Christian doctrine of God," and grew out of the expanded idea of Deity which was necessary when "Jesus as well as the traditional God came to be regarded as divine." [1] Knudson defends the doctrine against the charge that it is dependent upon ethnic or other triads; these are not really parallels and in any case parallels are irrelevant, for Christian trinitarianism is rooted in the facts of Christian history and experience. The doctrine is not something alien, superimposed on the Christian idea of God, but an explication thereof. Its vitality comes from the religious ideas expressed in it and these are the source of the doctrine. Chief among those religious ideas is the fundamental concern of the Church with the redemptive activity of God in Christ, hence the unique divinity of Christ.

In its traditional form, Knudson observes, trinitarianism has a decided advantage over all deism or unitarianism in giving us a living God and a near God, in providing for his moral absoluteness (in the notion of inner love, which eliminates egoism), and in supporting the doctrine of Incarnation. In addition to these three religious values, the doctrine has a definite philosophical value: it gives a differentiated unity containing a principle of action, and protects against pantheism by the self-sufficiency of God.

Having thus apparently gone to some lengths to affirm the value of the doctrine, Knudson begins to note some of the difficulties of the classical doctrine, which are due to "later speculative elaborations": the danger of tritheism, if the three are *persons*; the dubiety of the need for more than two persons; or if the three

[1] A. C. Knudson, *The Doctrine of God*, 370. Cf. 370–428.

are less than persons, then the loss of the religious advantages of the idea of divine society and the inconceivability of a something between substance and attribute (cf. Tennant); the dependence on Platonic realism, which subordinates personality to essence, whereas we now affirm that personality is metaphysically ultimate; the doubtful value of the identification of the ego of Christ with God, in comparison with the modern view of God's indwelling in Christ; and the modern abandonment of the thought of redemption as a mystical-metaphysical process.

In view of these criticisms Knudson agrees with what he takes to be the general feeling that while "this creed enshrines great values that must be conserved," in its older form it goes beyond the limits of both reason and faith and is no longer final. He wishes to hold to the underlying motives—"that God is immanent in the world and that he was in some real sense incarnate in Christ," that he is redeemer and creator, and sanctifying spirit, and essentially sacrificial love.[2] But Knudson is not at all sure that the classical trinitarianism (which he takes to teach three *persons*, centers of consciousness) is the only or even the best way of conserving these values. Given the modern movement from Platonism to personalism in philosophy, he sees three ways of retaining the essential truths of trinitarianism, without the personal distinctions. The Trinity may be regarded as a symbol of the richness of the idea of God. Or we may adopt a revised Sabellianism, in which Father, Son and Holy Spirit are three eternal manifestations which describe God's essential nature. Or we may consider the doctrine as an assertion of the "Christlikeness of God." It is the last alternative which seems most congenial to Knudson because it focuses on the essential thing in trinitarianism, the new ethical concept of God as Christlike, it associates our knowledge of God with the historical revelation in Christ, and it points to God's ethical and metaphysical unity. In such a Christlike God, there may be eternal and necessary distinctions, but this is not essential to the absoluteness of God's love and ethical nature.

What, then, is the usefulness of the doctrinal symbol itself? It

[2] Ibid., 422 f.

is clear that Knudson does not think it essential to the statement
of the Christian idea of God. Here (as in the case of Baillie, Mc-
Giffert and Macintosh) the distinction of the "religious values"
of the doctrine from the form of the doctrine indicates that another point of view has been assumed from which it is presumably
possible to explicate the truth of the Christian idea of God and
to judge the value of the doctrine of the Trinity in relation thereto. Further, the doctrine is not held to be truly descriptive of God;
it is rather a symbol constructed by the human understanding
as an attempt to express the nature of divine love; it is wholly a
category of the finite mind, not essential to the revelation of God's
inmost being. Yet, while Knudson is embarrassed by the doctrine,
he is unwilling to let it go entirely. The doctrine has not yet out-
lived its usefulness: there are some weighty theoretical considerations which can be offered in its support, and it has a definite
practical value in that it "does unquestionably dramatize the divine
love in a way that appeals to the imagination and that makes it an
effective symbol of the divine grace." [3]

3. *Contemporary Monarchianism*

Probably the most widely held concept of the Trinity among
contemporary "liberal" theologians, especially those who have
been influenced by the renewed emphasis on revelation in Continental theology, may be designated as "monarchian" or
"modalist." Sharing much of the distrust of the classical formulations of the doctrine to which we have called attention, these men,
nevertheless, are willing to go considerably beyond Knudson in
the extent to which the notion of Trinity is held to be descriptive
of the essential nature of God. But all are suspicious of talk of
"immanent Trinity" or of "internal relations."

Two aspects of this type of thought may be distinguished.
One is seen in a willingness to accept a concept of "economic"
Trinity, or Trinity of manifestation or experience, combined

[3] Ibid., 428.

with a great hesitation regarding any notion of "essential Trinity" or "Trinity of being." This may sometimes be put down as nothing more than agnosticism or Ritschlian suspicion of metaphysics, but it is more likely to be the case that behind this attitude lies the belief that what we designate as *personæ* are not original or substantial or essential to God's being, but belong to or arise from the relations which God sustains to the world. Going somewhat further than this is the other view, that the Trinity of manifestation is rooted in the being of God in the sense that the *personæ* represent eternal aspects (or even simply attributes) of God's nature, or perhaps types or departments of the divine activity, or distinctions in the "content" of divine action. The first of these tendencies may technically be designated "modalist," the word "monarchian" being reserved for the second (and we shall occasionally utilize the terms in this way). But since "modalism" has been used so broadly as to include even Augustine, it is probably wiser to let the term "monarchian" serve to designate all the representatives of the type of thought which we have in mind. This will also be simpler, since the two tendencies so frequently appear together.[1]

Hastings Rashdall might be cited as an example of the simple identification of Father, Son and Spirit with divine attributes, though in his general estimate of the significance of the doctrine he is very close to those who would dispense with the whole formulation as unnecessary. Writing in opposition to the British exponents of the social theory of the Trinity (notably Charles Gore), he contends that the Abelardian theory of the Trinity is the proper interpretation of the classical doctrine, as expressed by Aquinas, Augustine, and even Athanasius. There is, according to

[1] It can be seen from the analysis in Ch. I that both of these attitudes come into the contemporary scene from the tradition of Schleiermacher and Ritschl, primarily by way of such men as Bushnell and W. A. Brown, though it is doubtful whether any of the thinkers considered here are fully aware of their dependence so far as the *form* of the doctrine is concerned. Many would consciously accept Schleiermacher's judgment of the *place* of the doctrine. Cf. above, 7 f., 25 ff.

Rashdall, nothing unintelligible or unreasonable in the doctrine of the Trinity, nor anything offensive to a unitarian: it simply means that God is Power, Wisdom and Love.[2]

Somewhat more favorable to the retention of the trinitarian symbol is the view expressed in D. M. Edwards' *Christianity and Philosophy*. Here the doctrine is explained primarily in terms of the threefold character of the divine activity, and its usefulness is clearly limited to the realm of manifestation. Edwards offers a negative judgment upon the traditional role and form of the doctrine, commenting that the notion of God as holy love has generally replaced the Trinity as the chief article of Christian faith in God. The Trinity is "not a primary affirmation of faith but an intellectual hypothesis" which arose from the need to correlate the received monotheistic faith with the experience of Christ as having the value of God and the experience of God's continued presence through his spirit.[3] The traditional development, especially the notions of *hypostasis* and *perichoresis* or coinherence, he finds altogether unintelligible (citing Tennant), and he thinks it presumptuous to try to analyze the internal structure of deity. Yet the doctrine has religious value when

regarded as a convenient summary of the chief aspects in which God may be known or experienced by men. Stated quite simply, it stands for the belief in the one personal God, the *Father* almighty, as revealed in the historic person of His *Son* Jesus Christ, and as ever present and active through His *Spirit* in the hearts and lives of men both individually and in their fellowship with each other.[4]

These aspects of men's knowledge of God, however, represent a genuine threefoldness of the divine functioning, believed to be grounded in God's eternal nature, and not just temporary roles. All of the dogma that goes beyond this is a product of Hellenistic philosophy and not essential to the New Testament experience of God in Christ.

[2] Cf. Hastings Rashdall, *God and Man*, ch. IV, esp. 117 ff.
[3] *Christianity and Philosophy*, 337 f.
[4] Ibid., 349.

Edwards appears at times to reduce the Trinity merely to a symbol for the great manifoldness and wealth of resources of the Deity: he sees no clear reason why other aspects or functions (personal activities) of God could not be hypostatized, e.g. his mercy, providence, or justice, and finds no religious reason for the finality of the number three. Yet the concept of Trinity does point to the three *outstanding* features of the divine self-giving. If, therefore, the doctrine is only a symbol for the richness of divine being, it nevertheless is genuinely descriptive of fundamental elements in that richness, as manifested in types of divine action.

A similar conception of the Trinity of manifestation as indicating aspects of divine activity may be seen in William Fulton's article on "Trinity" in Hastings' *Encyclopædia of Religion and Ethics*.[5] In his historical summary, Fulton makes much of the "transition" from the Trinity of experience to the Trinity of dogma. The former referred to the experience of God as Creator or Legislator (Father), as Redeemer (the Son), and as Sanctifier (the Holy Spirit). The Trinity of dogma, he avers, loses touch with the historical Christ and moves "entirely in the transcendent realm." Modern theology, thrown back on the historical revelation, is less concerned with the "essential" or "immanent" Trinity than with the basis of trinitarian doctrine. The modern tendency is therefore to think of the Trinity as a summary of the "different ways in which the knowledge of God may be held": 1) God as self-disclosed only as ultimate and absolute, 2) God as self-disclosing in Christ, and 3) God as self-imparting and communicating. Such a doctrine may be defended against the charge of Sabellianism, Fulton holds, in that the elements are here said to be "rooted eternally in unseen reality, . . . although known through the threefold self-manifestation or not known at all." [6]

The pattern of exclusive attention to the Trinity of experience or manifestation is characteristic also of such popular interpretations of the nature of God as those offered by H. F. Rall, Georgia Harkness, and W. M. Horton. In Rall's most recent work the

[5] XII (1922), 458ff.   [6] Ibid., 461.

doctrine is seen as an effort to sum up the Christian conception of God. That conception stems from a threefold experience: faith in the one living God, plus the new revelation of God in Christ, and the presence of God in the Holy Spirit. Thus faith is threefold, yet plainly in one God. Beyond this, Rall does not think it necessary to go; formal statements are not as important as the experience and faith.[7] Miss Harkness interprets the doctrine as meaning that God has manifested himself in three ways—in "creating and sustaining work as Father . . . within the conditions of human life as Son . . . within our lives as Holy Spirit." [8]

George F. Thomas may be taken as representing a view which is essentially "functional" or monarchian, yet more insistent on the grounding of manifestations in the essential being of God. "The doctrine of the Trinity," he argues, "is an assertion of the reality of these ways in which God shows Himself to Christians, and an insistence upon the source of them in the eternal being of God." The doctrine means "that God was truly and fully revealed both in Christ and in the Spirit, that no mere *temporary modes* but *eternal aspects* [or functions] *of the Divine Being* were manifested in them." [9] The doctrine has thus a definite religious importance, and also has philosophical value in freeing Christianity of abstract monotheism. But while Professor Thomas is willing to defend the doctrine against tritheistic misunderstanding and explain it as a development of the experience of reconciliation in Christ, one is constrained to infer that the notion has only secondary and derivative significance for him. The Trinity is not mentioned in the section of the essay on God, but appears only in the discussion of Christ and the Creeds.

Certain elements of the "modalistic" conception of the Trinity may be seen to appear even in a work so widely different from

[7] H. F. Rall, *The Christian Faith and Way* (1947), 83f. It is perhaps significant that the doctrine of the Trinity does not appear at all in Rall's earlier book on *The Meaning of God* (1925). Here it comes at the end of the chapter on the Holy Spirit and the Trinity.

[8] G. Harkness, *Understanding the Christian Faith* (1947), 74. Cf. also W. M. Horton, *God* (Hazen Books), 25 f.

[9] G. F. Thomas, "Central Christian Affirmations," in *The Christian Answer*, ed. H. P. Van Dusen, 154 f.

those just mentioned as Gustaf Aulén's *Faith of the Christian Church*. Aulén does not see that the trinitarian element in Christian faith adds anything new to his previous discussion of divine love; it only "defines more accurately certain affirmations about the mode of God's revelation . . ." [10] It must be noted, however, that Aulén's prior discussion of God's love is so Christologically oriented as to make the mode or form of revelation essentially related to the content of the revelation of love. The doctrine of the Trinity has, therefore, the dual significance of 1) indicating the distinctive and living content of Christian faith, the distinctiveness coming from faith in Christ and the immediate and living nature of faith from faith in the Spirit, and 2) guarding monotheism by indicating that reference to Christ and to the Spirit is always to the one true God. In its original intention the doctrine contains the essential and inalienable ideas of Christian faith: "That Christian faith in God is at the same time faith in Christ and in the Spirit." [11] All unitarian conceptions tend inevitably to become deistic or pantheistic, thus impoverishing and weakening the content and vividness of Christian faith in God.

At the same time, however, the essential elements to which Aulén here points are aspects of *faith*, and the title of this section of his work is "The Trinitarian Element in Christian Faith." The doctrine represents the threefold *viewpoint*, which preserves the unified and organic character of Christian faith in God. This is consistent with Aulén's conception of the business of theology, which is not to describe God in himself, but God as related to man in revelation and man as related to God in faith. Thus, while Aulén speaks of "abstract speculations" about the immanent Trinity as relatively harmless (at least in comparison with the tritheistic suggestion of the formula "three Persons"), in the Excursus on "The Boundary Line of Faith" he makes it clear that the trinitarian element in faith refers only to the revelation of

[10] G. Aulén, *The Faith of the Christian Church*, 255.
[11] Ibid., 258. The formula "three Persons" tends to violate this original intention, Aulén thinks, by dividing the conception of God; this tendency becomes stronger with the modern elaboration of the concept of personality. (Cf. 256f.).

God, and he reminds us that no affirmations can be made which
are not based on the revelation.

This definition of the boundary of faith is not to be taken in
a subjectivistic sense, for Aulén consistently insists on the completely theocentric character of faith: the purpose of theology is
the elucidation of the characteristically Christian idea of God. The
avoidance of "abstract speculations" and the suspicion of talk of
God-in-himself are rather to be associated with Aulén's characteristically Lutheran theme of the *Deus absconditus,* and with his
conviction that the modern conception of personality makes the
traditional statement "three Persons" inescapably tritheistic in its
implications. It is in view of these considerations that Aulén is led
to conclude:

Faith can . . . say nothing else about the revelation in Christ and
in the Spirit except that it originates in the eternal being of God.
. . . [With] the symbolical statements that the Son is "born of
the Father before the worlds," and that the Spirit "proceeds from
the Father and the Son," . . . faith touches that line of demarca-
tion which it cannot cross without passing beyond the area of
revelation and thereby becoming something else than faith.[12]

The variety and ambiguity of the views here classified as
monarchian illustrates vividly the sort of embarrassment which
the doctrine of the Trinity occasions for large areas of contemporary theology, and especially for that type of "liberal" thought
which seeks to maintain essential continuity with the historic
Christian theological tradition. All of these authors believe the
doctrine to stand for something (or some things) very important
in Christian faith and to be a valuable way of stating those essential elements. While they express great dissatisfaction with portions of the classical formulations, none of these theologians would
support the view (e.g. of Baillie or McGiffert) that the doctrine
is essentially an alien and "speculative" imposition upon religion.
Nor are they willing to reduce the doctrine simply to a symbol
for the richness of the idea of God or an assertion of the "Christ-

[12] Ibid., 258f.

likeness" of God (Knudson). The concept of Trinity is for them really rooted in the essential nature of the Christian faith.

Yet it is clear that in the case of each of those whom we have considered here, the trinitarian concept plays only a secondary and sharply limited role in the explication of the Christian understanding of God. The doctrine must be dealt with because it has been so important in historic Christianity and because it does have a permanent value, but it always appears as something extra—not extraneous or unimportant but, as Fulton puts it, a doctrine which "does not usually fit well into the general doctrine of God, and often bears the character of a doctrine apart." [13]

Certainly one fundamental reason for this hesitance with regard to the doctrine of the Trinity is to be found in the difficulty involved in the application of the term "person" to Father, Son and Holy Spirit. This usage seems to suggest such plurality in God as to conflict with monotheism. The writers with whom we are here concerned do not believe that in classical use *persona* meant what we mean by "person," and they will have nothing to do with the "social" concept of the Trinity as elaborated by the school of Illingworth and Gore.

One solution to the problem (viz. modalism) is to limit the significance of the doctrine of the Trinity primarily to the area of revelation or manifestation, with only the vague assertion that the threefoldness is truly rooted in the essential nature of God. With this assertion, modalism goes further than (e.g.) Knudson, but still stops short of the crucial question which the doctrine of the Trinity has historically sought to answer, namely, *in what way* are we to say that this threefoldness of revelation is rooted in the being of God? If the threefoldness is not simply a matter of our apprehension, what does it mean as applied to God himself? If we are able to say nothing about the nature of God in himself on the basis of his mode of revelation to us, then one is entitled to ask to what extent we can speak of the full or decisive revelation of God in Christ. Pure modalism, which speaks only of a Trinity of manifestation or revelation, *inevitably calls into question the*

[13] Fulton, op. cit., 462.

reality and truth of revelation by separating God's revelation or act from his Being. If the revelation is not a revelation of the being of God, then it is conceivable that God might be ultimately other than his revelation.

The writers considered here (especially Thomas) are not unaware of this latter problem, as is shown by the other (monarchian) feature of this type of thought. This is seen in the reference to eternal divine "aspects" or "functions"—to God as Creating, Redeeming, and Sanctifying (Edwards, Fulton); or to his Sovereignty, Redemptive love, and Presence (Thomas). Now it may well be the case that this sort of threeness of activity or function points or draws attention to the problem of the threeness of God, but it can hardly be said to correspond to the classical understanding of Trinity, for at least two reasons. First, to the extent that the terms "aspects" and "functions" are said to be descriptive of the being of God and not simply of his relation to the world, they seem in context to denote little more than the terms "attribute" or "qualities." And if this be the case, then it must be noted that it was precisely to exclude such an interpretation that the terms *persona* and *hypostasis* were introduced. In view of modern attempts to overcome the Aristotelian duality of substance and attribute and to reinterpret substance in terms of activity, such designations as "functions" seem less open to suspicion than "qualities," "aspects" or "attributes." Yet the way in which even the former term is used almost always connotes a certain externality rather than the inmost and essential being of God, or the inner determination or structure of the divine act. This is consistent with the fact that for the viewpoint under consideration, the trinitarian conception is of only secondary importance in the statement of the Christian notion of God (e.g. when compared with the concept of the personality of God).

Second, it must be recalled that at least after Augustine and the formulation of the doctrine of the indivisibility of the outward works of the Trinity, *opera trinitatis ad extra sunt indivisa*, the Catholic theology quite definitely rejected the association of the *personæ* with different aspects of the divine activity except with the most careful qualifications (i. e. by way of the notion of appropriation).[14] That is, classical trinitarianism has insisted on a coinherence not only of the divine *personæ*, but also of the divine activities. The extreme consequence of an unguarded identification of Father, Son, and Spirit with different divine functions may be seen in the sort of moral opposition between Father and Son (Judge and Redeemer) which arose in Protestant scholasticism. I do not suggest that this sort of dualism characterizes any of the persons here considered, but only that the attempt to explain the distinction of *personæ* simply by distinctions in the content of divine activity may, from the point of view of classical formulations, be said to make the distinction either too sharp or too shallow! The distinction is too shallow if it refers only to attributes or qualities or aspects of God's relation to the world. But when pressed, this kind of distinction becomes too sharp by leading to a separation of God's creative activity from his redemptive activity, or a division of his ethical nature. Since most of the theologians in question also assume that God is known as Father or Creator apart from his revelation of himself in Christ as Redeemer, this distinction of the *personæ* as departments of divine activity raises the question also of the unity of the ground of the trinitarian understanding of God, a question to which we shall return at a later stage of the discussion.

4. *The Trinity as "Defensive Doctrine"*

In some of the statements of Thomas and Aulén we come close to a type of thought which regards the doctrine of the Trinity as of importance to Christian theology, as indeed necessary, but only in a defensive way. The classic contemporary expression of this

[14] Cf. St. Augustine, *de Trinitate*, bk. I. cc. 4, 5, 8, 9; II. 10; IV. 21; V. 14; also *Enchiridion*, ch. 38. St. Thomas, *Summa Theologica* I. Q. 39. It should be noted that Aulén specifically affirms the entire unity of the works of God and points out the danger of tritheism which results from ascribing the works severally to the three persons of the Trinity.

view is undoubtedly that of Emil Brunner, who specifically designates the doctrine of the Trinity as *Schutzlehre*—defensive doctrine.[1]

1) The first point to be noted by Brunner, and in a way the
decisive point, is that while the doctrine has traditionally been
asserted to be the distinctive Christian doctrine of God—distinguishing it from Jewish, Moslem and rationalist monotheism—
nevertheless the doctrine was neither a theme of the New Testament proclamation, nor a central item of the content of the faith
of the primitive Christian community. Because of this, he concludes that

The ecclesiastical doctrine of the Trinity . . . is not the biblical
kerygma, hence also not the *kerygma* of the Church, but a theological defensive doctrine [*Schutzlehre*] for the biblical and ecclesiastical faith-center. It therefore does not belong to what the
Church has to preach, but it belongs to theology, where the Word
of God given to the Church may be considered with the aim of
examining [*Prüfung*] the Church's proclamation. For this theological reflection at least the doctrine is the center.[2]

From the outset, then, the doctrine of the Trinity is made secondary. It will become clear as we go along that this "primitivism"
regarding the content of Christian preaching (and presumably
worship) is by no means the sole explanation for Brunner's attitude toward the doctrine, but it is of real importance.

While the doctrine of the Trinity is not found in the New
Testament, nevertheless the *problem* of the doctrine is there,

---

[1] The exposition here follows Brunner's treatment in the *Dogmatik*, Bd. I:
Die Christliche Lehre von Gott, 213–255 (Eng. tr. by O. Wyon, *The Christian Doctrine of God*, Philadelphia, The Westminster Press [1950], 205–240).
In *The Mediator*, Brunner expressed essentially the same view, but in very
brief form. Only in the *Dogmatik* do we see the implications of the concept.
There are some suggestions in *The Mediator*, however, of a more favorable
judgment upon the doctrine of the Trinity than appears in the *Dogmatik*. In
the former, Brunner says that "the dogma of the Trinity . . . exists the
moment that we really believe that God was in Christ," whereas in the
Dogmatik, he will only allow that the *problem* of the dogma is raised by the
scriptural proclamation. (*The Mediator*, 275. Cf. 276.)

[2] *Dogmatik*, 214. (Eng. tr., 206.)

according to Brunner. The problem is presented in the revelation of God's name as Father. This name was from the beginning the name given to God by the Christian community, yet this is not a self-evident truth. Rather God is known to us as the Father of the Son, of Jesus Christ, and becomes our Father by the witness of the Holy Spirit. If God is revealed as Father, it is by stepping out of his mystery and showing himself in the Son and stimulating men to recognition of his revelation by the Holy Spirit. This is the starting point of the doctrine of the Trinity. The problem of the doctrine is likewise presented in the Church's confession that Jesus is the Lord, for there is only One who can be called Lord— the Father, the Lord of heaven and earth. The affirmation of the true divinity of Christ confronts us with the problem of reconciling this with the oneness of him who is Lord. The same problem is posed with respect to the Spirit, since it is *God's* Spirit working in us which effects the inward realization of the historical revelation.

Therefore it can be said that the biblical witness is not to the doctrine of the Trinity, but in the *direction* of the doctrine. God discloses himself in a threefoldness of names, and these names stand in a definite order: "from the Father through the Son to the Spirit." Brunner wishes to emphasize this order, this succession (*Hintereinander*), for he holds that the Church has not understood its decisive meaning and has taught instead a coexistence (*Nebeneinander*), which has involved the doctrine of God in serious difficulties. He admits that in certain passages the three names are put in juxtaposition, but insists that the biblical doctrine goes no further (i.e. to the concept of a triune God), and is governed throughout by the order.

The biblical witness may be summarized: "Only through the Son do we have the Father, only through the Son do we have the Spirit, only through the Spirit do we have the Son. In all, however, the one God reveals himself and gives himself to us."[3] What the *doctrine* of the Trinity is concerned with is the basis or ground of this testimony, the transcendent background of the work of

[3] Ibid., 229. (Eng. tr., 217.)

reconciliation and revelation, the *whence* of Christ, which belongs to the *what*. The doctrine is therefore to be designated as a product of reflection on the *kerygma* of revelation.[4] The importance of such reflection is not to be underestimated, for its purpose is to defend the reality of revelation by affirming the "unity of the *nature* and the *revelation* of God."[5] The doctrine arose as a defense against doctrines which would destroy that unity, namely, monarchianism and subordinationism, and the Church was justified in throwing all its strength into the battle, for it concerned the life and death of the whole gospel. Any doctrine which dissolves the identity of revealer and revelation, or of God's essence and his revelation, contradicts the decisive biblical message. Christ must be truly God, else there is no revelation and reconciliation. Yet insofar as Christ is God present to us and concerned with us, he is as revelation (Son) other than the revealer (Father). Hence the origin of the doctrine of the Trinity, as a defense of the divinity of Christ.

2) Having thus approved of what he takes to be the prime intention of the trinitarian doctrine, Brunner feels constrained to raise the question whether the doctrine as finally formulated "was really in accordance with that which it sought to defend," and replies that "this question can be answered affirmatively only in a very restricted sense."[6] The chief difficulty with the trinitarian formulations seems to be that they focus interest on the transcendent background rather than on the historical revelation. In the biblical witness the historical revelation always stands in the center of interest. It is the *work* of Christ which is central, the work of reconciliation and revelation. Of course, this work has its transcendent background and is inseparable therefrom; but all affirmations about the whence of Christ, the preëxistence and eternity, *must always be derived from the historical center.*

---

[4] Ibid., 229, 236, 252. Here is Brunner's chief complaint against Barth, that Barth "does not distinguish between the trinitarian *problem* and the *doctrine* of the Trinity"; he confuses the revelation with reflection on the revelation. Cf. 251f. (Eng. tr., 236.)

[5] Ibid., 232. (Eng. tr., 220.)   [6] Ibid., 232. (Eng. tr., 220.)

"Through the Spirit we see the Son as the Son of the Father; and through the Son, the Father as the Father of the Son and our Father. The three names do not stand as coexistent but in succession. The background can be seen and understood only as background of the foreground." [7]

But in the main stream of theological development, from Origen and the Alexandrine school, this focus of attention was spoiled by the introduction of the *logos* doctrine. For that led to speculations on the internal relations and to the shift of the interest-center from the historical to the eternal background. Out of this shift of interest come the formulæ of the classical doctrine of the Trinity. This means that a false mystery is substituted for the mystery of faith. The "mystery" of the three Persons is a mystery of thought, a *"mysterium logicum"* which lies entirely outside the biblical message. The only mystery which has a place in the proclamation of the apostles is the mystery of the Incarnation and the Cross. Just as the Trinity is not the *kerygma*, but a reflection on the *kerygma*, so the scandal of thought of the doctrine of the Trinity is not the scandal and folly of the gospel, but an "artificial scandal." What has been proclaimed by the Church since the fifth or sixth century as the mystery of the Trinity is a pseudo-mystery, an aberration of theological reflection from the biblical line. Therefore a theology which operates wholly from the biblical revelation has little sympathy for the doctrine of the Trinity.

Just how much, we may ask, is to be rejected on these grounds? To what extent does the classical doctrine go beyond the bounds of proper theology? Brunner makes it clear that he is not affirming a merely economic Trinity as against an immanent Trinity. The distinction he would make is not that of remaining in the historical and eschewing the eternal background: on the contrary, only when we know that Christ comes out of the mystery of God, out of the transcendence, do we know what and who he is. But he does emphatically renounce all doctrines of the inner-trinitarian relations of divine "persons," and also the classical formula

[7] Ibid., 237. (Eng. tr., 223f.).

una substantia tres personæ. The latter, he says, is to be suspected at once. "What place has the concept of *substantia* in a Christian theology?" [8] It denies the basic concept of revelation that God is known only as Lord and makes him a neutral object of speculation. This is a philosophical and speculative intrusion into the area of theology. Similarly, the concept of "Three Persons" is to be suspected because of its tritheistic suggestions. The transformation of the revealed truth that the Lord God reveals himself as Father through the Son, into a triunity of persons, is a construction of speculative thought which ought to be rejected.

The primary sin of orthodoxy, however, which is evident in this formula, is the substitution of the concept of *Nebeneinander* for the biblical message of the *Hintereinander* of Father, Son and Spirit. The Bible always maintains the order of successiveness of Father, Son and Spirit, and when the ecclesiastical definitions speak of the triune God they depart from this order. Brunner makes it clear that he does not mean to uphold a notion of *historical* successiveness—that is Sabellianism and surely to be rejected. He means the successiveness or order which is given with the movement of the divine self-communication, the *order* of Father through Son to Spirit, so that through the Spirit we have the Son and through the Son we have the Father.[9] We are bound to assert the preëxistence and eternity of the Son, i.e. that the revelation is truly from the mystery and transcendence of God, *but* "This assertion should be the *last* point of this movement." [10] Beyond this point we pass into interest in inner-trinitarian relations and place the three names as Persons beside one another, and in so doing we pass into speculation which is improper for truly biblical theology.

[8] Ibid., 240. (Eng. tr., 227.)

[9] Ibid., 236–238, 229, *et passim.*

[10] Ibid., 238. (Eng. tr., 225.) "We have the Father *through* the Son, *in* the Son: but we should not have the Father beside (*neben*) the Son and the Son beside the Father." The latter is a "logical mystery," a construction of thought to be rejected (241). It may be noted here that the classical doctrine of the co-existence is not adequately expressed by the term *Nebeneinander,* but (especially in view of the doctrine of Coinherence) *ought to be expressed also by the terms* Miteinander *and* Ineinander.

3) We have suggested that there are strong overtones of primitivism here. This is not simply a testing of doctrine by the New Testament, but a rigid limiting of the doctrines to be preached to those explicitly stated in the *kerygma*—this is an arbitrary business, as all primitivism is arbitrary. The *kerygma* cannot be so easily separated from theological reflection, for it includes such reflection. Also, the tone of the diatribe against theological "speculation" recalls the attitude of Ritschl. But beyond these aspects of Brunner's thought, there appears to be a more far-reaching reason for the rejection of the traditional formulæ of Trinity. It is to be seen in Brunner's association of the mystery of God with the doctrine that the Father is the "principle" or source of Godhead. Christ is truly the revelation of God, of the essence *of* God, but this revelation does not exhaust the mystery of God.

But all that can be said about God, all that the Son can disclose to us of the Nature of God, still leaves a residue of mystery: something which can never be said; something unfathomably mysterious. Even the revealed God remains a hidden God, and he wills to be worshipped as the one Who is hidden and unfathomable. . . . *Pater est fons totius trinitatis.* The mystery of God stands at the beginning and at the end of revelation.[11]

Brunner's repeated emphasis, in this connection, on the *Hintereinander* and on the rule *Pater est fons totius trinitatis,* implies that the mystery of which he speaks is to be associated with God the Father, and therefore that it is the Father who is ultimately God. He means much more than (e.g.) St. Thomas, when the latter asserts that the Father is the *principle* of deity. Brunner can only be interpreted as meaning that while the Son is truly of the essence of God, of the Father, he is not revelatory of the *entirety* of that essence. The Son is not, as the scholastics would put it, an adequate image of the Father.

To be sure, Brunner insists that from the unity of Revealer and Revelation (which is emphasized by the doctrine of the Trinity)

---

[11] Ibid., 239. (Eng. tr., 225f.)

we are to understand that God the Father is actually as he reveals himself in Christ. The love of Jesus is the love of God and reveals that God is love. But at once this affirmation is seriously qualified in relation to the distinction between Father and Son, which is to be understood in the sense of *Hintereinander*, and is directly related to the concepts of the hiddenness of God and God's wrath. God is revealed in Christ as Word, light, love, etc., and we know in Christ that this is God's own work. But there is also in God a "strange work," which is God's holiness working as wrath. As wrathful, God is not present in Jesus, but outside Jesus; the God whom we have in unbelief, outside of Christ, is the wrathful God. There is thus a double sphere of God's activity; the sphere in which he is revealed in Christ, and the sphere in which he is other, wrathful. These two spheres, Brunner insists, are actual, and "God is actual in both spheres, as loving in one, as angry in the other." [12] Why must this be the case? Because otherwise neither salvation nor lostness would have reality or seriousness. Brunner summarizes the point thus:

There are therefore works of God, which are not works of the Son. This non-identity of God and Son is grounded in this, that God alone is the creator, the Son however is called simply and solely the mediator of the creation. . . . God *gives* to the Son divinity from eternity, as he is the Father, who sends the Son as the reconciler of the world. This subordinationism, which does not abolish the *homoousios*, is inseparable from the Biblical witness and thought. God determines himself in freedom in the Son, in fellowship and love: therein he has also the freedom, where the Son is not received, to determine his holiness as wrath and . . . to work condemnation. This freedom of God, to work salvation and damnation . . . life and death, is the unfathomable mystery of God, which remains in the revelation of the Son. The mystery of God is not dispelled by the Son; for *pater est fons totius trinitatis*. God *can* be other than he revealed in Jesus as light and life, namely the hidden God, who as such does not work in the Word and his light, but in Not-word, in non-acknowledgment, in dark-

---

[12] Ibid., 245. (Eng. tr., 231.)

ness. This is that bare God, who does not veil himself in the form of the son of man, the terrible majesty, which is unbearable to all creatures.[13]

Several things are evident from this passage. When Brunner speaks of "God" he means the Father, who can be loving or who can be wrathful, and who is the locus of divine mystery and hiddenness. Obviously, Brunner can have nothing to do with the "rule" *opera trinitatis ad extra indivisa sunt:* for him "there are works of the Father, which are most certainly not works of the Son. The scriptures never speak of the wrathful work of Christ, but only of the wrath of God." It is not by the Son that Pilate is given power to put Christ to death, but by the Father; and it is the Father who stokes the eternal fires.[14]

At this point the consequences of Brunner's argument are exposed: redemption is the work of God as Son, damnation is the work of God as Father. It is hard to escape the conclusion that Brunner is moving back toward Protestant scholasticism with its sharp distinction of moral nature between the Persons of the Trinity. For Brunner the contrast between wrath and love is clearly a distinction in the nature of God himself. He calls it a "dialectic" between the wrath and compassion of God, "between the holiness which is identical with love, and the holiness which stands in contrast to it as the wrath of God." [15] This "dialectic" is necessary, he thinks, if we are to avoid either the Calvinistic doctrine of double election or universalism, and it is therefore important to an adequate doctrine of election as well as to a proper representation of the biblical differentiation between the work which the Father does in the Son and that which he does outside the Son.

[13] Ibid., 247. (Eng. tr., 232.)   [14] Ibid., 249. (Eng. tr., 234.)
[15] Ibid., 250. (Eng. tr., 234.) The defense of this dialectic from the standpoint of the problem of election and predestination, as well as Brunner's later discussion of that problem (Chs. 22, 23), shows clearly an anthropocentric orientation of his thought. For him, the primary point of reference is not the fulness of revelation and reconciliation in Christ, but the absolute seriousness of man's faith-decision.

It seems fair to conclude that Brunner does not really wish to affirm the classical doctrine of Trinity. He finds value in it as "defensive doctrine" because the doctrine of *homoousios* asserts the truth of the revelation of God's love in Christ, and because the distinction of Son from Father can be used to support the distinction between God's love and his wrath. That is, the doctrine can be used for the latter purpose when the concept of *Nebeneinander* is given up for *Hintereinander*. But here the position breaks down, for in this sharp subordination of Son to Father, the fulness of revelation is at once called into question. Brunner says this is not such a subordination as to destroy the *homoousios*—but, we may surely ask, how is it possible to use the term *homoousios* when the Son can be said to represent only a portion of the essence of God? The Son is for Brunner only that aspect of God which is love, revelation, reconciliation—he is not equal to the Father insofar as to the Father alone belong the mystery and the wrath. The Father here is not only the "source" of the Trinity, but in truth is himself alone God. Though the Father chooses to define himself as love in the Son, he remains outside this self-definition. He is free to define himself otherwise, where the Son is not received, i.e. where he is not known in his revelation. The distinction between Revealer and Revelation, therefore, means that as Father God can *be* other than as he has shown himself in the Son. Then the revelation is not truly adequate to his nature.

We may concur, of course, in saying that God remains mystery in his revelation, but it must not be said this way. Certainly we cannot parcel out God's mystery and his revelation, his wrath and his love among the "Persons" of the Trinity in this way without introducing a sort of subordinationism worse in its way than Arianism. For the Arians (at least the Semi-Arians) were willing to say that the Son was in all things *like* the Father. But Brunner appears to be saying that while the Son is of the essence of the Father, he is *not* in *all* respects *like* the father.[16]

[16] In support of his distinction between the works of Father and Son, Brunner appeals to the "Augustinian qualification" of the rule of the indivisibility of the work of the Trinity (*de Trin.*, I, 4). (Cf. *Dogmatik*, 249; Eng. tr., 234.) But this passage will not bear in any way the sort of con-

Given this understanding of Brunner's use of the doctrine of the Trinity, we are forced to ask whether he takes seriously his assertions that the *problem* of the doctrine really arises in the biblical *kerygma*. The problem of what doctrine? Apparently only a doctrine which asserts the divinity of Christ and recognizes some distinction between Revealer and Revelation. But here the halt is called. We are not to inquire further into the transcendent background, nor to ask further about the relation of Son and Spirit to the Father or to each other, nor to raise the question of the coexistence of Father, Son and Spirit. This limitation, however, implies that God-in-himself might actually be other than God-in-revelation. This is the same problem which is presented in modalism, and it is precisely the latter which the doctrine of the Trinity has historically denied.

Brunner, then, must be classed with the others treated above as an example of the difficulty and embarrassment which the doctrine of the Trinity occasions for contemporary theology. This embarrassment is mainly a characteristic of "liberal" theology, but by no means entirely so, as shown in the case of Brunner. The persistence of the difficulty is shown in the tendency even of those who would dispense with the doctrine to find in it a germ of religious value and truth. It is shown in the variety of methods which are used to conserve the doctrine, while yet relegating it to a clearly subordinate place in the scheme of doctrine. In general, we have to say that in all those types of thought, Schleiermacher's judgment is substantially reaffirmed: the doctrine of the Trinity is not a primary affirmation of faith, but secondary and dependent—though some here would allow it a relatively more important place than he did. It is also characteristic of these views that they assume the validity of Schleiermacher's contention that the doctrine is a "combination of utterances" rather than a direct

---

struction which Brunner wishes. Augustine only says that because of the relation of Son to Father, it was appropriate that the Son should become Incarnate, and that neither Father nor Spirit can be said to be Incarnate, etc. This does not imply that Father and Spirit are not equally at work with the Son in redemption, and conversely that Son and Spirit are not equally at work with the Father in creation and judgment.

utterance of the Christian consciousness. We shall have more to say about this latter assumption and further criticism of this whole subordination of the doctrine (cf. esp. Ch. VII). For the present, we must turn to another sort of approach to the doctrine of the Trinity, which also is basically a continuation of a nineteenth-century pattern of thought, though it seeks to give a much more central place to the doctrine.

CHAPTER III

Philosophical Trinitarianism

There is really no line of thought in the contemporary period which can be said to be a *direct* continuation of the philosophical trinitarianism of Hegel and his disciples. The sort of alliance between theology and philosophy which was envisaged by both German and British idealism in the nineteenth century has been effectively dissolved, on the one hand by the contemporary repudiation of idealism in philosophy, and on the other by a theology which was not content to remain the servant of philosophy. Even the sort of philosophical defense of the doctrine of the Trinity which we saw to be characteristic of the rise of the social theory of the Godhead,[1] seems to have been abandoned, though, as we shall see in the next chapter, this type of argument has found considerable favor in contemporary fundamentalist and conservative theology.

It is possible, of course, to find some efforts to fit the notion of Trinity into essentially philosophical analyses of the nature of God. Charles Hartshorne, for example, finds in the trinitarian idea a certain correspondence to his philosophical description of God. The three elements in his conception of God (Reflexive Transcendence, absolute perfection or unsurpassibility, and relative perfection or surpassibility), he thinks correspond "in a manner" to the traditional understanding of Father, Son and Spirit, as regards their equality and relation. But, as Hartshorne points out, these elements in his system are not at all "persons." There are, in his view, many "persons" in God in the sense that the self-states of God in the temporal series are distinct (and unequal, each being superior to its predecessor). From the purely logical

---

[1] I.e., the argument that plurality of persons is necessary to protect the personality of God and his independence from the world. See Ch. I, § 4, above. Cf. however, E. L. Mascall, *He Who Is*, 186; F. R. Tennant, *Phil. Theol.*, II, 167f., and esp. L. Thornton, *The Incarnate Lord*, 396 (see below).

and philosophical point of view, then, the notion of Trinity is more intelligible than the supposedly rational concept of God as sheer unity without inner distinction—however, as Hartshorne recognizes, this "correspondence" does not constitute a justification of, or really reflect, the idea of the Triune God in anything resembling its classical forms.[2]

The chief heir to nineteenth-century philosophical trinitarianism, however, is not to be found in incidental efforts to bring the trinitarian concept into relation to an altogether independently established conception of God, but rather in a way of thinking which emphasizes the philosophical usefulness of the doctrine as an added justification or validation. One may detect in certain quarters a pronounced unwillingness to rest the case for the doctrine of the Trinity on the grounds of revelation or religious experience alone, and a strong interest, therefore, in justifying (and defining) the doctrine on other grounds. This is an *additional* argument in the sense that the doctrine is admittedly rooted in revelation, but the additional philosophical validation often appears to be of such importance as to be crucial for the acceptance of the doctrine. If this be the case, then regardless of its origin, the doctrine must be said to be essentially a doctrine of natural or philosophical theology—and if that is so, then we are not so very far (formally at least) from the nineteenth-century efforts to absorb theology into philosophy.

1. *The Trinity and Organic Philosophy*

This way of thinking is reflected in Fr. Lionel Thornton's Christological essay, *The Incarnate Lord*. To what extent, in the attempt to restate the doctrine of the Incarnation in relation to the categories of Whiteheadian philosophy, Thornton lets the philosophical categories become determinative of the content of the revelation it is not easy to say. Leonard Hodgson thinks it perfectly clear that Thornton does in no wise fall "into the temp-

[2] Charles Hartshorne, *Man's Vision of God*, 351f.

tation to assimilate the historic revelation to the demands of the philosophical system, as so many of the idealistic theologians had done."[1] I am not so sure. I do agree that Thornton does not *intend* to do this. He surely means to start with the revelation and sees the organic philosophy as serving it. But the question can be raised whether he really succeeds in escaping the danger of reversing the relation.

We may approach the problem in a preliminary way from some of Thornton's assertions regarding the general basis and justification of the doctrine. There can be no denying the importance of the passages in which he stresses the "revealed" character of the doctrine of the Trinity, i.e. its basis in the experience of the Christian community as recorded in the New Testament. We could never know except through revelation that "the actuality of God is differentiated in the Persons of the Trinity."[2] But once given, the revelation sheds light on "the whole structure of the universe and of history as apprehended by man through successive domains of experience."[3] Therefore it is possible and necessary to set Christ and the Spirit in their cosmic role, i.e. to translate the religious affirmations into "larger" terms of philosophical or metaphysical universality. To affirm the true deity of the Son and the Holy Spirit means for Thornton to conceive them in terms of cosmic significance and transcendent reality. Thus the evolution of the idea of the deity of Christ is equated with the progressive assignment of the Son to the New Creation, the First Creation and finally Transcendent Reality itself: and the failure of the early Church to affirm the full deity of the Holy Spirit is interpreted as a failure to work out the cosmic aspect of the Spirit's activity.

[1] L. Hodgson, *The Doctrine of the Trinity*, 228.
[2] Thornton, *The Incarnate Lord*, London, Longmans, Green (1928), 415. Cf. 315f.: "The principal foundation for our faith in the Incarnate Lord must always be the gospel revelation of the Son of God together with the apostolic experience of His redeeming activity." Also Ch. XI; Ch. XII, §§ 1, 3, 4; and Ch. XIII, § 1. The revelational basis of the doctrine is developed also in Thornton's article in *Essays Catholic and Critical* (ed. Selwyn), "The Christian Conception of God," 139ff.
[3] Ibid., 416.

The process of the development of the doctrine of the Trinity is therefore the process of conceiving the Persons in their cosmic function or metaphysical reality.[4]

The implication of this argument is that the categories of cosmic order are of greater significance and closer to the essence of deity than the more biblical categories of lordship, revelation, reconciliation, new creation, and sanctification. We need not raise the question at this point whether the exploration of the "cosmic" implications of the ideas of Father, Son and Spirit may not be a valuable and perhaps necessary enterprise. The crucial point is that the successful translation of the religious affirmations into cosmic categories is for Thornton an *essential* part (if not *the* essential part) of the *justification* of the doctrine of the Trinity as such:

If the doctrine of the Trinity is accepted as true, the rational justification of this acceptance cannot depend simply upon the correct interpretation of certain passages in the New Testament. For the value of such passages must depend upon the degree of divine guidance which we ascribe to their authors; and this consideration compels us to fall back upon much wider grounds of acceptance.

The doctrine of the Trinity is the ultimate differentiation of the Christian conception of God from other theistic systems of thought and from other forms of religious monotheism. Its *ultimate rational justification*, therefore, insofar as such a thing is possible at all, can only take the form of showing, or seeking to show, that it includes, guarantees and illuminates all positive elements of truth concerning the principle of individuality, disclosed within the cumulative wholes of man's spiritual experience.[5]

In the latter passage, Thornton guards himself against asserting absolutely the possibility of an *ultimate* philosophical justification of the doctrine, and he has also emphasized that "the rational justification for accepting this doctrine can only appear in its full

---

[4] Cf. esp. Ch. XII, § 2 (329ff.); Ch. XI, and Ch. XIV. The main intention of the book is of course to effect such a translation with respect to the Incarnation.

[5] Ibid., 380, 381. (Italics mine.)

force *within the order of experience which the biblical revelation itself created*, that is to say within the New Order of the Spirit." [6] Even this, however, permits us to conclude not only that the philosophical grounds are a necessary supplement to the witness of Christian experience, but that the former have some independent validity.

The tendency to assimilate the testimony of revelation to the demands of the metaphysical system appears more unambiguously in Thornton's discussion of the *form* of the doctrine, particularly in his argument for the necessity of using both the psychological and social analogies for the Trinity. Here again we must note that Thornton seeks in detail to show that both analogies are rooted in the New Testament—the psychological in the interpretation of Christ as the glorified Son of Man and the Johannine logos theology, the social in the synoptic and Johannine idea of Christ's sonship to the Father. *However*, "For those who accept the biblical revelation of God as a revelation of Ultimate reality, . . . it must inevitably follow that absolute individuality in God is regarded as the eternal archetype, ground and end of the finite principle of individuality in all its significant aspects." [7] On the basis of this perspective, Thornton elaborates (in Ch. XIV primarily) what seems to be a parallel argument for the necessity of both analogies, from the viewpoint of metaphysical adequacy.

This argument takes the form of an attempt to show the inadequacies of the alternatives of modalism and tritheism. Modalism [8] is to be rejected partly because it violates the New Testament record of Christian experience, but that conflict is *not* for Thornton the major difficulty. "There is," he insists, "much more involved in the issues raised by modalism than the bare fact of its conflict with New Testament experience. It actually weakens the

---

[6] Ibid., 379.

[7] Ibid., 378f. We shall return to Thornton's biblical analysis in Ch. V, and I therefore omit any detailed statement of it here.

[8] Thornton does not define modalism. Sometimes he equates it with a purely economic view of the Trinity, i.e. one in which the Persons are regarded as "no more than modes through which an undifferentiated deity is manifested" (389). But also he seems to apply the condemnation to all views which deny that Father, Son and Spirit are *persons*.

religious conception of individuality in God." [9] All religion is concerned to portray God as having concrete character, i.e. to draw the analogy between absolute and finite individuality. Such use of analogy is of the "very life-blood" of all religion, and the error of modalism is its refusal to apply the analogy in thorough-going fashion. It inconsistently selects only one aspect of individuality (viz. unity) to apply to God, whereas "at every stage in its manifestation the created principle of finite individuality is seen to have two aspects, unity and plurality. It moves steadily towards higher forms of unity. But at no stage in the organic series is the aspect of plurality eliminated." [10]

In the first instance, therefore, the objection to a modalist interpretation of the Trinity is drawn from the entire range of our experience of the principle of finite individuality. The argument may be summarized: modalism seeks to be an interpretation of monotheism; monotheism, if it is not to pass over into an absolute monism which relegates all plurality to appearance, must attribute "absolute individuality" to God; but if this is done consistently, then both unity and plurality must be included in the analogy, and modalism therefore be rejected as inadequate.

Thornton does go on, to be sure, to show how he believes modalism to violate the specific domain of religious experience, especially as found in the Hebrew-Christian tradition. The monotheism of the Old Testament is crowned by the New Testament revelation of the social aspect of individuality as belonging to God's eternal reality. But it is significant that the primary weight of the argument falls on the first, more general domain of experience. Furthermore, Thornton holds, modalism runs afoul of difficulties regarding the problem of creation, for

Creation, as a religious conception, involves the idea of a self-giving of God to His creatures . . . if then the idea of self-giving is essential to Christian theism, the principle of self-giving must find its eternal expression in the life of God. This is precisely what the doctrine of the Trinity secures when it is understood to mean "hypostatic" distinctions and "personal" relations within the God-

[9] Ibid., 389.   [10] Ibid., 390.

head. But if the Trinity be understood in a purely economic sense, so that the distinctions correspond only to aspects of God manifested in His activities of creation, revelation, inspiration or the like, then there are no eternal relations of self-giving within the divine life of Absolute Actuality. Thus the principle of self-giving in God, which is acknowledged to be essential, can find expression only *ad extra*, in relations with creation. But this is to make creation necessary to God, in the sense that the full actuality of God's life is incomplete apart from creation. This is to place God under a necessity *external to himself*.[11]

That is, unless there is a subject-object relation within God, then the creation is the necessary object of the divine love and activity. But this would mean that God is something less than the eternal order, which is utterly transcendent. Or, if God is to some extent transcendent over creation, then the object of his love and self-giving is less than himself, and it follows either that self-giving is not basic to the divine life, or that it never finds adequate expression—which would mean that something is lacking from the fulness of the life of God. Therefore, Thornton concludes, modalism is to be rejected as involving the denial either of God's self-giving nature, or of his ultimate reality.

We are not concerned at this point to assess the validity of this sort of argument, but rather to indicate the importance which Thornton attaches to it. It is significant that this is precisely the same kind of argument which was developed in the late nineteenth century by Illingworth and Richmond, in the attempt to defend the personality of God against the attacks of the idealism of Bradley and Bosanquet.[12] Both the argument from the nature of finite individuality and the argument from the problem of creation are characteristic of the effort to incorporate the doctrine of the Trinity into a general program of philosophical theism. Thornton apparently believes that these contentions can stand on their

[11] Ibid., 396.
[12] See above, Ch. I, § 4. Criticism of the social analogy will appear in Chs. V and VIII. As far as this particular sort of argument is concerned, Tennant's comment seems to me to the point: "obviously unless Trinitarianism becomes tritheism it cannot make use of such speculative support." (*Philosophical Theology*, II, 170.)

own feet (with only a little support from general religious experience and the affirmation that God is love) and that they are decisive. Both require that the doctrine of the Trinity be understood to affirm a genuine plurality of persons in God.

Thornton is less confident of the ability of reason to apply the analogy from finite individuality in such manner as to avoid tritheistic suggestions. He attempts to show that the plurality of *individuals* and the externality of relation of persons in human society does not invalidate the analogy whereby God is said to be one individual. It is, says Thornton, the conditions of "organic externality," of finitude, and of imperfection which result in the externality of human personal relations—whereas in God none of these conditions are present, and there can be perfect interpenetration of persons within one absolute individuality. The difficulties presented to reason in this aspect of the analogy are so formidable, Thornton avers, that it can be applied *fully* and with confident assurance only within "the illuminating context of the new fellowship in Christ," where the problems of attaining perfect mutuality and interpenetration "have been in principle, already solved." [13]

In sum, Thornton holds that fundamental arguments against both the modalist and the tritheistic interpretations of the Trinity can be drawn from "much wider grounds" than the mere record of New Testament experience. The important point for our present purposes is that he appears to believe these more general considerations to be essential both for the acceptance and the understanding of the doctrine. Since Thornton sees no conflict between the implications of the New Testament evidence and the analogy from the general experience of finite individuality, the question whether we can speak of his assimilating the revelation to the demands of the metaphysical system depends upon the validity of his analysis of the biblical witness—viz. his view that the witness of the New Testament implies a plurality (fellowship) of *persons* in God. We shall seek to show at a later point that this understanding of the New Testament witness is in fact in error—and if

[13] Ibid., 413. Cf. 407ff.

this can be shown, then it can be affirmed that Thornton is indeed involved in the subordination of the revelation to the philosophical system. This contention is supported by the fact, already noted, that the interpretation of the Trinity as a society of persons arose partly if not primarily out of the demands of idealistic philosophy.

But even apart from this problem of the form of the doctrine, while Thornton speaks frequently of the general analogy as only *confirming* the revelation, it seems that his primary interest is in setting the New Testament evidence in the "larger" context, and that on the successful performance of this task, the validity of the revelation is ultimately dependent. That is, it is the conformity of the New Testament witness to the Triunity of God with the evidence of our total experience of finite individuality which justifies our acceptance of the former. The point may be illustrated by contrast with Augustine's development of the psychological analogy. The analogies which Augustine draws from the finite self (in Bks. IX–XV of *de Trinitate*) are offered for the sake of illustrating a doctrine of Trinity already formulated, and are judged on the basis of their conformity or lack of conformity to that concept. For Thornton, however, the analogy from finite individuality is a positive and necessary factor in the defense of the trinitarian concept and in the determination of its form. It is argued that since God is the "eternal archetype, ground and end" of finite being, his individuality must include all the significant aspects of the highest level of finite individuality, i.e. both the plurality and the unity. With this, the development of the analogy tends to pass over into a supplementary and relatively independent validation and formulation of the doctrine.

2. *The Trinity and Artistic Experience*

In sharp contrast to Thornton's insistence on the pluralistic aspects of God's nature and his understanding of the Trinity as a fellowship of persons, stands Miss Dorothy Sayers' extraordinarily interesting study, *The Mind of the Maker*. Miss Sayers, too, endeavors to work out in detail an analogy for the Trinity in finite being but she finds the analogy exclusively in the *single* human self. Moreover, in the course of the analysis, her argument also goes significantly beyond an (Augustinian) attempt to find an analogy for the divine Triunity and becomes an argument from the trinitarianism of finite creativity to a Divine Trinity.

Since the characteristic common to God and man may be viewed as the ability and desire to make or create things, Miss Sayers proposes to consult the human maker who comes closest to making something out of nothing, viz. the creative artist (and in this case the literary artist, since she herself is a writer). On the basis of her experience and understanding of the process of human creativity, she suggests that there is no reason for considering the Trinity as obscure or remote from human experience. On the contrary, it is likely that "the Trinitarian structure of activity is mysterious to us just because it is universal." [1] The crux of the argument is that

every work (or *act*) of creation is three-fold, an earthly trinity to match the heavenly.
First, (*not in time, but merely in order of enumeration*) there is the Creative Idea, passionless, timeless, beholding the whole work complete at once, and the end in the beginning: and this is the image of the Father.
Second, there is the Creative Energy (or Activity) begotten of that idea, working in time from the beginning to the end, with sweat and passion, being incarnate in the bonds of matter: and this is the image of the Word.
Third, there is the Creative Power, the meaning of the work and its response in the lively soul: and this is the image of the indwelling Spirit.
And these three are one, each equally in itself the whole work, whereof none can exist without other: and this is the image of the Trinity. [2]

These things are not simply present in the material production, the book: they are in and *are* the mind of the writer. By *Creative Idea*, Miss Sayers means that pattern of the entire work, which

[1] From *The Mind of the Maker*, copyright 1942 by Dorothy L. Sayers, 27.
[2] Ibid., 28.

enters space and time and is actually known to the author only as expressed in Creative Energy. But the expression in space and time reveals an idea or pattern which is prior (not temporally, of course) and which is seen as a complete and timeless whole. *Creative Activity* is the creator in the common sense of the word, it is the sum total of the activity which brings a book into actual existence in space and time—"something distinct from the Idea itself, though it is the only thing that can make the Idea known to itself or to others, and yet is . . . (ideally) essentially identical with the Idea." [3] That is, the Activity is consubstantial with the Idea. The *Creative Power* proceeds from both Idea and Energy as that which returns to the author from his activity and produces a response in him, and which also communicates the activity to other readers. It is that by which they see the book as a whole and as a process and react to it. These three are of course inseparable. Each is the complete book, yet in a complete book all exist together. That is, they can be distinguished but not separated: the Idea is known by Power interpreting Activity, Activity by its revelation of Idea in Power, and Power as it reveals the Idea in Activity. It is important to add that all this may be complete in the author's imagination, i.e. without any material creation, though there may be an urgent desire for material manifestation. This guards the analogy against any confusion of creation with the Word: creation is the material manifestation in which there is reproduced the Trinity of Idea, Activity and Power which is in (or *is*) the author's mind.

In terms of the writer's communication to the reader, we may discern a sort of economic trinity. A book is threefold to the reader: the latter is aware of the book as Idea, as thought in the author's mind, but this is known only by the Incarnation of Word or Activity (the image of the Idea) in the book as written; finally the book is known as read, i.e. in the Power of its effect and the response it calls forth. [4]

---

[3] Ibid., 30.
[4] Cf. ibid., 88ff. Miss Sayers sees that the difficulty of understanding the Power is much like the difficulty of analyzing the Holy Spirit, because "our

Given this understanding of human creative activity, two sorts of consequences follow. The first consists in the implications for human life. If this triunity is in fact the very structure of the creative mind, then it follows that creative art is successful to the extent that it maintains the proper pattern of Idea, Activity and Power. But perhaps more important, this analysis of the structure of mind suggests the necessity of a creative approach to the problems of human life in general. The "problem solving" view of life is meaningless when applied to the creative act, and if it be true that the mind is essentially creative, practical problems ought to be handled as a writer deals with the material of a book—he takes them and uses them "to *make a new thing.*" It is this aspect of the consequences of the trinitarian nature of creativity which in the first instance lends weight to Miss Sayers' introductory discussion of the creeds as expressions of laws of nature, i.e. as "statements of fact about the universe as we know it." [5] The words of the Athanasian Creed regarding the Trinity "which except a man believe faithfully, he cannot be saved" are thus wholly intelligible. If the trinitarian understanding of creative mind is correct, then it is indeed the case that whoever does not faithfully believe this is flouting a law of the nature of the universe, not simply an arbitrary edict, and therefore "cannot be saved."

We are not concerned here to pass judgment upon the validity of this analysis of human creative activity—certainly not on its application to literary art, though even a layman may be permitted to discern suggestions of profound importance and usefulness in the application of the creative outlook to the ordinary problems of life. What is more relevant to our argument is the second consequence which Miss Sayers apparently draws from her analysis, namely, the implication that from the trinitarian structure of finite creative mind we are justified in arguing to the Trinity of God.

---

own perception of the thing is precisely what we are trying to perceive."
"We cannot really look at the movement of the Spirit, just because it is the
Power by which we do the looking" (91).
  [5] Ibid., 14. Cf. 146ff.

The implication is that we find the threefold structure in ourselves (the Book-as-Read) because that is the actual structure of the universe (the Book-as-Written), and that it is in the universe because it is in God's Idea about the universe (the Book-As-Thought): further, that this structure is in God's Idea because it is the structure of God's mind.[6]

The artist's experience *proves* that the Trinitarian doctrine of Idea, Energy, Power is, quite literally, what it purports to be: a doctrine of the Creative Mind.[7]

Miss Sayers is far too acute and too much of an Augustinian in her view of the Trinity to be guilty of resting her argument for the doctrine wholly on the analogy. But she does affirm the validity of two different ways of approach. First, we may begin by analyzing the workings of the artist's mind and then compare our conclusions with the pronouncements of the creeds, with the result that we discover a difference only of phraseology, a difference of degree and quality only between the mind of the human maker and the Mind of his Maker. Or, second, we may analyze the creedal statements, then translate them into the terms of the artistic analogy. In either case, the correspondence can hardly be held to be accidental, and the doctrine itself is certainly not obscurantist or apriorist or without relation to our experience, for either the Church Fathers unconsciously portrayed God from a human model, in which case the notion of Trinity is taken directly from human experience, or else the doctrine "derives from a purely religious experience of God, as revealed in Christ and interpreted by abstract philosophic reasoning about the nature of the Absolute"—in which case this religious experience turns out to be (as shown in the analysis of the creative artist) no isolated phenomenon, but "the very grain of the spiritual universe." [8]

But in her concern to show the doctrine of the Trinity to be intelligible in terms of our experience, Miss Sayers seems to feel that, given the creedal statements and an understanding of artistic

---

[6] Ibid., 98.   [7] Ibid., 102. (Italics mine.)
[8] Ibid., 148, 149. Cf. 146ff. and 97ff., which are most significant for Miss Sayers' methodology.

creativity, it is relatively a matter of indifference whether we begin with the finite creative mind and argue to God analogically, or begin with the Creeds and discover the analogy in finite mind. For her own primarily practical purpose this may be a matter of little moment, but theologically it is of the greatest consequence, for it is not altogether clear precisely what is the doctrine of the Trinity of the Creeds. Miss Sayers accepts the Augustinian formulation in the Athanasian Creed as normative, and the psychological sort of analogy as obvious. But this interpretation would be rejected by many within her own communion (e.g. Lionel Thornton).

The basic difficulty which confronts all attempts to bring analogy to the defense of the doctrine of the Trinity is the question of what aspect of experience is to be chosen as the finite analogate. Unless we know already what the doctrine means, we have no way of determining which element of human experience can best serve as the basis for argument. Of course, we can affirm that the Trinity is a pure anthropomorphism, which means, as Miss Sayers says, that it is wholly *intelligible*, but this leaves us quite without any way of affirming that it is descriptive of God—unless we say that the anthropomorphic construction is validated by the implications of a revelation in Christ, in which case the revelation is returned to the position of ultimate criterion (and source), and the analogy selected to conform to it. It is therefore wholly necessary that we begin with what Miss Sayers calls the Book-as-Written—i.e. the "actual structure of the universe," or better, the Incarnation and the gift of the Holy Spirit which reveal to us the structure of God's mind or being—and from the vantage point of this revelation be able to see an analogy in the threefold structure of our own minds.

It is significant that we are unable to cite from contemporary literature any noteworthy example of a purely philosophical trinitarianism, that is, any argument for the trinitarian nature of God which claims to be independent of revelation. This means that not only has the Hegelian form of the doctrine been rejected by contemporary Christian thought, but also the Hegelian effort to make theology captive to philosophy. Nevertheless, the views sketched here do reflect something of that philosophical attitude. Father Thornton and Miss Sayers both appeal to their respective analogies not only for the purpose of illustration, but in an effort to reëstablish the validity of the doctrine. And we have seen that what begins as an attempt simply to *confirm* the revelation of the triune nature of God, passes very quickly into a relatively independent argument and thence into a determination of the content of the doctrine by the analogy—and with this, theology is once more subsumed under philosophy. *To the extent,* therefore, that these writers hold such an appeal to analogy to be necessary, or relatively independent of revelation, and determinative of the form and content of the doctrine, the question may be raised whether they do not in effect abandon the revelational base of trinitarianism—that is, whether they do not call into question both the adequacy and finality of the basis of the doctrine in revelation and Christian experience.

In justice to Miss Sayers and Father Thornton, it must be recognized that they both do explicitly affirm the revelational basis for the doctrine, therefore we may for the present focus the problem somewhat differently. Insofar as they make good that affirmation, it is relevant to ask whether the "defense" of the Trinity from analogy is not (at the very least) premature, from the point of view of the contemporary theological situation. We have seen that the crucial question for contemporary theology is: What is the basis of the doctrine of the Trinity in revelation and faith, and further, how is the doctrine to be developed from that basis and what does the doctrine affirm? The fact that this problem does not seem very troublesome to Miss Sayers or Father Thornton may have something to do with the fact that they speak from the relatively conservative wing of the Anglican Church, which was not so deeply influenced by the radical questioning of the nineteenth century. But the problem is inescapable. Schleiermacher, Ritschl and Barth all bear testimony to the primacy of the problem of theological methodology and to the necessity of theological reconstruction on the basis of a new understanding of

revelation. This means that any analogical development or "justification" of the doctrine of the Trinity must wait upon a restatement of the root or basis of the doctrine in Christian faith.[9]

This point may be emphasized by playing Miss Sayers and
Father Thornton off against each other. Both find strong corroboration of the trinitarian concept in finite analogies, but the analogies are so different that it is hard to see how thay can be used to
defend the same concept of Trinity. The Trinity clearly means
for Miss Sayers a triunity within one Creative Mind, on the analogy of a *single* human person: for Father Thornton, however, the
analogy from finite individuality requires a *plurality* of persons
in God. The inference to be drawn from this contrast is that all
efforts to find finite analogies for the Trinity (whatever their
intent) must be subsequent to doctrinal reconstruction on the
basis of the specifically Christian experience of God. It is the
latter task with which some of the theologians discussed in Chapter II have tried to deal, though with doubtful success; and it is
this effort with which we shall be primarily concerned in subsequent chapters of this work. For this reason, it is impossible to
assess now the relative merits of Father Thornton's philosophical
analogy from the plurality of persons, or Miss Sayers' analogy
from the creative artist. We can pass judgment on such analogies
only after careful reconsideration of the revelation to which the
New Testament bears witness.

[9] Father Thornton, to be sure, does restate at some length what seems to
him the basis of the doctrine in the New Testament, and we shall say more
about this analysis at a later point.

CHAPTER IV

The Trinity in Authoritarian Christianity

1. Fundamentalist and Conservative Protestantism

It was suggested at the conclusion of our survey of nineteenth-century thought that the doctrine of the Trinity does not play any very live or central part in the thought of "conservative" Protestants. Yet it is unquestionably the case that those who rally to the banner of the infallible and inerrant scripture consider themselves defenders of the trinitarian faith. This doubleness of attitude can be seen, for example, in E. J. Carnell's *Introduction to Christian Apologetics*, which is sub-titled "A Philosophic Defense of the Trinitarian-theistic Faith." The reader might expect the trinitarian understanding of God to be central in such a work, yet the argument which is actually developed really gives very little attention to that doctrine.

Carnell asserts that the logical starting point, the highest principle or "over-all synthesizing element which unites the particulars," is for Christianity the Trinity.[1] But he gives only incidental indications of what this means: he rejects Aquinas' "empirical" proof for the existence of God because it does not prove the Trinity; and he asserts that "without the Trinity the problem of the one and the many cannot be solved," and that therefore the Trinity is necessary to a rational view of the universe.[2] But the latter point is mentioned only in passing and nowhere is it shown *how* the Trinity solves the problem of the one and the many. At another point, Carnell suggests that the biblical view of God as

---

[1] Op. cit., 124.   [2] Ibid., 130, 133f.

three persons in one essence gives us a personal God, hence one who can be the object of fellowship.[3] But apart from these few references, the trinitarian understanding of God does not figure in the discussion at all. What Carnell is really defending is the coherence and adequacy of the idea of a God who has given man an infallible revelation in the Bible. It is only by virtue of the belief that the Bible teaches a trinity of persons in God that Carnell is able to claim his work to be a defense of the "trinitarian-theistic" faith.

The first thing to be noted, then, is that fundamentalism is trinitarian primarily by virtue of its loyalty to the tradition (or what it believes to be the tradition). Orthodox Protestantism accepted the doctrine of the Trinity as one of the truths revealed in the Bible, and contemporary fundamentalism does likewise. While the fundamentalist would claim to be the true defender of the trinitarian faith, since he cannot conceive of the Trinity being defended on any view of the scriptures other than that of verbal inspiration, yet the Trinity is not at all the center of his interest. It is not central in his polemic against liberalism: there the argument revolves chiefly around the inspiration of the scriptures, the divinity of Christ, the "blood-atonement," and the Second Coming. Nor is the doctrine central in his "constructive" theology, for the essential outlines of the doctrine have long since been laid down and nothing has happened or could happen to require revision. Thus the systematic theologies of contemporary conservative Protestantism usually simply restate what was said about the Trinity in conservative nineteenth-century theology.[4]

On the other hand, it would be quite unfair to doubt the sincerity of conservative Protestantism's defense of the doctrine of the Trinity, or to imply that no positive approach to the doctrine can be found among conservative writers. Two works which attempt to deal systematically with the doctrine are worthy of

---

[3] Ibid., 181.
[4] Cf. for example H. Orton Wiley, *Christian Theology*, I, 394ff.; John T. Mueller, *Christian Dogmatics*, 149; Albert F. Gray, *Christian Theology*, I, 171–196.

special consideration, the more so because both show the influence of the late nineteenth-century development of the social theory of the Trinity—C. Norman Bartlett's *The Triune God*,[5] and John B. Champion's *Personality and the Trinity*.[6]

Both Bartlett and Champion accept the view that the Trinity is explicitly taught in the scriptures, which are the authentic and inspired revelation of God—though Champion finds the revelation of the Trinity given also in the process of redemption, the incarnation and Christ's death on the cross being "the clear and unmistakeable revelation of the Persons of the Trinity ministering in their holy offices to those receiving the Divine Redemption. . . . Since Jesus Christ is nothing less than the revelation of God in Person, He could not possibly be this without revealing that God is more than one Person." [7] With respect to the basis of the doctrine of the Trinity, it is evident that neither Champion nor Bartlett finds any real problem. The important facts about the Trinity of persons in God are clearly stated in scripture. The problem for them is one of understanding and appreciating the reasonableness and intelligibility of those facts, of explaining as adequately as possible the threeness and the oneness.

In the way in which Champion and Bartlett approach the latter problem, we begin to see the influence of Illingworth, Moberly and Richmond—to whom Champion appeals frequently. Champion insists that the problems of theology must be approached from the "adequate viewpoint" of "redeemed personality," though precisely what this means is not at all clear. Personality is defined as "*the highest conceivable form or type of life in correspondence or reciprocity with its counterpart or kindred environment which thus enables it to complete itself.*" [8] On the basis of this definition, Champion proceeds to show the necessity of tripersonality in God. It is, he says, "absolutely impossible" for only one person of a kind to exist in any order of personal life. God could not fulfill

---

[5] N. Y., The American Tract Society, 1937.
[6] N. Y., Fleming H. Revell, 1935. Champion cannot be as easily identified with fundamentalism as Bartlett, and takes more account of liberal and contemporary thought.
[7] Champion, op. cit., 33.   [8] Ibid., 51.

himself if he were only one person, for fulfilment is possible only in another. Unless God is social, then man surpasses him—and if he is social, then he contains more than one person. God cannot be personality if he is only one person, for a person cannot exist in isolation: "*a self-existent life* [person] *is a contradiction in terms.*" [9]

It should be evident that this understanding of personality as *essentially* complementary and inclusive, rather than exclusive,[10] becomes, for Champion, more than a means of understanding the triunity of three persons; it is also an argument for their necessity. The argument presupposes the personality of God, and the essential likeness of divine and human personality, as well as the notion that interdependence is the defining characteristic of human personality, though Champion nowhere examines the first two of these premises. The case also, of course, rests on the assumption that the scriptures clearly teach that Father, Son and Spirit are three distinct *persons*.

Bartlett offers a similar proof of the "necessitation" of the Trinity. This is divided into a number of different arguments: that a unipersonal God would tend to become depersonalized through relation to a mechanical universe, and that a God who deserves worship must have an object equal to himself as an adequate object for his satisfaction; that a God able to find full satisfaction in his own perfection would be infinitely egotistical, hence imperfect; that as infinite creative activity, God requires an "infinite foundation of inspiration external—in one sense at least— to Himself"; [11] that God's perfection requires him to seek and find infinite perfection to admire in another; that God could not know himself apart from fellowship with another being; that God could not be perfectly happy without another person to love; that his self-fulfilment requires self-sacrifice or effacement in and through another—and so forth. All these may be summed up in the general

Ibid., 103. Cf. 18, 33, 102, 218f.
[10] Here Champion goes beyond Illingworth and Moberly, who felt that exclusiveness was an essential characteristic of *finite* personality. Cf. Champion, op. cit., 105.
[11] Bartlett, op. cit., 55.

contention that God must possess all perfections, hence personality; personality requires personal qualities, therefore commerce between persons. The argument is predicated on a relatively uncritical use of analogy (really univocity, since it practically ignores the finite-infinite distinction), but Bartlett thinks it sufficient to show that theistic personalism inescapably involves plurality of persons in God.

We have seen that Bartlett and Champion assume the Trinity which is taught in the scriptures to be a trinity of *persons*. They are thus both violently opposed to "modalism" and to any use of the psychological analogy. *"True Trinitarianism,"* says Champion, *"is unalterably a Trinity of Persons."* [12] The real problem is therefore to show *how* the persons exist in absolute unity. Here the two writers take somewhat different lines. Champion denies any distinction between "person" and "personality": God could not be three persons and one personality; he is three personalities in triunity. The author seeks to avoid the tritheistic implications of this language by denying that self-consciousness is normal or central in personality: it is simply consciousness which is central. Self-consciousness as simple awareness of self is not normally habitual; habitual self-consciousness is evil and represents a diseased state of the self. God is therefore not self-conscious, but in him the three persons are other-conscious or inter-conscious.[13] All personality is co-personal, i.e. social as well as individual, and in God we find the highest form of the co-personal, the "inter-existent."

The Three Interpersonalities as infinite other-selves exist in corresponding interrelations, forever living in the perfect harmony of mutual interpenetration of interexistence. Each Divine Interpersonality is absolutely inseparable from the other Two, and has interconsciousness or other-consciousness rather than self-consciousness.[14]

[12] Op. cit., 227.
[13] Ibid., 177ff., 125. There is an apparent confusion here of self-consciousness with self-love or preoccupation with self.
[14] Ibid., 66f.

Whatever the precise meaning of this phraseology, it appears to rest on an extension of the notion of the interpenetration of personality which was exploited by Richmond and Illingworth. Champion finds further protection of the "social trinity" against the charge of tritheism in the assertion that the divine society is constitutional and beyond free choice. Man is social only voluntarily and can act contrary to his society, but "God does not choose to be God: He is God. He does not choose social unity: He is that unity to infinite degree." [15]

Bartlett, on the other hand, does draw a distinction between "person" and "personality"; God is three persons in one nature or personality. "Personality in God is the sum total of the infinite attributes resident in the inmost depths of His one divine nature; while the Persons in God are His threefold individuality, the three personal centers of consciousness, three separate self-conscious and self-determining persons or selves." [16] This is not tritheism, he asserts, for these persons share perfectly the common nature, in a manner analogous to the sharing of nature by three brothers. Of course, three human persons could never achieve perfect sharing of spirit, because of sin and finitude, but in perfection there are no barriers to unity.

The unity and trinity of God may perhaps be explained this way:

the distinction between substance and Persons in the Deity is the distinction between a more or less subconscious nature possessed in common, and three active Self-consciousnesses freely exerted and yet absolutely controlled by the power of this underlying nature subconsciously and yet irresistibly dominant.[17]

Here again the argument involves a thorough-going acceptance of the concept of the permeability of personality. Bartlett asserts that the whole trend of modern discovery is in the direction of enlarging the bounds of personality and of breaking down the walls of individuality, but offers no evidence for this except to assert that "even in ordinary experience we find that there is con-

[15] Ibid., 75.   [16] Bartlett, op. cit., 79f.   [17] Ibid., 81.

stant interpenetration of personality without any demolition of separate individuality." [18] Assuming, however, that this understanding of personality is valid, Bartlett is free to break new ground in the discussion of "the problem of a quadruple consciousness in each of the three centers of consciousness." [19] Here he offers some suggestions as to how each person of the Trinity experiences himself as living in the other two, how each person experiences the indwelling of the other two in himself, and how each person is aware of the distinction between his indwelling and his being indwelt.

In sum, the center of the problem of the doctrine of the Trinity, according to both Bartlett and Champion, is the explanation of how three persons can exist in one being. Though with substantial differences of terminology, both find the solution to this problem in a doctrine of infinite interpenetration or interexistence of personality, which in turn rests upon the denial that exclusiveness or individuality is an essential part of personality.

Apart from the question of the validity of this notion of personality, a prior question must be raised—whether the sort of development represented by Champion and Bartlett indicates a fundamentally constructive approach to the doctrine of the Trinity in terms relevant to the problem of the doctrine as we have outlined it in the preceding discussion. The answer to this question must be "no." In spite of their use of some of the conceptions developed by the British defenders of the "social Trinity," neither Bartlett nor Champion recognizes the necessity of any serious reconsideration of the basis or formal terminology of the doctrine. Both assume without question that the formula "three Persons in One God" means and has always meant three "persons" in the ordinary sense of the term. The belief that God is a Trinity of three persons is held to be based on the explicit teaching of the scriptures. This interpretation of the doctrine is further defended in terms of a Christology which may be suspected of too simple an identification of Jesus Christ as a "Divine Person." Thus Bartlett:

[18] Ibid., 87.   [19] Ibid., 92.

Jesus constantly referred to God as His Father, a Person distinct from Himself. He also promised to send the Comforter from the Father. How could Jesus pretend to be in relation with a God above, to be divine Himself, and to send the Holy Spirit as a third divine Person, if God were only one Person showing Himself in three different ways? [20]

Finally, in spite of the talk of "interexistence" or "interpenetration," it is hard to see how this version of the social Trinity can escape the charge of tritheism—especially when the distinction between Father and Son is directly equated with the distinction between Father and Jesus Christ, and the Persons are defined as "separate self-conscious and self-determining . . . selves" (Bartlett). One can only conclude that unless and until Conservative Protestantism is willing to undertake serious reconsideration of the basis of the doctrine of the Trinity in revelation and Christian experience, and therefore of its own theological method, there is little reason to expect from it any genuinely significant and productive restatement of the doctrine.

2. *Roman Catholicism* [1]

A. THE THEOLOGICAL PLACE OF THE DOCTRINE OF THE TRINITY

Roman Catholic theology provides an excellent illustration of the ultimate and pervasive importance of theological method for both the role and the form of the doctrine of the Trinity. Given the Catholic conception of revelation as the communication of an eternal deposit of truth, which is entrusted to the Church and which can be infallibly defined by the Church, and given the declaration of the Church that the fact of and the reason for the

---

[20] Bartlett, op. cit., 15. Cf. Champion, op. cit., 33 (quoted above).

[1] I make no pretense here to a full statement of the Catholic doctrine of the Trinity. It will be sufficient for our purposes to sketch only the main outlines of the doctrinal development and to place it in the perspective of the general problem of contemporary theology.

existence of Three Persons in one God are a part of the "immediate deposit of faith," [2] there cannot be for Catholic thought
any serious questioning of the validity and the essential form of
the doctrine of the Trinity. Therefore, it would be technically
improper to speak of any crucial decline or revival of theological
interest in a doctrine which is consistently maintained to be the
central article of faith.

But one may perhaps detect a renewed effort to make the doctrine more meaningful to the non-theological Catholic, i.e. to point
out its relevance to the rest of the faith and to the devotional life.
This is probably best illustrated in Klein's *The Doctrine of the
Trinity*,[3] which, although a fairly elaborate and complete statement of the doctrine, is nevertheless expressly aimed at encouraging popular devotion to the Trinity. Klein seeks to show that there
is no reason for the Christian to be silent about the Trinity because
of its mystery. The Trinity is a fact which can be grasped by all,
at least to the extent that we may properly worship the Persons,
and that we may understand the central place of the Trinity in
the liturgy and prayers of the Church. Similar, though less ambi-
tious, efforts are to be found in Richard Downey, *The Blessed
Trinity*,[4] Valentin M. Breton, *Trinité: histoire, doctrine, piété*,[5]
and John P. Arendzen, *The Holy Trinity*.[6]

It is quite unfair to say simply that the doctrine is recommended
to Catholics only by appeal to ecclesiastical authority, or that, as
William Adams Brown remarked, the Trinity is important to

[2] Joseph Pohle, *The Divine Trinity*; adapted and revised by A. Preuss,
3rd rev. ed., 9. (Hereafter referred to as "Pohle-Preuss.")
[3] Felix Klein, *The Doctrine of the Trinity*, N. Y., P. J. Kenedy & Sons
(publishers to the Holy Apostolic See), (1940) tr. by Daniel J. Sullivan, of
Le Dieu des chretiens, notre foi en la Trinité. Klein claims to see a definite
increase in the devotional importance of the doctrine. His work is designed
to increase further the number of those "who thoroughly understand the
preponderant, or rather the unique place which the Trinity holds in dogma,
in the liturgy, in the life of the spirit . . ." (p. 1).
[4] N. Y., Macmillan (1930). This essay is reprinted as Ch. IV of G. D. Smith
(ed.), *The Teaching of the Catholic Church* (I), N. Y., Macmillan (1949).
All page references to Downey refer to the latter work.
[5] Paris (?), Bloud et Gay (1931).   [6] London, Sheed and Ward (1939).

Catholics primarily because it expresses the mystical (and mysterious) conception of God which is characteristic of Catholic piety.[7] It is quite true, of course, that the doctrine has been defined as dogma and therefore must be believed, whether it is understood or not.[8] Nevertheless, in both popular and systematic expositions of the doctrine a serious effort is made to show that the doctrine is at every point truly rooted in scripture, that it is in no sense *contrary* to reason, and that the trinitarian understanding of the nature of God is intimately related to all the other essentials of the faith.

Theologically speaking, at least, the Catholic Church is committed to the view that "the essential characteristic which distinguishes Christianity from every other religion, even Judaism, is explicit belief in the Trinity." [9] R. Garrigou-Lagrange contrasts the attitude of the Church with the view of those Protestants who attribute to the concept of the Trinity only an indirect importance by virtue of its usefulness in guarding against contradiction in the more essential beliefs of Christianity:

On the contrary, in the eyes of the Church, if this single mystery is a safeguard against contradiction in the other mysteries, this is so because it is their supreme principle, the very center of the whole faith, having for its primary object the intimate life of God. If this supreme mystery were to become evident for us, as it is for the blessed in heaven, then all the other mysteries would be illumined from this sublime source. This mystery is the one toward which all the truths of the faith converge, the one toward which, in this mortal life. the saints in their contemplation aspire with increasing ardor. . . . [The revelation of the Trinity] confirms our natural knowledge of God and raises it to a higher plane by manifesting the infinite fecundity of the divine nature.[10]

[7] W. A. Brown, *Christian Theology in Outline*, 149.

[8] Cf. F. J. Sheed, *Theology and Sanity*, 88: "What we must realize is that success in finding answers to this and such like questions [about the inner nature of the Trinity] has a bearing upon our *understanding* of the doctrine of the Blessed Trinity, but none at all upon our *acceptance* of it."

[9] Klein, op. cit., 1.

[10] R. Garrigou-Lagrange, *God: His Existence and Nature*, II, St. Louis, B. Herder Book Co. (1936), 173f.

B. THE BASIS OF THE DOCTRINE

1) We have called attention to the view of the Church that the doctrine of the Trinity is a part of the immediate deposit of revealed truth which has been imparted by God to man. That deposit of truth is to be found in the first instance in the scriptures, which are held to be divinely inspired and therefore to contain infallible truths. It is not necessary for us to trace out in detail the Catholic view of the scriptural basis of the Trinity, but it is important to see something of the general pattern of the appeal to scripture, for this exemplifies the traditional mode of development. Klein's discussion is most helpful here. As is usual in Catholic treatises, Klein holds that the Trinity is suggested or foreshadowed in the Old Testament—in certain passages which directly imply a sort of plurality in God,[1] in the angel of Jehovah theophanies, in the Messianic portions of the prophets, and in the tendency toward hypostatization of the Spirit and Wisdom of God. It is recognized, of course, that the main emphasis of the Old Testament is on the unity of God, and that therefore the full force of these suggestions can be seen only in the light of the truth explicitly revealed in the New Testament.[2]

In treating the New Testament, which is held to be saturated with the thought of the three divine Persons, a division is commonly made between passages which treat of the Persons collectively and those which emphasize the divinity or distinctness of the Persons separately. The former are notably found at the beginning of Christ's earthly history (the Annunciation), at his baptism, at the Last Supper, at the first visit after the resurrection and in the last commission.[3] The latter passages are more numerous. Texts are cited in which "God is designated as the Father of Jesus in an entirely particular sense," thus teaching the literal divine sonship

---

[1] E.g. Gen. 1:26; 3:22; 11:7.

[2] Klein, op. cit., 50ff. Cf. Pohle-Preuss, op. cit., 1ff.

[3] Klein, 54ff. Cf. Downey. 116f.; Pohle-Preuss, 22ff., 43ff. Both Pohle-Pruess and Downey, especially the former, discuss the problem of the authenticity of the "Johannine comma" (1 Jn. 5:7) and are plainly disposed to reject it on textual grounds, though admitting its dogmatic authority.

and fatherhood, in which the Holy Spirit is referred to as a Person in the literal sense of the word (here, of course, the case rests heavily on the Paraclete sayings), and in which Jesus is specially revealed as the Son. The heart of the New Testament revelation of the Trinity is the teaching of Jesus—regarding himself, his real sonship and equality with the Father, the distinctness and procession of the Paraclete, etc. "We cannot emphasize too often that we gain our knowledge of the Trinity from Him [Jesus], and from Him alone." [4] Klein takes account of the objection that the important passages here are mainly from John by insisting that these sayings represent, "save for incorrigibly obdurate critics, a tradition close to the beginnings of Christianity," and also by extensive reference to corroborating passages from the other Gospels and from Acts and the Epistles.[5]

In sum, it is held that the essential elements of the doctrine of the Trinity are explicitly taught in the New Testament—the fact of the existence of three divine Persons, their equality, their distinctness, unity and *coinherence*, and their mutual relations as expressed in the doctrine of the immanent processions, generation and spiration—i.e., three Persons and two processions. All that the Councils have done is to give language of technical precision to the faith clearly expressed in scripture. It was necessary, to combat erroneous interpretations, that the Son should explicitly be declared to be consubstantial with the Father and that the Holy Ghost be said to proceed from the Son as well as from the Father—these and other technical matters of terminology were determined by the Councils, beginning with Nicea and Constantinople. But all of the essentials were present in the mind of the Church from the first. On the *fact* of the Trinity and the necessity of belief in it, there was from the beginning "no hesitation, no variation, either in practice or in teaching." [6] That faith which was from the first lived in all its exactness, in acts of worship and ado-

[4] Klein, 123. This means from Jesus' own words, not simply from the fact of the Incarnation.
[5] Ibid., 126f. Cf. 70ff.   [6] Ibid., 91.

ration, is most clearly and most completely stated in the Athanasian Creed, which may be taken as basic for any exposition of the Catholic doctrine of the Trinity.

2) The scriptural revelation is the primary and ultimate basis of the trinitarian dogma, but the elaboration of the doctrine rests also upon rational analogy. The fundamental meaning and terms of the doctrine of the Trinity may be regarded as definitely fixed by ecclesiastical and theological usage: they were chosen with extreme care in the language of the time, and must not be changed. The terms, however—and this is the task which occupies the bulk of Catholic treatises on the Trinity—"are susceptible of analysis, explanatory additions, deepening, and even, provided the essential meaning is in no way altered, to a certain degree capable of being adapted in successive ages to the mental habits and philosophical language of the time." [7] We shall see in the next section the particular importance of this possibility in relation to the meaning of the term "Person" in Catholic usage. For the present, however, it is important to note that while the Trinity may be referred to as an "absolute mystery," i.e. a mystery which is wholly indemonstrable, which can neither be discovered by reason nor an *adequate* idea of it be formulated by reason; nevertheless, reason can achieve "a very useful understanding" of the mystery, and it can offer auxiliary conceptions to aid in the perception of the precise nature of the mystery. We could never know this mystery apart from revelation, and reason can never seize it fully, but reason can penetrate it indefinitely, "always further without meeting any limits." [8]

Probably the most important aspect of this work of reason is the development of the analogy whereby it is asserted that the generation of the Son is by the mode of understanding, and the spiration of the Holy Ghost by the mode of will. This is the point at which St. Thomas begins his treatise on the Trinity, and may not unjustly be called the "Thomistic analogy," though it comes originally from Augustine's *de Trinitate*. Because of the impor-

---

[7] Ibid., 90. [8] Ibid., 4. Cf. Pohle-Preuss, 194f.

tance of the analogy in the concrete exposition of the doctrine of the Trinity, we may introduce it here as an at least supplementary basis of the doctrine as developed in Catholic theology.

The validity which is to be assigned to this analogy must be carefully defined. Klein first introduces it almost as if he were working out a rationalistic deduction of the necessity of Trinity in God: God is, and he must know himself truly, for it would be absurd to say that existent Absolute Being did not know itself. His idea of himself is true, a perfect, coexistent and adequate representation of himself. Yet his thought is distinct from himself. Thus he engenders "another self . . . the likeness of His substance, His true image, equal in all things to Himself, subsisting and living, like Himself," and interior to Himself.[9] And Klein sometimes speaks as if reason could by itself have an intimation of the Trinity from the necessity for Absolute Being to know and love itself; the dogma then "confirms, fixes, vivifies this true intuition of the human mind."[10] Yet he vigorously insists that we could never know the fact of generation and spiration in God except by revelation, and that this mystery can never be fully understood. The correlation of generation and spiration with the understanding and the will is *only* by way of analogy from the human soul.

This suggests the possibility of two ways in which the relationship between the roles of reason and revelation may be put. First, we may speak of a rational deduction of the necessity for absolute Being to know itself and love itself, but we can know only through revelation that this absolute knowledge and love constitute distinct subsistences in God. Or, second, we may refer simply to the (scriptural) revelation of the generation of the Son and the spiration of the Spirit and then seek an analogy in the human soul as the image of God. In either case, the correlation is only an analogy, but it is an exceedingly important one. It has a twofold basis: 1) in the scriptural terms Logos and Spirit, which suggest intellectual and volitional processes,[11] and 2) the Augustinian analogy

---

[9] Klein, op. cit., 117.   [10] Ibid., 193.

[11] Cf. Downey, op. cit., 126: "The second person is called the Logos, that is, the word or concept, something begotten by an intellectual process; whereas the third person is called the Holy Spirit. Here the term 'spirit,'

from the soul in terms of memory, understanding and will, an analogy which has been accepted by all the greatest minds of the Church, because it is "the closest image of the Trinity we have been able to find, and the one which helps us best to understand the generation of the Son especially." [12]

While, therefore, the beliefs that the generation of the Son is by the mode of understanding and that the spiration of the Spirit is by the mode of will are not articles of faith, they are sure theological conclusions rooted in scripture and tradition, and not to be denied without temerity. As Abbé Penido puts it, the analogy rests upon the faith of the centuries that there is an ontological similitude between the image of God in the soul and the Trinity. This is not a vulgar analogy or an anthropomorphism; it is, after metaphysical analysis, "an analogy of proper proportionality, able to compass formally the divine reality." [13] The method is psychological only in origin; we do not apply to God the concept of *human* word or angelic word, but "*the analogical notion of word as such.*" Therefore we may affirm that the analogy gives us *certain truth*, that this emanation of word and love in us represents the divine processions as they are. This is not the whole truth, of course, but we can claim for the analogy that minimum of objectivity which suffices to distinguish it from simple metaphor. Certainty applies here at least to the affirmation that there can be only two sorts of processions, and to the association of generation with the intellect and of spiration with the will. In more technical terms,

the so-called "psychological" theory is not a simple point of comparison, but a true metaphysical analogy—analogy of proper proportionality of the dynamic order, with a simply infinite distance between the two terms—compassing truly and formally, although

---

derived from the Latin *spirare*, to breathe, is used by analogy with the manner in which we draw a deep breath or sigh as expressive of the attraction of the will to some loved object."

[12] Klein, op. cit., 148. Cf. Garrigou-Lagrange, op. cit., 185.

[13] M. T.–L. Penido, *Le Rôle de l'Analogie en Theologie Dogmatique*, 300. This is a very precise work, worthy of careful attention.

imperfectly, the reality of the mystery of the Trinity, at least in certain points.[14]

C. THE "PERSONAL" DISTINCTIONS

It is hardly necessary to emphasize the fact that the terminology of the Catholic doctrine of the Trinity is definitely fixed, and not to be changed. The formula *"una substantia [natura, essentia] et tres personae"* is here to stay. But as Klein has suggested, reason may properly interpret and even adapt the terms to the different understandings of the ages. It is therefore proper for us to inquire what is intended by this formula, especially by the term *"persona"* or "Person."

We are told by Klein that a "person" is "an intelligent being which makes up, by itself alone, a complete and non-communicable whole; a being conscious and master of itself, which says *I* and *me*, which is aware of what flows from itself and what it receives from elsewhere. . . . Spontaneous and free in its actions, an independent centre of rights and responsibilities, . . ."[1] Downey's view is similar, and follows the traditional pattern of beginning with Boethius' definition, *"rationalis naturae individua substantia*—an individual substance of a rational nature." This is interpreted to involve three requisite qualifications for personality: 1) subsistence or substantiality, a "person is first and foremost a substance, that is, something which exists in itself, . . . and not something which merely inheres in something else"; 2) distinctness or "complete individuality, so that it is not in any sense part of, or common to, something else"; and 3) rationality. "By a person, then," he says, "we mean a distinct substance endowed with the faculty of reason."[2]

Of course, both Klein and Downey emphasize that we apply the term "person" to God only analogically. But the difference which is to be recognized in using the term with respect to God lies mainly in the relation of person to nature. That is, in God, plurality of persons does not mean plurality of natures; human

[14] Ibid., 311.
[1] Klein, op. cit., 9.   [2] Downey, op. cit., 112.

persons have only *like* natures, the divine persons have one nature in the numerical sense. Both Klein and Downey give the impression that there is no real difficulty in applying the term person to God, since we can readily state what a person is. The mystery lies in the difficulty of conceiving how the three divine persons can possess one nature which is simple and indivisible and possessed in entirety by each of the persons.

So far, it would appear that this view of the Trinity corresponds primarily to the "social" interpretation which we discussed earlier. This is especially suggested by the more popular definition of person offered by Klein. The transition from human person to divine person is felt to be fairly easy. The tendency toward a societal conception of the Trinity is seen also in the concept of the mutual love of Father and Son, and particularly in the assumption that Christian devotion and adoration are directed to the divine persons *severally*. While, says Klein, I can hardly understand how the three persons are still only one God, I have no difficulty conceiving the idea of the Father, and of the Son and of the Holy Ghost, and of acting "towards each one in my thoughts, feelings, and actions as I act towards God." Nor is there anything to prevent me from bowing before the Father, or approaching with gratitude and love the Son, or appealing within to the Holy Ghost.[3]

But along with these "pluralistic" suggestions must be put the whole emphasis on the analogy from the human soul, the "Thomistic analogy," and the definition of person as a distinct "subsisting relation." In the latter connection Catholic thought universally follows Augustine's contention that the *personæ* of the Trinity differ only by their relations to one another. This assertion is supplemented by the "law of the Trinity" (formulated by Anselm, and approved by the Council of Florence in 1439) that "in God all things are one except where there is opposition of relation."[4]

This second approach to the problem of the nature of the divine

---

[3] Klein, op. cit., 271. Cf. Chs. XIV, XV. Downey, op. cit., 135.
[4] Relations of opposition, as applied to God, means relations of origin.

persons is most clearly seen in Penido. Having concluded on the basis of detailed discussion of the divine processions and subsistent relations, that "in God there is intellectual and volitional emanation, ending in two terms, Word and Love, subsistent all together and relative; consubstantial in all perfections, but in all in which they are distinguished from each other, purely relative, because the substance unites and the relation divides," he *then* raises the question "three what?" [5] We reply, he says, three "persons," by which we mean that "the Father, the Son, and the Spirit appear to present some characteristics which correspond, when quite properly guarded, to our concept of personality." [6]

In order to guard the analogy, we must first understand the true concept of personality, and to do this, we must distinguish carefully *psychological* personality from *metaphysical* personality. Psychological personality refers to the empirical self, the personality subject to all the vicissitudes of empirical things and events, birth, development, change, etc.: it is the concrete "me-substance," independent in its being and action. *Metaphysical* personality is a *mode of being*; its concept synthesizes a series of perfections, signifying a nature which is substantial, individual and incommunicable, complete, subsistent, existing in itself and for itself, in full independence and liberty. Metaphysical personality is, as Aquinas puts it, individual intellectual substance. It is this rather than psychological personality which is the basis of the analogy to the divine persons. Note that what is stripped away from psychological personality here is essentially the element of self-consciousness, and perhaps even individual consciousness: "in reality, that which we affirm to exist analogically in God, is not an experiential [expérimentale] reality, it is a mode of existence, it is not a 'personal consciousness' [personne-conscience], it is a 'personal-being'." [7]

Together with this conclusion of Abbé Penido, we may put the rejection by Pohle-Preuss of Locke's definition of personality. Locke held "that personality is constituted by continued consciousness." But, argue Pohle-Preuss, "if consciousness were the

---

[5] Penido, op. cit., 323.   [6] Ibid., 323.   [7] Ibid., 333. Cf. 326ff.

only essential and formal note of personality, it would follow that where there is but one consciousness, there is but one person, whereas a double consciousness would constitute two persons, and so forth. Inasmuch as the Triune God has but one (absolute) consciousness, while Christ the Godman has two, Locke's theory would destroy both the Trinity and the uni-personality of Christ. . . ." [8]

In other words, the personality from which the analogy to the divine persons springs is to be understood strictly in the archaic sense of the term *persona*. Metaphysical personality is essentially distinctness, individual subsistence, incommunicability—*in a rational nature*. To have analogy instead of equivocation, says Penido, there must be maintained, in the midst of radical diversity, "a minimum of unity (proportional) of signification. That minimum here is substantiality and incommunicability: provided that the two notions prove themselves in an intellectual nature, there is personality." [9]

Penido is here striving (of necessity) to come to terms with Boethius' definition, which would appear to be more relevant to the social analogy for the Trinity. But notice how this definition is used by Penido (and Pohle-Preuss as well). He begins with the doctrine of the divine processions and the development of the "Thomistic analogy." Accordingly, Father, Son and Spirit are first and basically defined as "subsistent relations." (Whatever our final judgment on the precise meaning of this designation, it is certainly to be understood in the context of the psychological analogy.) Given this definition, an analogy is drawn between the divine "subsistent relations" and created personality, whereby

[8] Pohle-Preuss, op. cit., 226. So also F. Diekamp, *Kath. Dogmatik*, I, 1930, p. 271: "In God, just as there is *one* nature, so also there is *one* knowledge, *one* self-consciousness." (Quoted by Barth, *Doctrine of the Word of God*, 411). The explicit doctrine that self-consciousness was *the* characteristic of the divine persons was formulated among Catholic theologians by Anton Günther. He held that the persons of the Trinity were subjects willing and thinking independently, and joined in the unity of one absolute personality. (This was developed on the basis of the Hegelian thesis, antithesis, synthesis.) Günther's view was condemned by Pope Pius IX in 1859.

[9] Penido, op. cit., 323. Cf. 331, 337.

Father, Son and Spirit are said to be "persons." But this is a long way from the relatively simple analogy which Klein would have us draw on the basis of his original definition of "person." Furthermore, in utilizing the classical definition—an individual substance (or subsistence) of a rational nature—Penido associates *self-consciousness and consciousness with rational nature.* Thus he is saying, in effect, that Father, Son and Spirit are distinctions (relations, modes of existence) within one divine consciousness or self-consciousness. Penido uses the reference to "individual substance" only to show that the trinitarian distinctions pertain to the essence of God. He usually speaks of incommunicability, or distinctness, or separate *subsistence* (and especially subsistent relation) in defining the "persons."

Actually, it may be said that the Boethian concept does not harmonize well with the position which Catholic dogmatics has had to take in relation to modern conceptions of personality as self-consciousness, or with the definition of the Persons as subsistent relations. Thus Pohle-Preuss hold that "the Divine Persons consist in, and are constituted by, 'subsistent relations'" in God; i.e. in one substance or essence or nature (one consciousness, will and intellect). But following the classical statement, they must define *hypostasis* as "an individual substance, separate and distinct from all other substances of the same kind, possessing itself and all the parts, attributes, and energies which are in it," and *persona* as a rational *hypostasis*, a subject, self or ego of a rational nature.[10] In Boethius' case the definition is guarded against tritheistic implications by a strong philosophical realism, and the same purpose is served by contemporary assertions that consciousness belongs to one divine nature. But the double difficulty remains— 1) how one can say that "individual substances, separate and distinct . . ." are identical with subsistent relations in one essence or substance; and 2) how one can speak intelligibly of three persons, selfs or egos yet not say three self-consciousnesses. The latter can be done only in disregard of modern conceptions of the term person. Indeed, it is hard to see how we can escape formal contradiction when

[10] Pohle-Preuss, op. cit., 220, 222.

Boethius' definition is put alongside the assertion that "the terms 'essence,' 'substance,' and 'nature' are applied synonymously to God." [11] We should then have to say that *una substantia tres personae* means three substances (or essences or natures) in one substance (or essence or nature). The scholastics, of course, felt this difficulty, and interpreted the *substantia* in Boethius' definition as meaning *subsistentia*.

This difficulty is probably at the root of the apparent divergence between popular and technical Catholic formulations of the Trinity. Careful examination of the more precise treatises discloses that the dogma of *tres personae* does not mean at all what in common parlance is intended by "three persons," nor perhaps even what was meant by the Boethian definition of *persona*, but distinctions in God which may best be called "subsistent relations." Yet in less technical works the tendency is (probably of necessity, since the terminology is fixed by ecclesiastical usage) to represent the Trinity more in terms of the societal analogy, and perhaps even to leave the door open to popular conceptions which are implicitly tritheistic. The latter may be seen in the use of the term person without careful qualification, in the emphasis on devotion to the Persons severally, and in the general assumption that the mystery of the Trinity is not in understanding the nature of the threeness but in conceiving the unity.

D. THE DIVINE RELATIONS

We have already mentioned the doctrine of the inner divine (or immanent) processions in connection with the "Thomistic analogy." This doctrine, the "principle of the Trinity," is in many ways the heart of the Catholic understanding of the Trinity. It is the immanent processions which properly constitute the mystery of the Trinity. For in the original deposit of revelation, not only the *fact* of the existence of three divine Persons, but also the *cause* of the three Persons is given us. We are told of the existence in God of two qualitatively distinct eternal processions: generation (*generatio, gennesis*) and spiration (*spiratio, pneusis*). The source

[11] Loc. cit.

of the processions is God the Father, who "proceeds from no one. . . . He is, simply and absolutely, Principle without principle. . . . He does not receive existence from another."[1] He is the principle of divine existence, therefore preëminently called God. This is seen in the fact that the Gospels present God primarily as Father, and Christ relates everything, including himself, to the Father.

We learn also from the scriptures that the Second Person of the Trinity proceeds from the Father by way of (spiritual) generation, since he is called Son and only-begotten. The central meaning of the notion of generation, "of a being drawing its origin from a living principle, with which it remains one in likeness of nature,"[2] is directly suggested by the name *Son*. This name occupies the place of primacy and guards against all suggestions of inferiority of the Second Person, while the term Word guards against suggestions of materiality. The scriptures do not tell us specifically what is the mode of the procession of the Holy Spirit, but since the Son is the *only* begotten, it is obvious that the Spirit proceeds in a different manner, and this is commonly termed spiration, representing the breathing out of the love of Father and Son for one another.

Thus far, Catholic doctrine does not recognize any significant controversy and the statement of the revealed doctrine of the two processions can occupy relatively little space in general treatises on the Trinity. The deliverance of revelation is held to be perfectly clear here. Great pains are taken, however, to defend the doctrine of the "double procession" of the Spirit—from the Father and from the Son—against the view of the Eastern Church that the Spirit proceeds *only* from the Father. No objection is made to the positive affirmation, characteristic of the Greek Fathers, that the Spirit proceeds from the Father *through* the Son (*ex Patre per Filium*), and it is recognized that this can be combined with the Western formula (*ex Patre Filioque*). But the necessity of the *Filioque* is most vigorously maintained.

---

[1] Klein, op. cit., 108.　　　　　[2] Ibid., 142.

The elements of the doctrine of the processions stated so far are all to be understood as a part of the immediate revelation, and are defended primarily on the basis of copious proof-texts from scripture and tradition. Beyond these basic elements we move into the area of speculative theology, the implications of dogma, where we are concerned with two groups of problems. The first is the identification of generation and spiration with the intellectual and volitional processes. This we have already discussed. The second is the development of the corollaries which follow (from the character of the processions *per intellectum et voluntatem*) regarding the divine Relations, Properties and Notions. Speculative theology here attempts to make the concepts of the inner processions clear to the understanding, to "harmonize the content of revelation with the findings of reason." [3]

From the fact of the two processions, it is argued that there are four *real* (subsisting) relations—paternity and filiation (or active and passive generation) and spiration and procession (or active and passive spiration). Of these, paternity, filiation, and procession (or passive spiration) constitute divine Persons: active spiration is common to both Father and Son and is therefore not an individual relation. On the basis of the judgment that a real relation cannot *inhere* in the divine essence, for this would introduce composition in God, it is held that a "real divine relation must subsist of itself, must be in fact the divine essence itself in its eternal intrinsic origins." [4] Thus we return to the definition of the Persons as distinct subsisting relations. The Persons differ, i.e. they are incommunicable, only by virtue of the relations of opposition (origin) between them, the relative opposition of generator to generated, and of spirator(s) to spirated.[5]

---

[3] Downey, op. cit., 134.

[4] Downey, op. cit., 136. A real relation is that between real objects which are really distinct and whose relation is founded on a "solid fact" (e.g. the act of generation or spiration).

[5] On this line of analysis, it.is apparent that the *filioque* is necessary to prevent the Son and the Spirit from dissolving into one. Cf. Pohle-Preuss, 230 ff. Here we may recall the "law of the Trinity," that "In God all things are one except where there is opposition of relation." This has been defined as dogma, though the number of relations has not been formally defined.

With the doctrine of Divine Relations, we ought also to associate the dogma of *circumincessio* or *perichoresis*, the coinherence of the divine Persons. This doctrine is "perhaps the most profound aspect of the Trinitary revelation and the one which best sums up all the others." [6] It refers to the mutual interpenetration or indwelling of the Persons, which is based on the divine processions and relations, but especially on the identity of essence, i.e. on "the fact that the divine Persons possess all three but one and the same nature, not merely a similar nature . . . but single, numerically one. Since each Person is present as a whole in His nature, He is clearly for the same reason present in the two other Persons. . . ." [7] The doctrine may be put either in static terms in which the Persons are portrayed as resting in one another (*circuminsessio*) or in more dynamic terms as indicating the eternal interchange and flow of life and activity (*perichoresis, circumincessio*), This is the ultimate and least penetrable aspect of the mystery of the Trinity; for it there are no analogies in the created world.[8] It is the final guarantee of the unity of God, resting not only on the doctrines of consubstantiality and procession, but also and primarily on the word of Christ himself, "I am in the Father and the Father is in me" (Jn. 14:11).

E. THE APPROPRIATIONS AND MISSIONS

A final aspect of the speculative theological development of the doctrine of the Trinity has to do with the theory of the divine Appropriations and Missions. This, we may say, constitutes the Catholic doctrine of the Trinity *ad extra*, the economic Trinity. It is significant that Catholic thought does not proceed from the economic to the immanent Trinity, but develops the doctrine of the immanent Trinity on the basis of the given revelation and adds

---

The concepts of Properties and Notions follow directly from the analysis of relations. The discussion of these items is taken over directly from St. Thomas. (Cf. *S. Theol.*, I, QQ. 28, 30, 32.)

[6] Klein, op. cit., 243.
[7] Klein, op. cit. 243f. Cf. Pohle-Preuss, op. cit., 283ff.
[8] Compare this assertion with the arguments cited earlier from the supposed interpenetrability of human personality.

to this the theory of appropriations and missions as part of speculative theology. The primary exception to this order is the argument from the sending (mission) of the Spirit by the Son to the doctrine of the Procession of the Spirit from the Son.

In contrast to the divine properties, which pertain exclusively to one of the divine Persons, the appropriations attribute to one of the Persons something which is common to all three. Certain outward works or attributes are ascribed to one of the Persons without thereby implying that what is appropriated really belongs to that one any more than to the others, though some intrinsic relationship must always exist between the hypostatic character of the Person and the attribute itself. This means that the appropriation is always based at least partly on the divine origins.

Whatever is appropriated to the Father will be found to imply in some way that he is the fount, the source, the principle which proceeds from none, but from which all else derives; whatever is appropriated to the Son will have necessarily some reference to the intellectual operation according to which he proceeds from the Father; and finally, whatever is appropriated to the Holy Spirit will be traceable to the actions of the divine will according to which he proceeds from both the Father and the Son, consubstantial with them, but distinct in personality.[1]

Thus power is attributed to the Father, wisdom to the Son and goodness and love to the Holy Spirit.

The doctrine of Appropriation is to be contrasted most sharply with those views (cf. above, Ch. II) which tend to equate the distinction of Father, Son and Spirit with types or aspects of divine activity (Creating, Redeeming, Sanctifying, etc.). On the Catholic view the identity of the divine essence directly implies a unity of operation. The Persons share fully in all of the divine works, in creation, in the Incarnation, in the effusion of grace, in *everything* except the relations which constitute and distinguish the persons. *Opera trinitatis ad extra indivisa sunt.* "Any attempt

[1] Downey, op. cit., 138f.

to go beyond mere appropriation is sure to result in a scission of the Divine essence." [2]

The temporal divine missions, *missiones ad extra* or "sendings," are of a quite different order from the appropriations, though they are related to the latter in that the missions conform strictly to the divine Origins and that a divine function is usually appropriated to the Person "sent." Obviously, only the Son and the Holy Spirit can be sent, since they alone proceed, and only the Father and the Son can send. A mission is defined as a going forth or procession of the Person sent such that the Person acquires a new relation to creatures; the Person sending is the *terminus a quo*, the effect in the creature the *terminus ad quem*. Regarded as an operation, a temporal mission is the work of the whole Trinity, though only one Person can be said to be sent and is spoken of as sent by one or both others. In the Incarnation, the preëminent visible mission, only the Son assumes human nature, though the whole Trinity shares in the work. Similarly all three Persons participate in the work of sanctification, though only the Holy Spirit is said to be the Gift to us.

It is, we have suggested, significant that in the Catholic statement of the doctrine of the Trinity, the concepts of appropriations and missions come at the end of the discussion and are classed as *implications* of the revelation. This does not mean that the "economic" aspects of the doctrine are unimportant or only superficially related to the immanent Trinity. On the contrary, the doctrine of the appropriations and (more especially) the missions are precisely intended to show the essential relation of the divine *oikonomia* to the internal trinitarian nature and life of God and the relevance of the latter to the life of the Christian community. But the order of thought which proceeds from the fully developed doctrine of the immanent relations of the divine Persons to the manifestations of the Trinity in history is directly contrary to the method which seems to be called for by the theological reorientation of the last century.

[2] Pohle-Preuss, op. cit., 280; cf. 275ff. Cf. Klein, op. cit., 151f., 155.

There is no need to labor the point that the Catholic view presupposes an understanding of revelation which is wholly untenable for contemporary Protestant theology, a view of revelation which conceives that the essential elements of the doctrine of the Trinity are divinely revealed truths recorded in the scriptures and infallibly explicated by the Councils of the Church. Here, in principle, Catholic and Protestant fundamentalism are equally unacceptable. Catholic theology is more subtle and elaborate (and also more careful) in its development of the scriptural revelation but no less "incorrigibly obdurate" in its attitude toward biblical criticism. Whatever our final judgment of the value of the doctrines of the internal relations of Father, Son and Spirit, or circumincession or the Thomistic analogy, we must agree with the objection of liberal Protestantism that these doctrines cannot be justified on the basis of biblical literalism and the method of proof-text, together with the fragmental and propositional view of revelation which it implies.

Only when and if we can restate the ground of the trinitarian concept in terms consonant with the contemporary theological insights will it be possible or worth-while to raise the question of the validity of many of these further elements of the doctrine. All Christian doctrine must continually be recreated out of the faith of the community, not on the basis of infallible deliverances of scripture but looking to the revelation of God in the concrete historical events to which the scriptures bear (finite and fallible) witness.

An illuminating and significant difference may be seen between the treatment of the Trinity by Augustine and Aquinas. Augustine assumes a literalistic view of the inspiration of the scriptures, but the basis and point of departure for his understanding of the Trinity was always the temporal sending of the Son and the giving of the Holy Spirit, i.e. the historical events from which the doctrine arises. Aquinas, on the other hand, begins with the received tradition, the doctrine, as authoritative. The proposition that God is a Trinity of Father, Son and Spirit is not for him a part of our finite reflection on the meaning of the revelation in

Christ, but is itself a part of an original deposit of truth, which may be explicated in abstraction from the historical events. Thus, and here contemporary Catholic theology follows his lead, Aquinas speaks of the mission of the divine persons only at the end of the *Tractatus*.[3]

In a sense our objection here is an objection to doctrinal authoritarianism in general. Regarding all the essentials of the doctrine—three coequal and coeternal Persons, two processions, *filioque*, coinherence—the result of the theological analysis is already determined by dogmatic definitions, and even in the area of "theological speculation" the use of the Thomistic analogy and of the concepts of relations, etc., is so largely fixed by tradition that we do not find here any basic divergence from the thought of the Angelic Doctor himself. Klein asserts, to be sure, that the terminology of the doctrine is susceptible "to a certain degree . . . of being adapted in successive ages to the mental habits and philosophical language of the time," provided, of course, that the essential meaning is not altered.[4] But in relation to the crucial problem of the term "person," which is seriously misleading if taken in the banal sense of self-conscious individuality, the "adaptation" which is allowed seems to be only a restatement of the archaic meaning of the term. Within the rigid structure of Catholic dogmatic definition and tradition, it is difficult to see how we can expect any vital reconstruction of the doctrine in terms at once meaningful to contemporary thought and life and accurately representative of the intention of the dogma. We see rather a restatement of the traditional forms and definitions with emphasis on the importance of the dogma for Catholic liturgy and theology.

The fact that the Catholic understanding of the Trinity rests upon revelation conceived in the form of revealed truths also involves serious difficulties for the appreciation of the relevance of the doctrine to the Christian life. While it is true that the doctrine of the missions establishes a connection between the trinitarian nature of God and the work of redemption and sanctification, it is also true to say that when Catholic authors attempt to empha-

---

[3] *Summa Theologica*, I, Q. 43.   [4] Op. cit., 90.

size the importance of the doctrine of the Trinity for Christian life they think primarily in terms of *devotion* to the Trinity. But devotion to the Trinity seems to mean devotion to the several Persons of the Trinity. Thus Klein writes, in a passage already referred to, that we ought to bow down "with humble, filial and confident respect before the Father," approach the Son with affection and gratitude, and appeal within ourselves to the Holy Ghost. If this be the religious or devotional significance of the doctrine of the Trinity, then Tennant's objection seems relevant, that the devotional value derives largely from (perhaps subconscious) tritheistic suggestions.

A final difficulty, which is by no means peculiar to the Roman Catholic view of the Trinity, has to do with the content of the doctrine. It is the general problem of the relation of trinity and unity. Klein, as we have seen, finds the real difficulty in conceiving the Trinity not in the fact of three Persons—the terms Father, Son and Spirit are readily conceived—but in the manner in which these are still only one God. Pohle-Preuss divide their discussion into two general parts, entitled "Trinity in Unity" and "Unity in Trinity," but this is misleading, for in the first part they really discuss the threeness (processions, persons, relations, appropriations, etc.) and in the second part deal with the unity (consubstantiality, external operation, *perichoresis*). One might expect to discover how trinity and unity contribute to each other, but this is not forthcoming. Threeness of Person and Oneness of Essence stand as dual assertions necessary to guard against monarchianism and tritheism. This is a doctrine of trinity *and* unity, rather than trinity *in* unity; it is the *mysterium logicum*, the "artificial scandal" which Brunner so vigorously attacks. The meaning of Person and Nature is carefully defined, but the relation of Person to Nature remains vague.[5] It is this relation, of course, which is held to be the essential

[5] Pohle-Preuss approach the problem, but only approach it, in their discussion of the one *summa res*, under the doctrine of consubstantiality. The one *summa res*, they say, "simultaneously exercises two separate and distinct functions,—the function of one Absolute and three Relatives." Op. cit., 259. Under the second aspect we speak of the Father who generates, etc. What, then, is the nature of the distinction between Nature and Person, *summa res* absolute and *summa res* relative? It cannot be a *real distinction*, for that

mystery of the Trinity. Nevertheless, the question may be asked whether some of the difficulty of conceiving a doctrine of trinity in unity and unity in trinity does not lie in a faulty conception of the basis of the doctrine in revelation.[6]

---

would leave only three modes of manifestation. The distinction must therefore be either modal (Durandus), formal (Scotus), or virtual (Aquinas). Since modal and formal involve a sort of composition inadmissable to God, most theologians adopt the notion of virtual distinction.

I say this only approaches the problem because it does not deal with the source of the difficulty, in the understanding of the revelational root of the doctrine of the Trinity. Pohle-Preuss also assert that the doctrine of coinherence is the final *summary* of the notion of trinity in unity and unity in trinity. But since this is identified as the most mysterious aspect of the trinitarian doctrine, it can hardly be said to illuminate the problem very much.

[6] Cf. below, Ch. V, § 5, and Chs. VI and VII.

PART III

CONTEMPORARY RECONSTRUCTION OF TRINITARIAN DOCTRINE

CHAPTER V

The Trinity as Synthesis and Completion of the Doctrinal System

In the first chapter of this study we saw that the pervasive indifference toward doctrine of the Trinity which developed in the nineteenth century and continued into the period of contemporary theology stemmed in part from the calling into question of the traditional concepts of revelation, and from the insistence of Schleiermacher and subsequent "liberal" theology that all Christian theology must be derived directly and immediately from the living experience of the Christian community and the historical events on which it rests. Schleiermacher, Ritschl and liberal theologians generally were profoundly suspicious of the classical trinitarian conception of God because they did not see how it could be derived from the new understanding of the basis of Christian affirmations. We have seen also that the continued suspicion of the doctrine of the Trinity in contemporary theological discussion rests mainly upon a similar judgment that the historical bases of Christian faith and life cannot be said to require the elaboration of a doctrine of the inner-trinitarian nature of God. There are those, we noted, who seek to maintain the traditional doctrine (though in varying forms) either with the assistance of general philosophical considerations, or from the point of view of an authoritarianism which does not recognize that the revelational basis of theology was ever called into question.

These are not, however, the only available alternatives, and while it would be rash to assert that there is any concerted movement in contemporary Protestant theology toward a reaffirmation of the centrality of the trinitarian concept, nevertheless it may be affirmed that in the main stream of contemporary theological development there is a strong current of thought in the direction of renewed recognition of the necessity and importance of a Christian doctrine of the Trinity. This is to be seen not only in the appearance of systematic studies like those of Karl Barth, Leonard Hodgson and Charles Lowry, but also in the place accorded to the Trinity in such works as J. S. Whale's *Christian Doctrine*, N. Micklem's *What Is the Faith?*, W. N. Pittenger's *Christ and the Christian Faith* and D. M. Baillie's *God Was in Christ.*

It is the genius of this renewed interest in the doctrine that it perceives trinitarian theology to be precisely derived from the experience of the Christian community—or better, from the revelation of God in those events to which the faith and experience of the community are a response. Without denying the real divergences in the understanding of revelation, we can say that for all those concerned, the data upon which the notion of the Trinity is based are the historical events to which the scriptures and the Church bear living witness. Revelation is not identified with the biblical texts but with that to which those texts point. This, broadly speaking, is a theory of revelation *in act*, rather than in proposition. The doctrine of the Trinity is not developed simply by piecing together trinitarian proof-texts, understood as divinely given truths, but is constructed as a consequence of the gospel taken as a whole. It is, as Micklem puts it, "a statement or necessary implication of the central and ultimately all-inclusive or all-involving revelation which we call the Incarnation." [1] The doctrine of the Trinity is thus not to be understood as *per se* a "revealed doctrine." but as a doctrine by which we seek to explicate the meaning of the revelation in Christ as it bears on the nature of God. These attempts to reinstate trinitarian doctrine in a key place in the dogmatic structure are genuinely *reconstructions* of the doctrine,

[1] Nathaniel Micklem, *What Is the Faith?* 99.

efforts to work out anew, from a new understanding of the form of the Christian revelation, the content of the distinctively Christian conception of God.

The new approach to the doctrine of the Trinity is characterized also by its emphasis on the "religious" significance of the concept. This means partly its significance for Christian devotion or worship. But it also means, and more fundamentally, the essential relation of the trinitarian understanding of God to all of the central elements of Christian faith. Roman Catholic and Fundamentalist theologies assert that the doctrine of the Trinity is true, because revealed, and *also* useful, i.e. of great *religious* importance. This way of putting the relationship is intolerable from the point of view with which we are now concerned. For the very ground of the renewed interest in the doctrine is the conception of Christianity as essentially a trinitarian *religion*. It is from the trinitarian nature of the revelation and redemption, which are the source and sustenance of Christian life and faith, that the notion of the triune God derives its support and meaning.

Thus far, we have been indicating certain very general characteristics common to all those to be considered in this and the next chapter as assigning the doctrine of the Trinity to a central place in the structure of theology. Now, however, we must recall the provisional distinction drawn at the beginning of Chapter II between those who view the doctrine as a "completion" of the doctrinal system, i.e. as an ultimate theoretically necessary implication of the primary data of faith and as a *synthesis* of those data, and those (notably Karl Barth) who consider the Trinity as an immediate implication of revelation, i.e. as essentially identical with the content of revelation. This distinction will be revealed as of primary importance in the understanding of contemporary trinitarianism and in our own constructive elaboration. Thus in this chapter we shall be concerned with the former approach, and in Chapter VI with the latter.

We may distinguish two stages or movements in the argument. First we need to consider the general conception of the trinitarian character of the Christian religion, i.e. the facts of revelation and Christian experience which require the development of a doctrine of Trinity. This is the question of methodology, of the theological place of the doctrine. Then we may proceed to a more detailed examination of what are considered to be the data and the way in which they are explicated in trinitarian doctrine as such. In the actual development of the doctrine, we find two quite different conceptions of the Trinity, the one reviving what we have earlier called the social or societal interpretation of the Trinity, the other adopting either the psychological analogy alone or a combination of the psychological and social analogies. These two types of thought will be described in sections 2 and 3 respectively. Then we shall be in a position to offer a critique of the conception of the *role* of the trinitarian doctrine which is common to all the theologians discussed in this chapter.

1. *The Basis of the Doctrine in Revelation and Christian Experience*

The common denominator of the views now under consideration—viz. the judgment that the doctrine of the Trinity is the ultimate and necessary consequence or synthesis of the data of Christian revelation and experience—finds expression in varying forms. W. Norman Pittenger approaches the Trinity as a presupposition and implication of the Incarnation. This doctrine of God is, he says, the "inevitable corollary of such an implicit belief and such an explicit assertion about the person of Jesus Christ," as has culminated in the Nicene and Chalcedonian formulae.[1] The converse affirmation may also be made, of course, that the Incarnation is a corollary of the conception of the Trinity. The doctrines of the Trinity and Incarnation are mutually interdependent and inseparable, but Pittenger's emphasis is clearly first upon belief about Christ. Beginning there, we proceed to the explication of the implications of that belief for the nature of God.

The doctrine of the Trinity is furthermore, he implies, based *solely* in the historic revelation in Christ. We shall see that this

[1] *Christ and the Christian Faith*, 134.

statement represents a characteristic motif of the whole pattern of thought with which we are now concerned. Contemporary reassertions of the necessity of the trinitarian conception reveal a fairly uniform willingness to let the case for the doctrine rest wholly on the basis of revelation and the experience of the community, quite apart from all "philosophical" justification (though there may be philosophical implications). This attitude is implicit in Pittenger's insistence that the doctrine of the Trinity is not at all to be derived from neo-Platonic trinitarian notions, but rooted (entirely) in a "complex event and experience":

Three experiences had come to men from one God; therefore three sorts of relationship were possible with one God; therefore some corresponding distinctions must exist within God, who as ultimate Truth does not reveal himself in any other guise than that which actually is of the essence of his being.[2]

Only by way of a doctrine of threefold distinctions in the very being of God could the Church preserve "the reality of its experience both as given by God and as giving God" and at the same time hold on to the valuable aspects of the concept of divine immutability. The metaphysical doctrine of the Trinity is therefore necessary to secure the absolute truthfulness of God's self-revelation.

Similarly, though from a more evangelical point of view, J. S. Whale understands the formulation of the doctrine of the Trinity to be a result of the Church's wrestling with three (apparently) mutually incompatible axioms: 1) monotheism, the belief in God holy and transcendent; 2) the divinity of Christ; and 3) God as Spirit, known formerly (by the Hebrews) as immanent in the whole creation, "but now newly experienced and understood as the Holy Spirit of the God and Father of the Lord Jesus Christ."[3] The doctrine of the Trinity is a further elaboration of monotheism, a new definition required by an *implicitly* trinitarian revelation. As a doctrine, this is not the heart of the gospel, nor

[2] Ibid., 138; cf. 143.
[3] Whale, *Christian Doctrine*, 112ff.

necessarily essential to piety, nor "to cite the almost blasphemous
error with which the *Quicunque Vult* opens—is belief in its dogmatic formulation necessary to salvation." But as a formulation,
the doctrine is "the ultimate *intellectual* implicate of the Christian
faith, and the historic monument to a mystery with which some
of the greatest minds have wrestled." [4]

Nathaniel Micklem puts the matter somewhat similarly in
terms of a distinction between dogma and theology. Dogma for
him refers to the gospel, which is always stated in (narrative)
terms of God's action, e.g. "God was in Christ reconciling the
world to himself," and includes the *necessary implications* of the
gospel. Theology includes the statements about the interpretation of the gospel and its implications, and is subject to change
and reinterpretation. The doctrine of the Trinity cannot therefore possess finality of language, but the "assertion of the Trinity
—that is, that the Deity is Three Persons in One God—is a dogma
of the Faith." [5] It cannot be denied without denying the Christian
revelation itself (provided, of course, that one understands the
consequences of his denial). Not every Christian must use this
formula, but every Christian must mean what this formula expresses. For the very essence of Christian experience is threefold.
It is the experience of God as Creator and Sustainer, the new
apprehension of God in Christ as the Redeemer (which involves
the apprehension that he was the same God, i.e. the acceptance
of Christ as the Incarnation declares the unity of the God of
Creation and Redemption), and the experience of the fellowship
of the Holy Spirit, the presence of the Kingdom, i.e. of God as
Sanctifier. To put it differently, we may say that the Trinity is an
answer to the question of what the Incarnation means for the
being of God. We cannot say either that "Jesus is God" or that
"Jesus was like God"—for he is not God simply, else his human
life was a masquerade; and yet he is not merely like God, for
God has come in him. Therefore we affirm the doctrine of the
Trinity, which does not solve the mystery, but succinctly states

[4] Ibid., 120. (Italics mine.)
[5] *What Is the Faith?*, p. 111. Cf. also 74ff.

it. The Trinity is a dogma, the only all-comprehensive Christian dogma, because the story, the gospel, centers around the three mighty acts of God—Creation, Incarnation and the giving of the Holy Spirit. The dogma asserts that these correspond to three modes or "Persons" of the divine Being.[6]

Formally, at least, Leonard Hodgson's conception of the basis of the doctrine of the Trinity in revelation is akin to the views just stated. In affirming that the Trinity is a doctrine of revelation, Hodgson wants it clearly understood that he does not mean revelation in the sense of communication of propositions, or "revealed truths." The tenability of that notion has now been destroyed by biblical criticism, and revelation must be conceived as given in *deeds*, in divine activity in history. Revelation provides a "key-feature," a sequence of events which reason interprets. The doctrine of the Trinity is thus not a "revealed mystery of faith," but the "product of rational reflection on those particular manifestations of the divine activity which center in the birth, ministry, crucifixion, resurrection and ascension of Jesus Christ and the gift of the Holy Spirit to the Church." We may properly say that it could not have been discovered by reason alone, because it depends absolutely on the happening of the events "which drove human reason to see that they required a trinitarian God for their cause." [7] The New Testament is therefore not the *revelatum*, but a record of the *revelatum*, i.e. of the key-feature which is composed of events in which God is apprehended to have acted. The doctrine of the Trinity is a "philosophico-theological attempt to grasp what must be the nature of the God who makes Himself known in this way." [8]

Hodgson is willing to speak of this procedure as essentially empirical, in the sense that it begins with certain empirical data and formally resembles the procedure of arguing from creaturely existence as such to divine existence, except that trinitarian theology starts from a specific feature of human experience. Hodgson

[6] Ibid., 126ff.
[7] Leonard Hodgson, *The Doctrine of the Trinity*, 25.
[8] Ibid., 139.

suggests that the concept of the Trinity has a definite philosophical usefulness, i.e., as the explication of an all-important key-feature it may be used to interpret the whole of experience; but he does not intend this to be thought of as a philosophical justification or validation of the doctrine itself. The trinitarian understanding of God depends entirely upon the specific events recorded in the New Testament and is accepted or rejected as man's eyes are or are not opened to see the theological significance of those events.[9]

Charles Lowry's analysis of the root of the doctrine of the Trinity follows in this same general pattern, though he is dissatisfied with any theory of revelation as simply an act or event, and he gives more weight to the character of religious doctrine as mythological and symbolic in form. He sees man as motivated chiefly by feeling and therefore requiring (in his religion) a "tenable and powerful myth." [10] The doctrine of the Trinity is evidently more scientific, general and further from immediate experience than the New Testament or the Apostles' or Nicene Creeds, but it still participates in the religious preference for analogy and symbol. This doctrine, like all others, must be stated in "symbolic and mythopoetic" fashion, in the form of a "realistic, dramatic, and mythological interpretation of the being and the relations of Father, Son and Holy Spirit." [11]

Apart from these (minor) variations, Lowry reasserts the view that Christian theology is the explication of Christian experience, the attempt to put essential religious ideas into rational and communicable formulations. Theology rests on religion, on faith, on empiricism; it is concerned with the real and the factual. The first fact which Christians added to the faith of Israel in the Father-God was the faith in Christ as the Son of God and the belief that through him they were related to that true God. The second was the fact, the experience, of the outpouring of the Holy Spirit. Christianity is therefore essentially a trinitarian religion, and "The doctrine of the Trinity is the one all-compre-

---

[9] Cf. ibid., 35ff., 110, 136ff.
[10] Lowry, *The Trinity and Christian Devotion*, 29.
[11] Ibid., 103. Cf. 19.

hensive Christian doctrine. It gathers up into the seam of a single grand generalization with respect to the being and activity of God all the major aspects of Christian truth. It is the formulation which the Christian facts in their totality compel." [12]

Among the various authors whom we have been citing, there is formal agreement that the doctrine of the Trinity is based directly (and solely) on the facts of Christian experience or history, that it is a necessary intellectual implication or consequence of those facts (i.e. that Christianity is a trinitarian religion), and that it is the central or all-inclusive doctrine of the faith. There is not the same degree of agreement, however, as to precisely what are the facts of Christian experience which compel the trinitarian formulation or as to just what is the content of the doctrine which is so required. To an analysis of this divergence we may now turn.

2. *Revival of the Social Analogy*

A. WEBB AND THORNTON

The revival of the social analogy for the Trinity in the contemporary period by Leonard Hodgson and Charles Lowry was given primary impetus by the writings of C. C. J. Webb (especially the first volume of his Gifford lectures, *God and Personality*) and of Lionel Thornton (notably his *The Incarnate Lord*).

Webb's analysis was in several ways a focal point. While he did not himself break much new ground, most of his argument having been anticipated and even worked out in some detail in connection with the late nineteenth-century social theory, nevertheless there are at least two main elements in Webb's argument which bore fruit in the subsequent development. The first is his historical analysis of the notion of personality as applied to God, in which he points out that the idea of the personality *of* God is a relatively modern development except in quite unorthodox thought. Classical Christian theology, Webb holds, spoke always of personality *in* God, of God as *tres personae* in *una substantia*. Until the modern period (i.e. approximately until the time of

[12] Ibid., 52. Cf. 18, 54ff., 62, 66ff., 79.

Schleiermacher) God was referred to as *a* person only by those who sought to deny the doctrine that he is three Persons, and then only negatively.[1]

The second element has to do with the reason for the affirmation of *tres personae*. The primary source of the application of the term *persona* to Father, Son and Spirit is of course Tertullian, who had in mind, Webb thinks, chiefly the grammatical associations of the word. In spite of Tertullian's questionable use of scripture, i.e. his literalism and his treatment of literature as dogma, Webb nevertheless finds indicated in his thought a solid foundation for this way of speaking: "This solid foundation is the profound impression made by the attitude towards God attributed in the Gospels to the Founder of the Christian religion and the inference to which it had led that the personal relation—I use the term advisedly—of loving sonship in which Jesus Christ was there represented as standing towards his Father in heaven was the revelation of a permanent and essential feature of the divine life, . . ." [2] Webb does not stress this second feature of his analysis, but it becomes of crucial importance in later thought.

In our earlier discussion of Lionel Thornton's trinitarian construction, as elaborated in *The Incarnate Lord*, we were concerned only with the relation of that construction to his philosophical orientation. Now, however, we must take account of his conception of the New Testament basis of the doctrine of the Trinity, for this is significantly reflected in the thinking of Leonard Hodgson.[3]

Briefly, Thornton distinguishes two lines of development in New Testament and patristic thought. One begins from the experience of redemption, of Christ as the mediator between God and man, the one who delivers man from his sin into the life of the Spirit in fellowship with God. This experience finds expression in the (apocalyptic) conception of Christ as the glorified Son of Man, whereby Christ is understood as "the beginning and fountain-head of a new creation. . . . The head of a new race, because

---

[1] Webb, *God and Personality*, 61ff.   [2] Ibid., 67. Cf. 141.
[3] Thornton, *The Incarnate Lord*, esp. Ch. XI.

He is the transcendent source of Christian experience in the New Order" of fellowship and communion.[4] The other line of development which Thornton discerns stems from that element of the New Testament witness which Webb had designated as the solid foundation for the use of the term *persona*—the unique relation of sonship which Christ bore to the Father. The idea of Christ's messianic sonship is traced in the first instance to the synoptics, being found in the baptism and temptation narratives, in the Q passage in Mt. 11=Lk. 10, and in the words heard by the disciples in the transfiguration vision. Thornton thinks that this tradition of thought, which presumably stemmed ultimately from Jesus' teaching about himself, "must have influenced apostolic thought profoundly, when we consider what immense development the theme of our Lord's sonship received in the fourth gospel," [5] but he has some difficulty in attributing this conception of the Son's fellowship with the Father to the Pauline epistles.

Both of these lines of development are carried further in the Fourth Gospel (and intersect in Jn. 1:14, 18). The conception of Christ as mediator and redeemer, previously developed in Colossians, Ephesians and Hebrews, is now continued in the Logos doctrine, where Christ is transferred from the headship of the new creation back to the first creation. The Logos theology of the prologue to the Fourth Gospel places "the creative [and redemptive] principle within the Godhead," but "did not make *explicit* the later trinitarian doctrine of a fellowship of Persons in the Godhead." [6] The latter function was performed by the Johannine elaboration of the concept of Christ's sonship to God, and later by Origen's notion of eternal generation. The Logos concept represents the New Testament interest in setting the redemptive mediator at the head of creation, and places the gospel on the background of a cosmic order.

But the redemptive experience demands a more ultimate background in the eternal fellowship in God, because the center of

---

[4] Ibid., 294. Thornton has reference here chiefly to the Pauline conception of Christ as the second Adam, a heavenly preëxistent being, etc. He does not associate this so much with the synoptic Son of Man passages.

[5] Ibid., 295.   [6] Ibid., 298.

that experience is *koinonia*, the fellowship of the Spirit, *agape*. "The law of ἀγάπη reigns in heaven, and only so can be translated to earth. Hence the Johannine doctrine of sonship is in reality the last word of the New Testament upon the doctrine of redemption." [7] The Johannine sonship doctrine is elaborated primarily in the assertion of the claim to equality with the Father (Jn. v) and the description of the mutual relations of Father and Son (esp. Jn. xiv to xvii). In the conceptions of the Good Shepherd, the Vine, and the Bread of Heaven, which are expressive of the mediatorial line of thought, this theme of sonship is woven together with the relationship of the Son to mankind as the representative of the Father. On the other hand, the redemptive activity is predicated upon Christ's unique relation to God. The fact that Christ dwells in the Father is the "underlying ground or cause" of his dwelling in his disciples. The fundamental direction of New Testament thought, according to Thornton, thus carries "apostolic interpretation stage by stage to the conception of a plurality of Persons in God, a conception which becomes fully articulate in St. John's Gospel, particularly in chs. xiv to xvii." [8]

The source of this conception of a divine plurality of Persons may be said to be twofold. There is, first of all, *Christ's own teaching*, and here Thornton affirms that "the transition from the primitive concept of sonship in Q to the developed concept of an absolute sonship in St. John was a true and legitimate development. For the Johannine concept does no more than abstract from its original form, an estimate of our Lord's Person and status which is required by the content of His teaching as given in the earliest tradition." [9] But the conception of plurality of Persons in God is also based upon the essential nature of *the Christian experience of fellowship, agape,* in the new community: "Since the new law of ἀγάπη flows down into the new community through the Spirit of Christ from the 'Father of our Lord Jesus Christ,' this law of ἀγάπη, revealed in the Messiah's life-story and reproduced by the Spirit as the inner principle of life in the New Order, must be referred back to its transcendent source in the life of God.

---

[7] Ibid., 312.   [8] Ibid., 304.   [9] Ibid., 305f.

. . . The fellowship, or κοινωνία, of the Spirit in the new community is referred back to a transcendent fellowship of Persons in the life of God." [10]

The two lines of development which he sees in the New Testament, Thornton also traces in subsequent theology. The doctrine of the Logos-mediator reached its culmination in Clement of Alexandria and was revived by Augustine. The sonship theology was basic to Origen's doctrine of eternal generation and determinative in the formation and defense of the Nicene position. The presence of these two types of theology in the developed Western form of the doctrine of the Trinity maintains a balance between the psychological and social analogies. Both types of analogy are rooted in the New Testament.

On the basis of these assertions, it seems that Thornton wishes to utilize both the social and the psychological analogies. But one cannot help wondering whether he takes the psychological analogy seriously. His whole analysis of the New Testament evidence is directed toward showing that it culminates in the conception of a plurality of Persons in God. Moreover, he assumes throughout that the developed doctrine of the Trinity refers to Father, Son and Spirit as Persons in the full sense of the word—though without the limitations of finiteness, physical organism or ethical failure, and thus in complete interpenetration.[11] And, in his constructive statement, Thornton speaks of three Persons or Personal Centres in One Absolute Individuality or Actuality.

It is true, of course, that the personal and social principles are *transcended* in God as well as included, so that in him the contrast between these principles, between the "self-regarding and outward-facing aspects of individuality," is "utterly transcended in eternal and unchangeable harmony, in perfect interpenetration of the Persons, and in fulness of beatitude which consists in absolute self-giving." [12] Moreover, Thornton is unwilling to use the term personality, which in its modern sense he thinks would mean

[10] Ibid., 304, 305.   [11] Cf. 297f., 366ff., 382 and *passim*.
[12] Ibid., 415.

either three Gods or unitarianism, and insists on the term "Person" because of its technical meaning in the history of the doctrine. He believes that the word *person* "can be clearly differentiated from the modern word personality" but he does not tell us how much of the connotation of the latter he would exclude from the meaning of *person*.[13] It is clear, though, that the Divine Persons are thought of as analogous to "personal centers of activity" and the Divine Individuality includes the social principle. The force of the argument is definitely on the side of the social analogy.

B. LEONARD HODGSON

   1) The Data of the Doctrine of the Trinity.

   Whatever elements of the psychological analogy remain in Thornton's conception of the Trinity are avoided in Leonard Hodgson's Croall lectures, *The Doctrine of the Trinity*. This is to be seen at the outset in Hodgson's focusing of attention exclusively on the experience of "adoptive sonship" as the central element of the New Testament revelation. This is the experience in which one is seized, or possessed, by the Spirit of God and lifted above himself to a higher level of power and activity. This experience, Hodgson says, is what Jesus had in mind when he counselled the disciples not to be anxious for words to speak in the time of judgment, "but whatsoever shall be given you in that hour, that speak ye: for it is not ye that speak, but the Holy Ghost" (Mk. 13:11). These words must have come out of Jesus' own experience of communion with and consecration to the Father, for his whole life exemplifies "the continual seeking to find and do the Father's will in guidance and strength of the Spirit." [1] While Jesus admittedly did not speak of the Spirit very often, according to the synoptic record, Hodgson regards the few references as of great importance, and holds that it was Christ's primary ambition that the disciples should share his outlook and experience of fellowship in the Spirit (on the latter, cf. esp. Jn. 16:7).

   The experience of Pentecost was the beginning of the fulfill-

---

[13] Ibid., 414.   [1] Hodgson, op. cit., 43. Cf. 38sq.

ment of that ambition. The disciples were no longer dependent on Christ's presence in the flesh for a "second-hand" experience of possession by the Spirit, but entered on the first step of a new relationship which was "nothing less than the taking of the disciples within the mind of their Master." [2] They began actually to share his relationship with the Father, i.e. they entered into a life of adopted sonship. Hodgson insists that we take this Pauline metaphor (Rom. 8:15; Gal. 4:4-6) seriously. The Christian life is truly analogous to an experience of adoption into a social life, as into a family. The life of a Christian "is that of a member of the divine society, looking out on the world from within it." [3] The Christian shares the Lord's relationship to the Father and the Spirit; he therefore shares in the divine life of the Trinity.

In accordance with this understanding of the nature of Christian experience, the doctrine of the Trinity is held to be a statement of the presuppositions, or setting, of the life of the Christian. The Trinity is the conception of God to which that Christian experience necessarily gives rise. Christ was held by Christians to have been the fulfillment of all the Messianic expectations, to have been the source of freedom from sin, of new knowledge of. God, and of new power. They concluded that these things could not have been accomplished by any human or semi-divine being, but only by One who was God himself.

What then of his relation to the Father? In the language of preëxistence—which, though technically inadequate, is permissible in the area of "imaginative elaboration"—we may interpret the incarnate life of Christ by the analogy of a son away from home. Jesus is "a sojourner whose true home is in another sphere. He retains on earth those relationships to the Father and the Spirit which are His eternally but He exercises them under the conditions of human life on earth." [4] With this conception of the Incarnation, we come to the heart of Hodgson's argument. Christ's life has been described as "a life of self-giving in response to the Father's love, through the Spirit. The Doctrine of the Trinity is

[2] Ibid., 47. [3] Ibid., 49. [4] Ibid., 68.

the projection into eternity of this essential relationship, the assertion that eternally the Divine life is a life of mutual self-giving to one another of Father and Son through the Spirit who is the *vinculum* or bond of love between them." [5]

Such is the essential basis of the contention that in God there exists a plurality of Persons, a divine society which is the ground, achetype and actual setting of the new life of Christians. Hodgson takes it for granted that no question need be raised concerning the nature of the eternal Son as fully personal. He assumes that from the personal relationship of the Incarnate Christ to the Father, it follows directly that the Son is eternally a "person." It is a serious defect of Hodgson's work that he nowhere defines exactly what he means by the term "person." He seems to mean what he thinks intended by the modern use of the term, viz. a distinct center of consciousness. He speaks of the three as "complete persons," of "distinct Person in the full sense of that word," and of "intelligent, purposive centers of consciousness." [6]

Thus, in treating of the Spirit, Hodgson indicates that he is not content to say simply that the Spirit expresses conscious purposive will—this is true of the conception of the Spirit of God in both Old and New Testaments—but insists that the Holy Spirit is to be thought of as a "He," a Person "distinct from and parallel to the Father and the Son." [7] He recognizes that the classical terms *persona* and *hypostasis* do not necessarily involve the idea of a distinct center of consciousness, which is implied in the use of the modern term, and also that there are both "He" passages and "It" passages as well as some ambiguous language in the New Testament references to the Spirit. Nevertheless, he holds that the "He" references are fundamental.

[5] Loc. cit. (italics mine). Cf. also Hodgson's discussion of the limitations which are assumed in the Incarnation and which may therefore be "thought away" from our conception of the eternal Son, 69–77.
[6] Ibid., 96, 140, 129.
[7] Ibid., 79.

2) Trinitarian Theology: the "Revision" of the Concept of Unity.

The *theological* question which is posed by the data of revelation, according to Hodgson, is the question, "what kind of unity must we postulate of the God who has manifested Himself in these activities?" [1] In order to answer this question, Hodgson wants to draw a sharp distinction between two different types of unity—*mathematical* or arithmetical unity, and *organic* unity. This is important because otherwise we are likely to approach the problem of the unity of God with an unexamined (and inappropriate) *a priori* concept of unity. In mathematical unity, "the criterion of unity is the absence of [inner] multiplicity." [2] Organic unity, on the other hand, exists by virtue of an inner multiplicity of the elements which constitute the living being. An organism exists by unifying various elements which can contribute to the life of the organism just because they differ from and complement one another. This sort of unity exists on all levels, of course, and the higher we go in the scale of being, the more complex the inner structure of the organism and the further from simple mathematical unity. The scale of organic unity is "a scale of intensity of unifying power," in which the unity is not lessened but heightened by the number and variety of the constituent elements. Thus this is basically a unity of intensity or an "internally constitutive unity," of which organic unity is only one type.

The prime example of this unity is the unity of the activities of thinking, feeling and willing in the human self, because in the self "the seat of unity is not to be found in any one of its constituent elements, or in some further entity of the same order of being." [3] The unity of the self is constituted by the unifying power of its constituent elements. It is a unity of "intensity." Hodgson sug-

---

[1] Ibid., 87.   [2] Ibid., 90.

[3] Ibid., 92. Hodgson is here depending on John Laird's contention that the self is constituted by the co-functioning and interpermeation of these three activities, i.e. no one of these is primary in the sense of being the ground or unity of the other two, nor is there any fourth entity which possesses these three. Cf. Laird's *Problems of the Self* (1917); Hodgson, 85ff., 91f.

gests that all attempts to find the unity of the self in one of its activities or in some fourth element really involve a mistaken effort to reduce the organic unity to a mathematical unity. Intelligibility does not increase with the approach to arithmetical unity. On the contrary, all existing unities of which we have experience are actually of the organic type, and if any concept of unity is to be called unreal or imaginary, it is the notion of mathematical unity.

Given these two types of unity, we are to understand the unity of the Trinity in terms of intensive, or internally constitutive unity. We learn from God's revelation in history that "there are three elements perfectly unified in the Divine life, and each of these elements is itself a Person." [4] This is a mystery. Faith is necessary for the acceptance of the concept of the Trinity. But this is not an irrational mystery because we see that the divine unity is analogous to all of the actual unities of our experience and that the latter are imperfect instances of the true unity of God. The mystery is furthermore one which is required by the facts of revelation. Thus we need "no longer think that because the elements in the Godhead are not sub-personal activities, but complete persons, the degree of unity must be less than in the human self and that consequently the doctrine is tritheistic. Seeing that the degree of unification demanded so far exceeds anything within our experience, how mysterious, tremendous and fascinating, we argue, must be the intensity of that unifying power which constitutes the unity of the Blessed Trinity." [5]

The history of the development of the doctrine of the Trinity may be understood, according to Hodgson, in terms of the tension between the two conceptions of unity. The Church Fathers, because of the revelation, had to revise both their conception of God and their philosophical notion of unity. The Church could not be other than monotheistic, both because of its heritage from Judaism

---

[4] Ibid., 95.
[5] Ibid., 96. Compare this conception of unity with the passages cited earlier from D'Arcy, *Idealism and Theology* (esp. p. 232). The similarity, even of phraseology, is striking, though Hodgson does not indicate any acquaintance with D'Arcy's work. Cf. above 31f.

and because of the requirements of Greek philosophical thought. But both of these traditions assumed that the only real unity was mathematical, therefore the Christian revelation required a revision of the conception of unity, or else had to be given up. The various heresies gave up the revelation in favor of the unrevised concept of unity, adoptionism and Arianism by denying the godhead of the Son, modalism by reducing the revelation to a theophany. The formulæ developed by orthodox Christianity involved a revision of the concept of unity, but the Fathers did not clearly realize this and therefore never wholly abandoned subordinationism (in which the unity is preserved by identifying deity ultimately with one of the Persons and making the others divine by derivation).

The Creeds of Nicea and Constantinople, as well as the accepted formula, formally repudiated subordinationism, but because of the persistence of the arithmetical concept of unity and the fear of tritheism, the notion has persisted in the doctrines of the *principium* and the processions. But with the view of the divine unity as a dynamic unity, actively unifying the lives of the Persons, there is no need or room for this: "The thought of the Father as the Source or Fount of Godhead is a relic of pre-Christian theology which has not fully assimilated the Christian revelation." [6]

There is, Hodgson allows, a sense in which unity is predicated of God in the mathematical meaning of absence of multiplicity, viz. when we are contrasting monotheism with polytheism. But when we speak of the unity of the Trinity, of the internal nature

---

[6] Ibid., 102. Hodgson finds in the Athanasian Creed the only explicit and unequivocal repudiation of subordinationism among the ancient creeds, but ignores the fact that the Athanasian Creed equally explicitly teaches the generation of the Son and the procession of the Holy Spirit.

The doctrine of the processions does involve a sort of "subordination," but this is qualitatively different from the subordinationism of Arius, in which the Son and Spirit are created, i.e. are not of the essence of God. Hodgson treats this difference as if it were one only of degree.

It is true that in some of the Fathers, e.g. the Cappadocians, the notion of *principium* is used as a guard for the unity of God, but this is not necessarily the only nor even the primary function of the concept, which stems ultimately from the relation of Father, Son and Spirit in the divine *oikonomia*. Cf. below, ch. VI, § 5; ch. VIII, § 5.

of God, we speak in terms of an internally constitutive unity. Revelation requires that we begin with the empirical data of the divine multiplicity, with the fact of three and only three Persons in the Godhead, and then seek to understand the nature of the divine unity. We must reflect on the given material without denying or distorting it, yet we must seek to show that the mystery of the divine unity is not an irrational mystery.

Additional help in understanding the mystery of the unity of the Trinity may be gained, Hodgson thinks, from the (personal) idealist argument for the "inclusiveness of personality." He rejects unequivocally the idealistic tendency to confuse the Son with the world, but believes that we may separate this error from the valid contention that the unifying personal life of the Absolute can include personalities—considered as intelligent, purposive centers of consciousness—without destroying their relative independence. In spite of their underestimation of contingency and evil in the world, the idealists have shown enough to suggest that "a personal unity of personalities might be possible if all the persons unified were perfect." [7]

Hodgson does not offer these conceptions of unity as final and perfect solutions of the problem. But the evidence of Christian experience, viewed from within, "requires us to believe in a God whose unity unifies three activities each of which is made known to us as a distinct Person in the full sense of that word." [8] The task of philosophy is to interpret the data, not to prescribe what is given or to explain it away. Therefore, even if it appeared that this evidence conflicted with the requirements of consistency, it would be better to suspend judgment than to distort the facts. But we can seek to show that "the idea of . . . an internally constitutive unity is not repugnant to reason," that "certain idealistic arguments . . . encourage us to believe that in God both the Unity and its Constituents may be personal," and that "it is generally characteristic of our earthly experience to know the ultimate unities

----

[7] Cf. ibid., 128ff., 133. Hodgson has in mind Lotze, the two Cairds, Green, Royce and Bosanquet.
[8] Ibid., 140.

not in their unity but in their multiplicity." [9] Even though we cannot go beyond this, there is nothing irrational or unphilosophical in holding to the data of the revelation we have received.

Moreover, Hodgson believes that in this attempt to formulate a concept of unity of three fully personal divine selves, he stands squarely in the main line of historical development. To be sure, much of what the classical theologians taught under the heading of the doctrine of generation and procession has now to be assigned to the realm of the imagination. Those doctrines rested upon the false conception of propositional revelation, which led the earlier theologians to think that the biblical evidence offered much more information than is really available. Apart from the assertion of the unity of the Persons, and the mutual self-giving of the Father and the Son through the Spirit, Hodgson thinks that "we have no evidence on which to say anything further with confidence about the inner life of the eternal Godhead." [10] But on the main point, the conception of Father, Son and Spirit as Persons in the full meaning of the word, Hodgson feels that he is in complete agreement with not only the Cappadocian fathers, who are well known for their use of the analogy of three men, but also St. Augustine, St. Thomas Aquinas and John Calvin. The teaching of these men is frequently claimed to be at least consistent with a view of the Trinity in which the *personæ* are less than full Persons. Such a view, Hodgson argues at length, rests on a misunderstanding of the theologians in question. In reality what they maintained was in essence the same conception which Hodgson is now affirming.[11]

3) "Trinitarian Religion."

The phrase "Trinitarian Religion" is intended by Hodgson to indicate the importance of the trinitarian conception for Christian life and devotion, and its implications for Christian thought. The distinctive and new element in the understanding of the Christian life as one of adopted sonship, he says, comes from recognizing

[9] Ibid., 141. [10] Ibid., 142. [11] See Appendix B.

"clearly and consciously" our "distinct relationship" to each of the Persons:

We may sometimes address ourselves to the Spirit or to the Son as well as to the Father, for each is a He, none is an it. But we shall not be confusedly addressing ourselves sometimes to One and sometimes to Another without knowing when or why. We shall speak to the Spirit as to the Lord who moves and inspires us and unites us to the Son; we shall speak to the Son as to our Redeemer who has taken us to share in His sonship, in union with whom we are united to His Father and may address Him as our Father.[12]

This is not to be taken to imply simply that we must understand the different activities of the Persons. Hodgson evidently means to say that the devotional value of the Trinity derives from the consideration of Father, Son and Spirit as Persons in the full sense of the word. Thus he counsels:

It is better that we should enrich our spiritual life by exploring *to the full* the possibilities of our threefold relationship to Him than that for fear of tritheism we should impoverish it and never enter fully into the heritage of our Christian revelation.[13]

On the philosophical side, Hodgson suggests that the type of unity which is implied in the trinitarian revelation furnishes us with a pattern by which we may judge all true unity—the unity of the elements in the self which produces harmonious and creative life, the unity of churches, of classes and of nations. We understand that true unity is not based on identity or uniformity, but brings together varied elements wherever there is the love which serves as the intensely unifying power. This conception of unity, unlike the mathematical notion, makes intelligible the notion of immortality. On the presupposition of a unity of simplicity, union with God can only mean absorption into his undifferentiated unity and loss of personal identity. But given the notion of the unity of love in the Trinity, in which the Persons yet remain distinct, we can see how it is possible that God takes "created souls to be one while remaining many in the unity of the Blessed

[12] Ibid., 179f.   [13] Ibid., 180. (Italics mine.)

Trinity." [14] Finally, this conception of the Trinity enables us to see how God can be truly personal without our falling into the error of making the created universe necessary to God. Hodgson argues that the "idea of personality implies a plurality of persons. We cannot think of any life as truly personal unless it be a life of intercourse between persons." If God is only one person, then there must be some object outside himself which is the object of his love, presumably the created world. But the doctrine of the Trinity teaches us that God has within himself "all the elements necessary for a fully personal life." Thus we can maintain the independence and full personality of God, and the freedom of his love for the world.[15]

C. CHARLES LOWRY

The Anglican tendency toward the view that the Trinity consists of a fellowship or society of persons is best represented in America by Charles Lowry's *The Trinity and Christian Devotion.* This book is intended as a basically popular work and shows clearly the influence of Hodgson, though at some points Lowry is more explicit (and perhaps more extreme) and more accurate in interpretation of the tradition.

Lowry is quite at one with Hodgson in holding that Christianity is a trinitarian religion, i.e. that the "facts" of the religion compel formulation of a doctrine of Trinity. The primary facts are: 1) Christ—on the question of his ultimate being hangs the integrity of the whole Christian revelation—and 2) the outpouring of the Holy Spirit, experienced in ecstatic prophetism, the *koinonia* of the community and new ethical and spiritual levels of life.[1] Lowry places great weight on the Matthean baptismal formula as indicating the trinitarian consciousness of the Church at a very early time. The fact that the Son and the Holy Spirit are included under a singular name with the Father, in a gospel which "by general consent is the most nearly official and authoritative

---

[14] Ibid., 189. Cf. 187ff.
[15] Ibid., 189ff. In this argument, Hodgson returns to one of the primary sources of the nineteenth-century social theory of the Trinity.
[1] Lowry, op. cit., 61ff., 66ff.

Church document of the first century," indicates that by *cir.*
85 A.D. "the Church as represented at least by a very influential
section of it, believed that the crucified and risen Son of God and
the Spirit of the Lord were *both* distinct entities or 'Persons' *and*
at the same time united in some very close way with the Father-
God of Israel and the Master's own teaching, and sharing in the
heavenly glory and universal authority of the Lord of Sabaoth." [2]

The way in which Lowry puts this last assertion is significant,
for it illustrates most vividly a point of view basic to the social
theory of the Trinity, namely, that the witness of the New Testament is primarily to the threeness rather than to the unity of God.
This was expressly indicated in Thornton's contention that the
religious interest is chiefly in the threefoldness and Hodgson's
observation that we know God most directly in his multiplicity
rather than in his unity. So also Lowry concludes from the New
Testament evidence that the Church looked "to Three . . . not
simply to one. At the same time there was, they knew, a perfect
unity of *will, thought* and *action* as among the Three, and there
was, *they must have assumed (though here we can only speculate), some kind of ultimate common Divine being,* since the Son
certainly was of his Father and the Spirit was the cosmically oper-
ative breath of the Lord Jehovah. At any rate, there was in this
Trinity none of the personal dissonance, active spiritual divergence, and conflict of wills characteristic of the many Gods
of paganism. And the idea of the single Divine name was retained." [3]

In his own formulation of the doctrine of the Trinity, Lowry
is willing to make free use of the phrase "centers of consciousness," which Hodgson seems to avoid. Whereas Hodgson speaks
vaguely of "complete persons" or "persons in the full sense of the
word," Lowry defines the Persons more precisely as "faces or
media of manifestation, and centers of consciousness." Father, Son

---

[2] Ibid., 54.
[3] Loc. cit. (italics mine). Note how little Lowry is able to say here of the
unity of God. He says elsewhere that in the NT the "distributive manifestation" of God is in the forefront; there is no thought of denying monotheism
or even questioning it, "but it remains in the background" (ibid., 83f.).

and Spirit are each personal agents, centers of will and activity, "distinct, individual, personal determinations and centers of God-head." [4] At the same time, Lowry speaks of the Persons as "constituted internally" by a "common Divine consciousness"—one God with one "being, life, mind, will, and consciousness." There is, he says, a "real sharing, a genuine communion, an authentic love" between the centers of consciousness and activity.[5] Furthermore, he holds that the unity of God is not an impersonal unity, as of essence or universal. It is more than mere unity of spirit of two people or the unity of a group. It is a "superpersonal union" of the Divine Persons, so that God in his unity may be spoken of as "Thou" or "He." There is no analogy for this Divine unity which is "more than weakly partial or faintly suggestive," though Lowry accepts Hodgson's concept of intensive or organic unity as a fundamental contribution to trinitarian thought. He also finds the unity guarded by the Augustinian conception of the unity of the action of the Trinity (*opera trinitatis ad extra indivisa sunt*).

In contrast to Hodgson, Lowry does not believe that the social conception of the Trinity has been central in the history of the doctrine. The definitions which he offers for *substantia, persona* and *hypostasis* indicate that he does not think of the classical formulæ as requiring the modern conception of person.[6] He thinks that Augustine, in analyzing the Johannine proposition "God is love," started out on the social analogy and occasionally came back to it in his conception of the Father and Son as united in the love which is the Holy Spirit. But because Augustine could not reconcile genuine sociality in God with his mathematical conception of unity he drew back and devoted most of his time to the exploration of the analogy from the single human personality. It was the analogy of the individual person which then became standard for thought about the Trinity until the nineteenth century when

---

[4] Ibid., 19, 79.   [5] Ibid., 106, 88.

[6] *Substantia* = "concrete being: including both the sum of attributes and the unique principle of individuality." *Persona* = "a permanent individual mode or manner of Divine existence." *Hypostasis* = "that which supports in being various attributes or a concrete individual determination of being." (Ibid., 81, 82.) Cf. also 99, where Lowry identifies the final Cappadocian view as a "modal" view.

there arose a definite trend toward a social understanding of God.

In view of this historical judgment, Lowry's reasons for accepting the social analogy are illuminating. He sees three possible alternatives for modern thought. One is what he calls "essential Sabellianism," i.e. the Trinity as one of appearance or experience only. This view he rejects as wholly inconsistent with any explanation of the Christian facts.[7] The "modal" view, which Lowry thinks was the final Cappadocian view and which was included in Augustine's scheme, expresses the belief that God is "one identical Divine being in point of internal content, but that this Being, God Himself, exists really and objectively in a threefold manner. . . ."[8] This second view Lowry himself held for a long time, but now rejects because of two serious "and possibly fatal" defects. It has "no clear analogy in human experience"; we can have a clear analogy from individual personality or from human society, but we know of no middle existence. Moreover, this view "leans too heavily on the relation of God to the world or creation (and redemption as a process set within it). It contains nothing within it that is intrinsically self-explanatory and intellectually satisfying from the standpoint of God-in-Himself."[9] The third alternative, which admits the analogy from the society or fellowship of persons, involves the thoroughgoing application of the view which Augustine suggested in his exposition of the thesis that God is love. It is consistent with the Christian facts, avoids the defects of the "modal" view, and expresses most adequately the central Christian conviction that God in his innermost nature is love. We must be careful, however, to safeguard the unity of God (by a conception of intensive unity) and to recall that all thinking about God is analogical and symbolical.

A good deal of what Lowry has to say about the Trinity and

---

[7] Lowry would not include in this view Sabellius's notion of temporal succession of the Persons. (Cf. ibid., 98f.)

[8] Ibid., 99. This view is, of course, to be sharply distinguished from "modalism," which term is often used to mean Sabellianism.

[9] Ibid., 100, 101. Lowry seems to allow that this "modal" view is not inconsistent with the NT.

Christian worship may be succinctly summarized in the assertion that all Christian devotion is at least implicitly trinitarian. Christian devotion is not simply self-surrender and dedication to God. It is that, of course, but more specifically it is "union with Christ in the power of the Holy Spirit," e.g. in Baptism and Communion.[10] The vision of God is the vision of the Three in One, for we see him who has revealed himself to us as Father, Son and Holy Spirit. Our encounter with God is with him "who is known as knowledge and love because of Jesus Christ and because of the Holy Ghost. It is in the Cross that we know that God is verily our Father and that we are sons and heirs of a matchless inheritance. It is in the power of the Holy Spirit that we know certainly that the crucified rabbi Jesus is Very God and Lord of History, and that His love for us is the love of God Himself." [11] Christian worship is thus inescapably worship of God as Triune. We apprehend him as Creator, Redeemer and Sanctifier, and we believe that God not only acts this way but actually is such a being, hence we worship him as eternally Father, Son and Holy Spirit. Moreover, in our affirmation that God is loving, we affirm that he is in himself eternally Love. As such, he alone is truly worshipful.

Beyond this, Lowry suggests certain "tactics" or techniques of the devotional life which he terms "practical devotional implications of the doctrine of the Trinity," or ways of making worship explicitly as well as implicitly trinitarian, especially in meditation, study and prayer. While Lowry agrees that prayer to God in his unity (as Lord and Father) ought to remain central, he thinks that there is good reason for addressing prayers to the Trinity as such and to the Persons severally. We may properly pray both to Christ and to the Holy Spirit, though of course with no thought of dividing the one substance or being of God, and provided the proper background of such prayer in the doctrine of the Trinity is kept in mind. The understanding of the Trinity is also important for Christian action, in vocation, in concern for the world, and in love.

[10] Ibid., 119.   [11] Ibid., 128.

3. *Interpretation of the Trinity via the Psychological Analogy or a Combination of Analogies*

Within the broad framework of the approach to the doctrine of the Trinity outlined at the beginning of this chapter, the development of the social analogy by Thornton, Hodgson and Lowry is undoubtedly the most fully articulated position in the contemporary theological scene.[1] There are, however, several major theologians who, while adopting the same general position concerning the basis and importance of the doctrine, differ sharply from Hodgson and Lowry in their conception of the relative usefulness of the social and psychological analogies. J. S. Whale, W. Norman Pittenger and Nathaniel Micklem may be taken as examples of summary statements of the doctrine of the Trinity either primarily along the lines of the psychological analogy (Whale), or in terms of a middle position (Pittenger), or by a combination of the two analogies (Micklem).

The divergence between the psychological and social approaches to the Trinity is rooted ultimately and directly in different understandings of the revelation which is held to be the basis of the doctrine. J. S. Whale, for example, summarizes the biblical witness as testimony first of all to the One only God, about whom it speaks "in three distinct ways which are normative for Christian thinking." [2] The development of the doctrine of the Trinity is thus a "further definition of monotheism," an elaboration of the unitary conception of God in terms of triunity. In other words, he understands the movement of the biblical testimony to be from unity to trinity—the New Testament speaks of the action of the one God by which he reveals himself to be threefold in his unity. Probably neither Hodgson nor Lowry would object strenuously to the actual phraseology used here,

---

[1] Of course, the by far most detailed and elaborate statement of a doctrine of Trinity in contemporary Protestant theology is to be found in Karl Barth's *Dogmatik*, where the psychological analogy is vigorously affirmed. But Barth's distinctive conception of the ground and role of the doctrine takes his work out of the general type here considered and requires that it be discussed separately (see below, ch. VI).

[2] Whale, op. cit., 114.

but the difference of approach is unmistakable. They begin by emphasizing the threeness and then move to the problem of unity —this we may call a doctrine of Trinity in Unity. Whale proceeds in the opposite direction, and we may describe his view as one of Unity in Trinity.

It is in accordance with his understanding of the biblical evidence that Whale asserts that the resultant doctrine of the Trinity "acknowledged in the Godhead, not one Individual nor three Individuals, but a personal unity existing in three eternal modes or functions." [3] The terms *hypostasis* (or subsistence) and *persona* (or person) he says were intended to have a common meaning, which was "more than 'phase' . . . and less than 'individual personality.' " [4] "Person" does not mean what is usually meant by "personality." The doctrine of the Trinity does not refer to three subjects; that would make tritheism inevitable. Whale's own suggestion is that God is one as subject, three as object. We cannot separate the activity of Father, Son and Spirit, yet these three terms stand for "distinctive and precious religious realities." [5]

Whereas Whale is plainly committed to the psychological analogy, Pittenger seems to adopt an intermediate position. The three experiences of God and relationships to him which comprise the complex event of revelation and the experience of the Church, require the affirmation that there is diversity in the unity of the Godhead. There are distinct yet interpenetrating "Persons," with peculiar operations or "economies" (though the whole Godhead is involved in all the divine activities). The "Persons," Pittenger holds, are not quite substantival (i.e. not univocally persons), nor merely adjectival, but half-way between. "If they are 'aspects,' " he says, "they are eternal and are as it were relatively distinct and different; if they are 'persons' they are so interpenetrating and so make up the one life which is God that they are also one together. Or we might say that as relationships subsisting in God, they have a certain 'prepositional' character: of him, in him, through him." [6] Later, he speaks of the Creative Source, Self-

[3] Ibid., 116.
[4] Ibid., 118.
[5] Ibid., 119.
[6] Pittenger, op. cit., 139.

Expression, and Response (terms strongly suggestive of the psychological analogy) as "inseparable eternal modes of being and activity, not merely 'adjectival' aspects of God but true subsistents." [7]

We have indicated that Micklem makes use of both the psychological and social analogies. The doctrine may be considered first as an assertion of true Personality in God. God's personality is analogous to ours; it includes three fundamental aspects or determinations—Father, Word and Spirit. The Word is associated with Wisdom and Purpose, and is embodied in Christ, hence called Son. Spirit refers to Creative activity or energy. Since God's thought gives actuality and substance to what he thinks, we may speak of the mutual love of the Father and the Word, and of the subsistence of that love. Micklem is obviously following in the lines of the traditional "Thomistic analogy" here. A second approach to the doctrine is by way of the religious basis in the experience of God as Creator and Sustainer, as the Redeemer in Christ, and as Sanctifier in the experience of the Holy Spirit. God is apprehended in three *modes*. From this apprehension we can pass to a conception of God in three mighty acts—"His creation, His coming, and His outpouring of the Holy Spirit." [8]

So far, we are still thinking basically in terms of the psychological analogy. But the classical doctrine, Micklem notes—and here he tends to move closer to the social analogy—teaches that God exists in three "Persons." "Person," Micklem points out carefully, is not equivalent in meaning to "person" in the ordinary sense, but means *persona* or *hypostasis*. There is no precise English equivalent for *hypostasis*, but two types of illustrations may be offered: the illustration of men as concrete individuations of human nature, and the illustration of ice, water, and vapor as concrete individuations of H_2O. The three *hypostases* are analogous to thinker, thought and will in man: yet these are "individual, subsistent determinations of His Being as distinct from one another as Peter and Paul." [9] Beyond this, Micklem will not take us. This is an insoluble mystery, but one which must be asserted. The Incarna-

---

[7] Ibid., 144.   [8] Ibid., 122.   [9] Ibid., 127.

tion necessitates the assertion that God exists in two *hypostases*, the Father and the Son, "for the Son is both God and at the same time not the Father," and the experience of God in the Church requires the affirmation of a third *hypostasis*, for "God's Spirit is God Himself, yet not identical with the Father." [10]

It is evident that Whale, Pittenger and Micklem are far from attempting any thoroughgoing restatement or reconstruction of the doctrine, after the fashion of Hodgson or Barth. They are content, by and large, to sketch what they take to be the central intent of the doctrine, and to show how that doctrine is necessitated by the nature and content of the Christian revelation. But it is equally evident that they do not conceive of the orthodox doctrine as teaching the sort of social Trinity advocated by Hodgson and Lowry, nor do they understand the biblical witness to require such a doctrine.

4. *The Problem of the Unity of the Doctrine of the Trinity*

We now have before us in some detail a variety of efforts to restate the doctrine of the Trinity and to reinstate it in a central place in Christian thinking. Already there has appeared a substantial divergence in the views of the *form* of the doctrine. But because of the brevity and incomplete nature of the statements of the psychological analogy, it would be difficult for us at this point to assess concretely the relative merits of this and the social analogy. All of these efforts, however, rest on a common understanding of the *basis* and *role* of the doctrine, and to this we must turn careful attention, for here lies a crucial aspect of the whole effort to rethink the doctrine of the Trinity in contemporary terms.

At the beginning of our survey of contemporary concern with this doctrine, we made a provisional distinction between two general concepts of the role of the doctrine in Christian theology.[1] According to the first, the trinitarian conception is a necessary combination or synthesis of several fundamental elements of Christian revelation and experience; it is therefore significant as the ulti-

---

[10] Ibid., 129, 130.   [1] Cf. above, 47f., 127.

mate and inclusive implicate, the final safeguard of the faith. According to the second conception, the doctrine is an *immediate* implication of the fact, form and content of revelation. With the material now before us, we can see more clearly the nature and importance of this distinction. In it lies the heart of the problem of the doctrine of the Trinity in contemporary theology.

That problem is one of the *unity of the ground or basis* of the doctrine of the Trinity, whence it also becomes a question of an integral relation to other Christian affirmations and the whole of the doctrinal system. This problem is posed in the first instance by Schleiermacher's insistence that all Christian theology be an organic whole and be at every point derived from the "immediate utterances" of the Christian consciousness. Schleiermacher's rejection of the doctrine of the Trinity was, of course, based partly on his subjectivistic understanding of religious experience; but also important was the fact that to him the trinitarian doctrine was only a *combination* of several direct utterances of the Christian consciousness, and that therefore the doctrine could never hold more than an indirect and secondary place in the system of Christian thought. In other words, the notion of the Triune God is not a part of the primary witness of faith, but is only the result of an attempt to put together or synthesize various elements of the primitive revelation. The problem is stated in similar form by Peter H. Steenstra, writing near the close of the nineteenth century. He writes that the Christian consciousness is certain of the fact of the divine power of Christ, and of the deduction therefrom that Christ is God Incarnate. Also the Christian experience of the Holy Spirit implies the deity of the Spirit. But, he comments, "it is possible to conceive of the facts as truly apprehended and truly described in single disjointed propositions, and yet entertain misgivings as to the validity and certainty of these elements in larger dogmatic statements." [2]

We may now suggest that this judgment on the place or role of the doctrine of the Trinity as a combination or synthesis of elements of faith clearly dominates contemporary thought. Those

[2] *The Being of God as Unity and Trinity* (1891), 177.

who defend the doctrine argue that it is a valid and necessary synthesis, but *they share with those who would reject the doctrine this common presupposition regarding its basis and development.*

This point of view is expressed in systematic form, for example, by Whale, who, it will be recalled, understands the doctrine of the Trinity to be an attempt to reconcile three apparently incompatible axioms: monotheism, which Christianity inherited from Judaism; belief in the divinity of Christ; and the new experience of God in the Holy Spirit.[3] Lowry, in similar vein, identifies the doctrine as a "grand generalization," which brings together all the Christian facts—or, more accurately, which results from the addition of the faith that Christ was truly God and the belief in the equal deity of the Spirit to the received faith in the Father-God of the Old Testament.[4]

This systematic judgment is often expressed as a corollary of the historical judgment that the development of the doctrine of the Trinity is to be understood as an effort to reconcile the experience of God in Christ, or the divinity of Christ, with the received and prior commitment to monotheism. Thus W. R. Matthews asserts that the doctrine is "historically the outcome of an attempt to preserve the two essential features of Christian experience—that God is one and that Jesus Christ is of right the object of worship, and hence neither merely human nor a demi-god." [5] And Knudson states that the doctrine grew out of the expanded idea of deity which was necessary when "Jesus *as well as* the traditional God came to be regarded as divine." [6]

In Thornton and Hodgson, the problem takes a slightly different form, which is typical of, but not limited to, the advocates of the social analogy. This is the tendency to separate the basis of the affirmation of the unity of God from the basis of the affirmation of the distinction of Persons. So Thornton holds that reason is pri-

[3] Whale, op. cit., 112ff.
[4] Lowry, op. cit., 54ff., 66ff. Cf. also Pittenger, op. cit., 138f.; and Micklem, op. cit., 120ff.
[5] Matthews, *God in Christian Experience*, 184f.
[6] Knudson, op. cit., 370 (italics mine). Cf. 385ff. See also Horton, op. cit., 25; Edwards, op. cit., 338; Rall, op. cit., 83f.; and not least Brunner, *Dogmatik*, 221f.

marily interested in the unity of God, whereas religious experience, which starts from the experience of personal communion with Father, Son and Spirit, is chiefly interested in the distinctions.[7] On the grounds of Hodgson's argument for the revision of the concept of unity, it might be held that he avoids this particular sort of division. Certainly his thought is largely free of the tendency to separate the revelation in Christ and the experience of the Spirit into different facts or elements. But, as we have indicated above, Hodgson does not really ground the *unity* of God in the "empirical facts" of revelation. His case for a new conception of divine unity comes close to a recognition of the "togetherness" and interrelatedness of trinity and unity, but he does not perceive the implications of this. He speaks of reason and revelation as uniting to insist that God is One, but as he explains this it means simply that revelation qualifies the type of unity which can be attributed to God. Essentially his point of view is that the affirmation of unity and trinity have different sources. Unity is required by reason and the Jewish heritage; trinity by the facts of revelation.[8] The revelation is thus something to be reconciled with the unity of God, and the latter we cannot know directly (as we can the plurality) but can only believe by an act of rational faith.

In discussing Roman Catholic thought, we called attention to the problem of trinity and unity in Pohle-Preuss's exposition. Pohle-Preuss approach the problem from the negative side, developing the concept of trinity in unity against monarchianism and unitarianism, and the concept of unity in trinity against tritheism. But this approach does not show us any way in which unity and trinity contribute to and require each other. It is a doctrine of trinity *and* unity: for certain reasons, God is said to be one; for certain other reasons he is said to be trinity. Both are to be affirmed, and neither to the exclusion of the other, but trinity and unity are always in a relation, if not of opposition, at least of parallelism in which neither contributes to the intelligibility of the other. We

---

[7] Thornton, *The Incarnate Lord*, 382ff. Cf. Selwyn, ed., *Essays Catholic and Critical*, 143f.

[8] Hodgson, op. cit., 97ff.

cannot be satisfied, however, with this negative approach if the doctrine of the Trinity is to be truly meaningful as an explication of Christian experience, or more than an intellectual "defensive doctrine" (to use Brunner's phrase). Nor can the problem be met adequately on the level of the discussion of the relation of "substance" and "person." This is undoubtedly important, but the real root of the problem of trinity and unity lies in the realm of the basis of the doctrine in revelation.

These illustrations should help to make clear the essential nature of what I have called the synthetic approach to the doctrine of the Trinity. Sometimes the doctrine is simply an intellectual attempt to reconcile and unite various independent propositions of the Christian revelation. This view is primarily characteristic of theology which rests on a literalistic approach to scripture. More important is the conception of the Trinity as a summation of three disparate experiences of God (as Creator, in nature, as Redeemer, in Christ, and as Holy Spirit, in the Church), or as the consequence of the need to reconcile the revelation of God in Christ and the Spirit with the prior commitment to monotheism. Interrelated with this, but distinguishable as a different form of the basic viewpoint, is the notion that the threefoldness is the specific interest of Christian revelation and experience, while the unity of God is grounded in the requirements of reason or the heritage of Judaism.

But if this is the real nature of the *doctrine* of the Trinity, it is hard to see how an adequate reply can be made to Schleiermacher's contention that the doctrine is not an immediate utterance of faith but only a combination of such utterances and therefore of secondary importance. No matter how strongly we affirm that such a formulation or synthesis is inevitable and necessary, either to ground the primary affirmations of faith in ultimate reality or to satisfy the intellectual demand for the completion of the system, the doctrine remains secondary in the order of the interests of faith. It does not stand on a par with the primary affirmations of God as Creator, of the divinity of Christ and of the deity of the Spirit; it stands on a plane once removed, in which these "immediate" conclusions of faith become the data for a further conclusion about the nature of God.

We may recall here Garrigou-Lagrange's charge that for many Protestants the doctrine of the Trinity has only "an indirect importance, by reason of its connection with the dogmas of the Incarnation in its redemptive aspect, and of the mission of the Holy Ghost, which presupposes three persons in God." It serves to guard against contradiction in these essential beliefs. On the contrary, Garrigou-Lagrange holds, "if this single mystery is a safeguard against contradiction in the other mysteries, this is so because it is their supreme principle, the very center of the whole faith, . . . If this supreme mystery were to become evident for us, as it is for the blessed in heaven, then all the other mysteries would be illumined from this sublime source." [9]

It would be better to say that if the doctrine of the Trinity is the center of the faith, it ought *now* to be a source of illumination for all the other doctrines. The Protestant theologians whom we have been considering in this chapter doubtless desire to establish the doctrine of the Trinity in just such a central place. But they are prevented from accomplishing this by the "indirect" (or "synthetic") method of developing the doctrine from its root in revelation. Given this understanding of the basis and elaboration of the doctrine, it is hard to see how the Trinity can be held to be a genuine *arché* or first principle of Christian thought. The synthetic view of the doctrine tends inevitably to suggest that it is essentially a kind of defensive doctrine, somewhat further removed from the life of faith than those affirmations which it is supposed to bring together.

[9] R. Garrigou-Lagrange, op. cit., 173f.

CHAPTER VI

The Trinity as the Immediate Implication of Revelation

The root problem in contemporary reconstruction of the doctrine of the Trinity is, according to our analysis, the question of its ground in revelation. We have seen that many recent attempts to reinstate the trinitarian conception in a truly central place in the Christian understanding of God are able to interpret this doctrine as only an *indirect* consequence of the revelation in Christ and therefore as subsequent to and an intellectual *synthesis* of other more primary and relatively independent affirmations. The question may be raised, then, whether this conception of the purpose and role of the doctrine of the Trinity does, in fact, represent the proper understanding of the biblical writers, or whether there is another way of approaching the materials which rests on a deeper appreciation of the unity of the gospel, and which might also prove sound the claim that this doctrine is in truth "the very center of the whole faith."

We suggested earlier that there might indeed be another way of looking at the doctrine of the Trinity, viz. as an *analysis*, an immediate implication of revelation, and therefore as essentially identical with the content of revelation. If such a conception can be shown to be more in harmony with the New Testament witness to the revelation in Jesus Christ, it will provide both explanation and validation for the classical judgments on the centrality of the trinitarian notion, and will show a way out of the difficulties entailed by the approaches to the doctrine which we have thus far considered. The possibility of just such a restatement of the basis and development of the doctrine is most notably to be seen, at least implicitly and in some places explicitly, in the work of Karl

Barth, whose treatise on the Trinity is by far the most elaborate and detailed statement in contemporary Protestant theology.

The difference between Barth's view and the views considered in the previous chapter is not that they hold the doctrine of the Trinity to be an intellectual formulation while he does not. If anything, Barth is willing to go further (than e.g. Thornton or Lowry) in recognizing that the Bible does not contain the dogma of the Trinity as such, any more than it explicitly contains any other dogmas. Barth is quite willing to say that this doctrine is an *implication* or an *interpretation* of the revelation and that the question is whether it is a *proper* interpretation. It is only the ground or "root" of the doctrine of the Trinity which is explicitly contained in scripture. The distinctive aspect of Barth's thought is the way in which he understands this root, so that for him the doctrine is not a synthesis or reconciliation of several elements, but what may be called an "analytical" development of the central fact of revelation. It is in this perspective that we shall find the most valuable contribution of Barth to the contemporary discussion of the Trinity.

1. *The Place of the Doctrine*

The most striking indication of Barth's judgment on the significance of the doctrine of the Trinity is the fact that he places it at the beginning of his dogmatics, not simply at the beginning of the doctrine of God or as the first doctrine, but actually in the *prolegomena* to dogmatics. This is not all, for the understanding of the doctrine which he delineates in *The Doctrine of the Word of God* is a continually recurring motif in the subsequent volumes of the *Kirchliche Dogmatik*. Barth turns again and again to relate the doctrines he is discussing to the trinitarian conception of God. The Trinity, he holds, is not an isolated affirmation about God, but is fundamental to all of the other aspects of the Christian faith.

This is seen especially, of course, in his treatment of the doctrine of God proper. The triunity of God is the basis, the inner truth and power of his self-disclosure as the Lord. His eternal Father-hood is the ground of his Fatherhood and lordship over us. It is as triune that God is in himself living and loving. His freedom consists in the "innertrinitarian" life of the Father with the Son through the Spirit. His freedom is not an abstract freedom or sovereignty, and his love is not an abstract seeking and finding of community; but his freedom and love are concrete in his being as Father, Son and Holy Spirit. God's triune nature is the ground of the perfections of his being—his eternity, his omnipotence, his omnipresence. The relation of Father and Son is the "type" of all relations of origination, whether of Creator-creature or inter-creaturely relations. The internal self-giving of God as Father and Son is the ground of the possibility of creation. The doctrine of the Trinity is the basis of a proper view of sin and reconciliation; and in particular the doctrine of the deity of the Holy Spirit is the presupposition of the doctrine of grace.[1]

The use of the trinitarian concept in later portions of the *Dogmatik*, while important as pointing to Barth's notion of the centrality of the doctrine and as providing an illustration of an attempt to make the Trinity truly an informing first principle of the doctrine of God and dogmatics generally, does not, however, add anything essentially new to the understanding of either the content or the place of the doctrine as Barth has elaborated these in the basic statements in the *Doctrine of the Word*. In that work, Barth indicates explicitly the primary reason why he places the doctrine of the Triune God at the head of dogmatics, and under the category of prolegomena. The doctrine must be found even in prolegomena, for as soon as we inquire into the revelation which the scriptures attest—this being the proper task of theology —we discover that a threefold question is involved. The revelation "absolutely insists on being regarded from the side of its subject, God." [2] And this means that we must ask not only *Who* is the

---

[1] Cf. *Dogmatik*, II/1, pp. 51f., 67, 535, 356f., 418, 743f., 364, 693, 595, 606, 627; *Dogmatik*, III/1, pp. 51ff.; *Doctrine of the Word of God*, 451, 469f., 535f.

[2] *Doctrine of the Word of God*, 339. (I am italicizing words which are emphasized in the original by spacing.)

self-revealing God, but also *how* this happens and *what* is the result. The statement "God reveals Himself"—by which we are to understand that it is *God* who reveals himself, that he reveals himself *through* himself, and that he reveals *himself*—is the identical answer which we are to give to all three questions.

Barth is correct in insisting that he is not here indulging in mere rationalistic deduction from a general proposition that God reveals himself; he is rather summarizing in a formula what the revelation means. The testimony to this actual revelation (which is Jesus Christ) is at one and the same time testimony to him who is the author of the revelation and to what is achieved in those who receive the revelation. It is testimony that God himself is the revealer and also his self-revelation and what he achieves in men; and it is the one God in "unimpaired unity" which does not dissolve the boundaries of these three forms of God in his revelation. Thus "by consideration of the unity and variety of God in His revelation attested in Scripture . . . we are confronted with the problem of the doctrine of the Trinity." [3]

Barth further justifies his beginning with the trinitarian doctrine on the grounds that the question of the significance of scripture, which is commonly treated first in dogmatics, cannot be answered "unless previously it has been made clear—naturally from Holy Scripture itself—who that God is whose revelation makes Scripture Holy." [4] Similarly, the questions of the existence and nature of God cannot be determined except on the basis of the decisive question, Who God is. And since the Christian conception of God (and of revelation) is distinguished from all other conceptions by the doctrine of the Trinity, it is proper that that doctrine should both externally and internally be placed at the head of dogmatics.

In these last two sentences, we approach the problem of the relation of Barth's view of the Trinity to his rejection of natural theology. Brunner claims that for Barth the decisive significance of the doctrine lies in its usefulness in opposing speculative "natural theology," in centering everything from beginning to end in

[3] Ibid., 344. Cf. 343f.   [4] Ibid., 345.

Jesus Christ. The God of the doctrine of the Trinity is the God of revelation, not the God of philosophy. Therefore Barth places it first.[5] It is undoubtedly true that Barth's emphasis on the doctrine of the Trinity may be taken as indicating his opposition to natural theology. But to say that for him the "decisive significance" of the doctrine lies here is to go too far. Barth attaches a supreme significance to the doctrine of the Trinity because (in contrast to Brunner) he really believes it to be an immediate implication of the fact, form and content of revelation; the doctrine is truly descriptive of God as he is in himself and therefore has a "practical, comprehensive significance" for all the rest of dogmatics. This can be said quite without reference to the question of the possibility of natural theology. The fact that Barth begins his *Dogmatik* by talking about the Trinity is in his case obviously associated with his attitude toward natural theology, but there is no necessary connection between the procedure and the attitude.

Brunner rather petulantly complains that Barth ought not in any case to have treated the doctrine in a discussion of prolegomena, which ought to be concerned with formal rather than material considerations. Here he has missed the point completely, not only of Barth's insistence on the unity of form and content, but of Barth's whole argument for the necessarily trinitarian nature of revelation. By treating the Trinity under the heading of Revelation, Barth achieves a double purpose. He emphasizes the exclusively revelational basis of this doctrine, developing the conception of the immanent Trinity at every point from the economic (and thereby avoiding the speculative approach to the immanent Trinity, of which Brunner is so much afraid). And by making the doctrine a part of prolegomena, Barth calls attention to the all-pervasive importance and influence of the doctrine. It is not just a part of the Christian doctrine of God but is integral to every aspect of the doctrine of God and to every other doctrine as well. Every Christian doctrine which purports to be based in revelation must be understood in terms of a trinitarian revelation

[5] Brunner, *Dogmatik*, I, 251.

(and thus the doctrine of the Trinity offers a crucial test for any theology which claims to speak of revelation).

In speaking of the interdependence of the problems of revelation and Trinity, it is well to recall Barth's readiness to affirm that the *doctrine* of the Trinity is not to be found in the scripture. The Bible presents us only with the *possibility* of the doctrine. Therefore, this dogma (like all others) must be continually recreated in relation to the language and concerns of the time. It did not originate in the historical situation of the scriptural texts. "It is the exegesis of these texts in the language, which means also in the light, of the questions arising out of a later situation. It belongs to the Church. It is a theologoumenon. It is a dogma." [6] This language reminds us of Brunner's description of the Trinity as a theological doctrine, but the implications are altogether different. Brunner assumes that because the Trinity is in the order of knowledge a product of theological reflection and not a part of the biblical *kerygma*, it is therefore for Christian faith only secondary and defensive. Barth sees that the significance of the doctrine is by no means determined simply by the time or circumstances of its elaboration.

Barth is quite willing to reckon with all the political, economic and other "profane" motives which were involved in the actual historical development of the doctrine of the Trinity. But when all this is admitted, there still remains the crucial question whether in this development the Church was not really confronted with a problem which we too cannot escape. Barth holds that the answer to this query is Yes! The question to which the doctrine of the Trinity is a reply is a question which arose directly out of the fact that the Church's proclamation is based on scripture, and was (and is) "a basic question, a life question of first rank for Church preaching and therefore likewise for Church theology." [7] It is the question of the Subject of revelation.

In other words, the question to which the doctrine of the Trinity is an answer is the question of the *reality* of revelation. This is indicated in Barth's assertions that the "predominant and decisive interest" of the doctrine "consists in stating adequately and completely that the Revealer is *God*"; and that the trinitarian dogma states this adequately and completely by "announcing that none other than the Revealer is God." [8] The two respects in which the doctrine goes beyond the biblical witness (and which therefore constitute the essential content of the Church doctrine as such) are, according to Barth, the denial of subordinationism and the denial of modalism. In both of these negative declarations, the doctrine asserts the reality of revelation. The denial of *subordinationism* is a denial that there is a "more or less in the Godness of God," i.e. a refutation of the notion that the God whom we meet in Jesus Christ or who is imparted to us in the Holy Spirit is somehow less than truly God. The denial of subordinationism is therefore the affirmation that as Son and as Spirit, God remains God. He is *Thou*, not an It or a He who can become an object and whose "thouness" can be limited and controlled. By being equally God as Father, Son and Holy Spirit, God remains equally Thou and therefore Lord. "The Subject of revelation is the Subject that remains *indissolubly Subject*." [9]

Modalism, as Barth understands the term, is the doctrine that Father, Son and Spirit are distinctions which only pertain to God for us, or God in his revelation, not to God in himself. But this is again a denial of revelation, a denial that *our* God, the God who makes himself known to us and makes himself ours in revelation, is really God. The doctrine of the Trinity, therefore, asserts that God is God only as Father, Son and Holy Spirit, i.e. that the three "elements" or "moments" of his self-revelation are not foreign or external to the Being of God. In opposition to subordinationism, then, the doctrine of the Trinity affirms that the God who reveals himself can be our *God*, "because He is equal to Himself in all His modes of existence, is one and the same Lord." In opposition to modalism, it affirms that the Lord can be *our* God, because his revelation, his willing to be our God, "is grounded and typified in His own essence, in His Godness itself." [10]

In sum, Barth is quite ready to agree that the doctrine of the

---

[8] Ibid., 436.   [9] Ibid., 438.   [10] Ibid., 440.

Trinity is not a scriptural doctrine, in the sense that as such it is not to be found in scripture. He declares it to be a *Church* doctrine. He is willing to speak of the doctrine as an "interpretation," an intellectual formulation only indirectly identical with propositions about revelation, and as an "objective presupposition." As against Brunner, who charges that because the doctrine is of this sort it is only a defensive doctrine and not to be preached, Barth stands on the side of all those who believe this to be a necessary and permanently valid formulation. He shares with them (in opposition to Brunner and to all modalism and monarchianism) the notion that the doctrine is the necessary implication of the revelation and redemption in Christ.

None of the elaborations of the doctrine of the Trinity considered earlier, however, are really able to meet the charge that the doctrine is in a measure secondary to other primary affirmations of faith. Barth escapes that difficulty because he understands the process of "interpretation" or "intellectual formulation" differently, viz. as "analytical" rather than "synthetic." The possibility of this alternative view rests upon Barth's distinctive understanding of the basis of the doctrine in revelation, and so to understand the crucial difference between Barth's view and the views considered in the previous chapter, we must turn to a careful examination of his conception of the root of the doctrine in scripture. It is this conception which lies behind and gives meaning to Barth's judgment concerning the primary and pervasive importance of the doctrine of the Triune God.

2. *The Ground of the Doctrine*

A. THE "FACT" OF REVELATION AND THE PROBLEM OF THE DOCTRINE

The revelation attested by scripture, according to Barth, means at least two things. First, it means that God himself addresses man as "thou," and therefore is himself immediately present in his speaking. His revelation is not something accidental to or less than himself which we can get behind and examine on the basis of a higher or more profound knowledge of God. In other words, the Bible purports to testify to a real revelation in which God himself has truly come to man. And, though we may speak of a great many implications and consequences which might be called reve-latory, he himself is the *content* of that revelation. Thus, second, God's revelation is a revelation of his Godhood, i.e. his coming to man as the Lord, which is to say that it is God's bringing him-self before the consciousness of another as a superior will, an I before a Thou.

The term "revelation" is, of course, being used here in a com-prehensive sense to describe *the whole of the existential relation-ship in which man is confronted by God.* Though Barth is Cal-vinistic in holding to the fundamental unity of the biblical wit-ness to revelation, it is quite clear that in his thinking the heart of the revelation and the pattern and norm for the whole definition of revelation is the event of God's coming in Jesus Christ. Thus "revelation" must here be understood to involve reconciliation, redemption, judgment—everything which is to be associated with the coming of Jesus Christ. This does not mean that these terms can be simply identified, but that the term revelation is used by Barth as the word which most readily characterizes the entire act of God's coming to man. Revelation is God's showing himself, his making himself present to man, his giving himself to man.

With this in mind, we can come specifically to Barth's designa-tion of the *root* of the doctrine of the Trinity by the statement *"God reveals Himself as the Lord."* [1] This sentence designates both form and content of the biblical revelation. Its meaning is to be analyzed in terms of the three concepts, Revealer, Revelation, and Revealedness. The chief theme of the Bible is evidently the second of the three, the Revelation, and similarly the historical construction of the doctrine of the Trinity centers mainly around the Son. But all three have equal weight in substance and logic, and the first and the third concepts come to expression as neces-sary counterparts of the second.

Thus, if we follow the "order" of biblical and historical inter-

[1] Ibid., 353, 360.

est, we may say that revelation means first God's *self-unveiling*, his becoming a Thou to men, his existing for them as God, his coming to them in Christ. This event is God's assuming a form. It is not something which goes without saying but an event, a move on God's part, "something novel in God, God's distinguishing Himself from Himself, a being of God in a mode of existence, not subordinate as compared with His first, hidden mode of being as God, but just different, one in which He can also be existent *for us* . . . God a second time. . . ." [2] The Lordship of God here consists in his freedom to be the Son, to be God for us.

But at the same time, the statement evidently refers equally to the Subject of revelation, the Revealer. Revelation is revelation *"of the God who according to His nature cannot be unveiled to man."* [3] He needs to be revealed; he does not belong to the realm of the creaturely knowledge of God. And his inscrutability is not abolished in the revelation. God speaks *in the form*; he remains free in it; the form does not take his place. Thus in revealing himself, he is both the Revelation and the Revealer. He reveals himself as the Father of the Son, and in so doing is Lord in his freedom to reveal or not to reveal.

Finally, the statement that God reveals himself as the Lord necessarily means that the self-unveiling is *imparted to men*. The revelation of which the Bible speaks is a concrete revelation to concrete men. It is an historical *revealedness*, which comes to men in quite definite historical positions. This is necessarily implied in the conception of God's Lordship as his becoming truly *Thou* to men. But this is *God's* revealedness, *his* being imparted to men so that their experiences and concepts are able to follow and respond to him. Thus there is a third sense in which God is Lord in his revelation: his freedom *"to become the God of such and such men."* God reveals himself as the Spirit—not just any spirit, not the "discoverable and arousable subsoil of man's spiritual life"— but *his* Spirit, the Spirit of the Father and the Son. [4]

There are two aspects of Barth's treatment of this statement about revelation which are crucial to the problem of the basis of

---

[2] Ibid., 363.   [3] Ibid., 368.   [4] Ibid., 381f. Cf. 373ff.

the doctrine of the Trinity. The first is the fact that, according to Barth, the doctrine of the Trinity "is an *analysis* of this statement, i.e. of what it designates." [5] The second is the establishment of a *single* ground of the doctrine. In the context of the first assertion, Barth is pointing out that the doctrine of the Trinity is not as such identical with the revelation, nor is it as such in the scriptures. It is an interpretation, an "ecclesiastically dogmatic" formulation. The point with which we are concerned, however, is the sort of interpretation which Barth has in mind. This becomes clear in his assertion that while statements about the Trinity cannot claim to be *directly* identical with the statement about revelation, nevertheless "the proposition or propositions about the Trinity of God, of course, claim to be . . . *indirectly, identical* with the proposition about revelation." [6] The doctrine is a theoretical formulation, but one which is immediately and directly required by the statement about revelation itself. It is a *"necessary* and *relevant analysis* of revelation." [7] Its content is essentially identical with the content of the proposition about revelation.

In using the term "analysis," Barth is pointing mainly to the necessity of the trinitarian formulation, but the way in which he uses the term calls attention to the second aspect of his view of the root of the doctrine. By deriving the conception of triunity out of the single summary proposition that God reveals himself as the Lord, Barth establishes at least a formal unity of the basis or root of the doctrine. The doctrine is not something arrived at by a combination of the revelation with other insights; it is not necessitated by the problem of relating the revelation to monotheism, or the deity of Christ to the deity of the Father. It is a doctrine arrived at by analysis of the one central fact to which the Bible bears witness—the act of God in revelation—and is therefore indirectly identical with this witness to revelation. Thus the doctrine of the Triune God does not rest merely upon what explicit indications of trinitarianism there may be in the Bible, nor in the piecing together of affirmations of the deity of Christ and the

---

[5] Ibid., 354 (italics mine). Cf. 356.   [6] Ibid., 355 (italics mine). Cf. 383.
[7] Ibid., 356 ("analysis" italicized by me).

Spirit and their unity with the Father, but *on that which unites the whole of the biblical witness.* This is implied in Barth's comment that the explicit indication of trinitarianism in the New Testament "first gathers weight from the fact that it is wrapped up in a perfect network of implicit indications, and above all from the fact that the entire theme of the revelation of God as it is handled in the Old and New Testaments, centrally in the New, cannot be touched, far less grasped, without encountering the preformation of these problems." [8]

The statement about revelation, then, is an attempt to sum up the whole witness of scripture to the dealing of God with man. It indicates that in this dealing there is both unity and variety. The statement has a "threefold [*dreifach*] meaning, yet a simple [*einfach*] content." It calls attention to the three "elements" of *"unveiling, veiling* and *impartation,* or of *form, freedom* and *historicity,* or of *Easter, Good Friday,* and *Pentecost,* or of *the Son, the Father,* and *the Spirit,"* but it also points to the indissoluble and unimpaired unity of the content of revelation. [9] These are not three "elements" in the sense they have to be added to one another or reconciled with one another, for they are clearly inseparable and interdependent. The whole biblical witness *in its unity,* "is implicitly, and in some places explicitly also, an indication [though only this] of the doctrine of the Trinity. In its ground-plan it must be interpreted as the ground-plan also of the doctrine of the Trinity." [10] It is because he understands the root of the doctrine in this way that Barth is able to speak of the doctrine itself as an *analysis* of revelation and as indirectly identical with statements about revelation.

B. THE CONCRETE TRIUNITY OF REVELATION

We have referred to the unity of the ground of the doctrine of the Trinity which is established by the statement "God reveals

[8] Ibid., 360. Cf. the citation from Harnack: "Confession of Father, Son and Spirit is . . . the unfolding of the belief that Jesus is the Christ." That is, the whole of the doctrine stems from the single root. (Harnack, *Lehrbuch d. Dogmengesch.,* 4th ed. 1909, Vol. I, 90.) Cited ibid., 361. Cf. also 384, 355.
[9] Barth, op. cit., 382.   [10] Ibid., 382f.

Himself as the Lord" as a *formal* unity. Both the unity and the variety implied by the conception of Trinity are developed out of the form of the proposition itself. But the value of this formal analysis of revelation depends on the validity of the interpretation of scripture which it summarizes—i.e. on the real unity and three-foldness of the New Testament witness. The proposition, in other words, is a formula which indicates that the revelation necessarily brings us to the doctrine of the Trinity, but which depends upon a proof already achieved. That proof is the exegesis of the concrete witness of scripture to revelation, thus we need now to indicate the outlines of the exegesis upon which Barth's conception of unity and variety in God is based. It will be evident that in this exegesis Barth brings the "formal" analysis of the statement about revelation into positive relation with traditional approaches to the doctrine—but always with the difference resulting from his conception of the single ground of the doctrine in the very nature of revelation.

1) We have said that God's revelation is, according to the biblical view, a revelation of his lordship. Thus he is primarily called *Yahweh* and *Kyrios*. But who is the Lord? The climax of the biblical witness is the statement that Jesus is the Lord. But this statement can never be taken alone or for granted, because throughout the New as well as the Old Testament, "true and real *divinity*, as expressed in the predicate *Kyrios*," is already ascribed "in the first instance to a completely *Other* than Jesus." [1] This Barth understands to be the meaning of all those passages in which Jesus' power, authority or dignity is regarded as derivative and quite subordinate as compared with that of God the Father. The lordship of Jesus, in this motif of the New Testament witness, is "merely an appearance, exercise, or application of the Lordship of God the *Father*. The essence of the Divinity ascribed to Jesus is to make clear, impart, and carry out who God the Father, God in the proper sense, is, and what He wills and does for man, to represent this God the Father." [2] This "subordinationism" is not to be denied, but is to be taken as an indication that in the logically

[1] Ibid., 442. [2] Ibid., 443.

material order, the revelation of God to which the scriptures bear witness is in the first place a revelation of the lordship of God the Father of Jesus Christ, and therefore our Father.

2) But the witness of the revelation in Christ to the lordship of God the Father is inseparable from the witness to the lordship of Jesus and the unity of that lordship with the lordship of the Father. Here we confront the question of the divinity of Jesus Christ. Regardless of the other connotations in the classical world of the term *Kyrios*, the Church, Barth insists, could not have been unaware of the significance of this word as a translation of the Old Testament name for God, and the application of it to Jesus could not have been unintentional. Its use was an affirmation that the lordship of Christ was the lordship of God. This is further indicated by the practical meaning of the name of Jesus in the early Christian community, where the name of Jesus takes on much the same significance which the name of Yahweh had in the Old Testament. Again the "intertexture . . . of word and deed" in the New Testament record of Christ points to the higher authority attributed to him. Finally, there are the explicit titles assigned to Jesus: Messiah, Son of Man, Son of God—all obscure but eloquent in the context—even *theos* and *ho theos*, and there are the various descriptive phrases (only-begotten Son, *arché* and *telos*, etc.) and indirect statements which contribute to this second motif of New Testament witness, that "Jesus is the Lord." [3]

Christ reveals the Father our Lord, but in so doing is himself our Lord and reveals himself. This is the one lordship of God, but it is different from the lordship of God the Creator.[4] It is "God's Lordship in turning to us." God deals with us as persons and establishes intercourse with us. He dissolves our sinful incapacity for his word in the miraculous event called revelation or recon-

[3] Cf. ibid., 457ff.

[4] It is important to note here that by "Creator," Barth does not mean simply "source or ground of existence." He means God's lordship (= thou-ness) over our existence as His Children. (Cf. 449f., 472.) Thus "creation" is the "first birth" which corresponds to the "new birth" in Christ. Since this original relation to God has been lost because of sin, the knowledge of God as Creator is inseparable from the knowledge of God as Reconciler and Redeemer. Cf. below, § 6.

ciliation. We cannot confuse God's lordship in the act of creation with his lordship in the act of reconciliation, or identify them directly; "we must in the former case (in view of creation) speak of a first mode of God's existence, in the latter (in view of reconciliation) speak of a second mode of God's existence." [4] The revelation discloses to us the infinite seriousness of the problem to which it is an answer. Thus we understand that reconciliation is not creation, but the lordship of God *in the midst of* our enmity towards *him*, whence we "surely . . . must assert that the Son is not the Father, but that the one God is here—in this work—not apart from the Father, but simply the Son or Word of the Father." But we must also say that the work of reconciliation is truly God's work, that it is a manifestation of *his* lordship in the midst of our enmity towards him, therefore that "*its Subject is identical with God in the full sense of the word.*" [5]

We must speak, then, of both unity and variety. God is the Father because he is the Father of the Son, and Jesus is the Son or Word because he *is* the revelation of the Father. Similarly, creation and reconciliation are "*utterly different*" in their meaning for us, but "*coalesce completely* in their origin." There is an order of subordination yet coordination here. The order of Father and Son or Father and Word corresponds to the order of creation and reconciliation. The Reconciler, as distinguished from the Creator, follows the Creator and is a second—but neither separate in lordship nor different in being, for the resurrection of the dead is no less a miracle, no less divine, no more readily conceivable, than

[4] Ibid., 469.
[5] Ibid., 469, 470. It should be noted that Barth's conception of the importance of the distinction between Creation and Reconciliation as a basis for the distinction between Father and Son is qualified by his insistence on the rule *opera trinitatis ad extra indivisa sunt* and on the doctrine of appropriations. (Cf. below, § 4.) The knowledge of the distinction and unity of Son and Father rests primarily and immediately on the confession of the lordship of Christ in his unity with and distinction from the Father; that knowledge rests "*also*" on the distinction between Creation and Reconciliation. (Cf. 472.) Barth should not be interpreted to mean that God's existence as Son is dependent on man's need for reconciliation, though our knowledge of God's Triunity evidently depends upon the revelation of One who was veiled and upon the reconciliation of men who needed to be reconciled.

creation *ex nihilo.* The difference is a difference only in "mode of existence."

3) Finally, Barth finds, the New Testament in its witness that "Jesus is the Lord" calls attention to the way in which men come to affirm this. It speaks of the historicity of the revelation, of a givenness to particular men in concrete historical situations. This special element is what the New Testament speaks of as the Holy Spirit. It is "the subjective side in the event of revelation." [6] This is God opening man up to receive revelation. It is God's reality, his spirit, his being subjectively present, from within, which enables revelation to be manifest. The Spirit is not identical with the Son, with Jesus Christ, who is the objective revelation, the object of faith. The Spirit is he in whom (or through whom) men confess and believe in the revelation. The Holy Spirit exists only "on the assumption of the conclusion and completion of the objective revelation." [7] Thus, while the Spirit is not the same as the Son, it is still the Spirit *of* Christ.

The Holy Spirit as an element in revelation is not a new content or revelation, but "simply . . . the instruction, illumination, stirring up of man *by means* of the Word, *on behalf* of the Word." [8] The Spirit completes the action upon man by guidance and instruction (the Paraclete doctrine). The Spirit empowers man to speak of Christ and enables his language to become testimony, the revelation to become actual anew. The Holy Spirit sets man free for the service of God, and by receiving the Spirit a man is a child of God. From all this, Barth concludes that the Holy Spirit is, according to the New Testament, no less than God himself, distinct from the Father and the Son, but no less God. According to the New Testament assertions, "the work of the Holy Spirit in revelation is a work which can only be ascribed to God Himself, and which is therefore actually and expressly

---

[6] Ibid., 515. Cf. 542.
[7] Ibid., 517. Cf. 513ff. The distinction made here between Christ and the Spirit has obvious similarity to the distinction drawn by Kirk (and utilized by Hodgson) between "communion" and "possession," and the distinction drawn by Thornton between content and agent.
[8] Ibid., 518.

ascribed to God." [9] It is the *Holy* Spirit. If Christ is not a demi-god and faith in him is faith in God himself, then that faith in him is not a human possibility, but is a "possibility coming from a mode of God's existence, a mode of existence which is on a level, in essential unity, with Him who in the New Testament is described as Father and Son." [10]

In all this analysis we find Barth bringing to light the *single* ground of the doctrine of the Trinity. That doctrine is rooted in the one act of revelation, which is yet internally threefold, so that the doctrine is developed by analysis of the meaning of the revelation. The revelation of God in Christ is not something which must be added to the knowledge of God the Father. On the contrary, "God the Father" in the New Testament means first of all God the Father of our Lord Jesus Christ. Conversely the Son is always to be understood as the Son of this Father. But neither Father nor Son is known except by the witness (possession, presence) of the Holy Spirit, which enables the believer to see Christ as the Son of the Father and the Father as his Father and our Father. The Spirit is the Spirit of the Father and the Son. In each of these "moments" or "elements" the one God manifests himself; each is truly God. Yet none can be reduced to one of the others.

The concrete exposition of scripture outlined here indicates clearly that Barth's preliminary analysis of the nature of revelation is not arbitrarily imposed on the biblical witness, but calls attention to a unity and variety in revelation which is both implicit and explicit in the New Testament. Whether we use the terms Revealer, Revelation and Revealedness, and the proposition "God reveals Himself as the Lord" to express this biblical witness is not a matter of the greatest importance. These phrases are at the very least indicative of the actual unity or integrity of the biblical testimony which they describe and which is the real root of the doctrine of the Trinity. Out of this root the doctrine of the Trin-

---

[9] Ibid., 534.
[10] Ibid., 528. Cf. 526ff. That is, as with the deity of Christ, so with the status of the Holy Spirit.

ity is developed as an analysis or interpretation which is at least indirectly identical with the biblical witness to revelation. As a doctrine, it is not the last but the first article of dogmatics. It springs immediately and necessarily out of the affirmation that "Jesus is the Lord," and adds nothing to the meaning which is implicit in that statement, therefore the content of the doctrine of the Trinity is nothing other than the content of revelation. "The doctrine of the Trinity is nothing else than the unfolding of the knowledge that Jesus is the Christ or the Lord." [11]

A final aspect of Barth's conception of the single basis of the trinitarian doctrine is his understanding of the way in which unity and trinity contribute to each other. We are not now thinking so much of the dialectical interrelation of unity and trinity in God, as of the way in which the revelation of trinity and the revelation of unity are related. This has been implied in what we have already said, but it comes to focus in portions of Barth's discussion of "God's Three-in-oneness." The relation is developed primarily from the side of the confirmation of unity by trinity. Here Barth emphasizes that the affirmation of the three-in-oneness of God is in no sense a contradiction or even a questioning of the unity, but "the final and decisive confirmation that God is *One*." The coming of God in Christ and the Spirit is an explicit affirmation of the one lordship of God. The Bible and the doctrine of the Trinity refer to the one Lord (*Yahweh, Kyrios*), "a single, unique Willer and Doer, whom Scripture designates as God." Baptism is not into three names, but into the one name. Faith is in one object.

God's "*numerical* unity of essence" is expressed in the threefold meaning of his self-revelation. In no sense is there a rivalry of interest between the deity of Christ or of the Spirit and monotheism. The New Testament does not think of belief in Christ as

[11] Ibid., 384. As noted above, Barth holds that the doctrine goes *beyond* the actual biblical witness in the express affirmations that Father, Son and Spirit are of equal essence and that God is God only as Triune. But these affirmations are what we have called "analytical," they are simply explicit statements of what is necessarily implied by the witness to revelation. See below, § 3.

anything other than belief in the one God and Lord. Thus the assertion of the equality of the essence of the Son with the Father is "at every point and pre-eminently to be regarded in the sense of *identity* of essence." [12]

It is from the point of view of anti-trinitarianism that the doctrine of the Trinity is held to be an attempt to reconcile the revelation in Christ with the principle of monotheism. Arianism (and all subordinationism), by making the object of faith something less than God, destroys the unity of God and is only superstition. Modalism, if it makes revelation only phenomenal form and posits a higher, more ultimate essence, denies revelation—or, if it takes revelation seriously, it takes seriously something less than God, an improper God, and thus denies monotheism. Both errors misunderstand that the point of the doctrine of the Trinity was not the reconciliation of revelation or the deity of Christ with monotheism, but "the whole point was and is also and precisely Christian monotheism." [13]

For our present purpose, the significant aspect of Barth's argument here is the conception that the Church doctrine is able to be an affirmation of monotheism just because the threefoldness of the revelation to which the New Testament testifies is itself an expression and confirmation of monotheism. Of course, the unity which is here given in and confirmed by the threeness is not just any unity; it is not singularity or isolation, but a unity which "includes a distinction (*distinctio* or *discretio*), an arrangement (*dispositio* or *œconomia*), in the essence of God." [14] And the dialectic of the formulæ, threeness in oneness and oneness in threeness, cannot be dissolved. Yet there is never an *opposition* between unity and trinity, because "according to the Biblical witness, in the revelation the one God is only knowable in the Three, the

[12] Ibid., 403.
[13] Ibid., 404. The aim of the Church doctrine of the Trinity, Barth contends, is not to obscure the *eis theos*, but to set it in the light. "From the very outset it is directed against the anti-Trinitarians as those who actually fail to confess the *one* God. The presumption and aim of the Church in this matter is the doctrine of the unity of God, the divine *monarchia* . . ." (401).
[14] Ibid., 407. Cf. 406ff.

Three only as the one God," just as "none of the Three is know-able without the other Two, but each of the Three only with the other Two." [15]

C. REJECTION OF ALL OTHER "ROOTS" OF THE DOCTRINE

The corollary of Barth's contention that the doctrine of the Trinity has a genuine root in revelation is the assertion that the doctrine is rooted *only* in revelation. The matter is argued particularly in the discussion of *Vestigium Trinitatis*, but an important aspect of the same problem is to be found in the contention that God is known as Father only in the Son. If the biblical witness is taken seriously, Barth avers, the revelation of the Father is wholly limited to its impartation in the Person of Christ. Jesus does not simply give the name Father to a philosophical Creator-God; he reveals the unfamiliar Father, *his* Father, and thus shows that and what the Creator is. That God is Father, in the Christian, trini-tarian sense, does not mean that God is first a universal Father and then the Father of Christ; it means that he is the Father of Jesus Christ and therefore our Father. The revelation of his Fatherhood (i.e. the "content" of the revelation, his lordship of our existence, his creatorhood) cannot be abstracted from the manner or form of that revelation in Jesus Christ.

Under the heading of *Vestigium Trinitatis*, Barth includes all the various analogues of the Trinity which have been discovered in creaturely existence, as presumably showing a similarity to or being a copy of the triune nature of God. These have been found in nature, in culture, in history, in religion and in psychology. But regardless of their type, all the *vestigia* are to be suspected, for inasmuch as they are held to be traces of the trinitarian God in creaturely existence as such, apart from revelation, they suggest the possibility of a second root of the doctrine of the Trinity, alongside the first. To admit such a possibility is to raise at once

---

[15] Ibid., 425. Cf. 423ff. This notion of the mutual relation of unity and threefoldness does not of course remove the mystery of the Trinity, but it states the mystery in the proper way and prevents the doctrine from becoming the sort of *logicum mysterium* which is a perpetual stumbling block to the understanding of the doctrine.

the question of which root is primary and therefore also the question of revelation itself and of theology being reduced to anthropology or cosmology.

Barth recognizes that the original function of the analogies for the Trinity was not to do this, but to find language for the expression of revelation, to show how the Trinity is capable of self-expression in created things. But this sort of illustration, Barth holds, always tends to pass into apologetics, into a second root or proof of the doctrine, and thus into a denial of the Trinitarian God of Holy Scripture. As soon as the notion of a *vestigium* is taken seriously it leads into the ambiguous sphere where it becomes a universal principle and therefore alien to the revelation. The door is left open and the *analogia entis* enters. Further, the passage from interpretation to illustration, which is involved in the search for *vestigia*, always sets something else than revelation at the center of attention and denies the self-evidence of revelation —this besides the fact that the illustrations are intrinsically unsatisfactory as analogies. Revelation will properly submit to interpretation but not to illustration.

Thus, with all due respect to the sincerity of the classical attempts to use the *vestigia* wholly in the service of revelation, Barth feels that we can escape the danger of their becoming a second root of the doctrine of the Trinity only by abandoning altogether the search for *vestigia trinitatis*. The only real *vestigium trinitatis in creatura*, which is better called *vestigium creaturæ in trinitate*, "consists of the form which God Himself in His revelation has *assumed* in our language, world and humanity." He creates a *vestigium* of himself, of his three-in-oneness, in the revelation, in the "triply one voice of the Father, the Son, and the Spirit."[1]

While we may be led to agree with Barth in rejecting the attempt to *ground* the doctrine of the Trinity in any illustration of three-in-oneness which may be discovered in creaturely existence, it does not seem to follow that we must forsake all attempts to *illustrate* the concept of Trinity, provided, of course, that we

[1] Ibid., 399. Cf. 384, 388ff.

understand the relative appropriateness of the illustration and that we recognize that we are engaged in illustration (or interpretation, which does not seem to be *qualitatively* different from illustration) and not in demonstration. After all, it cannot be too strongly emphasized that all of our language about the Trinity is analogical, including certainly the terms Father, Son or Word, and Holy Spirit and all trinitarian formulæ—and Barth recognizes this to be the case. Furthermore, it is evident that the notion of the subjectivity of God, which plays such an important place in Barth's thought, is to be understood by analogy with human subjectivity. Since he associates personality or subjectivity with the essence or unity of God, Barth cannot escape the use of an illustrative analogy for the divine unity. Why not also, then, for the divine variety or the divine three-in-oneness? Of course, it may turn out that no finite analogy can be discovered which is not intrinsically unsatisfactory as an analogy for the divine triunity. But in principle, the attempt to find such an analogy, at least as an aid to communication, cannot be altogether rejected.

3. *The Ultimacy of the Doctrine*

Of the two ways in which Barth understands the Church doctrine of the Trinity to go beyond the witness of scripture—viz. the explicit affirmation that the Father, Son and Holy Spirit are truly and equally God, and the affirmation that God is God only in these three modes of existence—we have emphasized the former in discussing the implications of the biblical witness. The latter is the denial of modalism, and together with the question of the relation of the doctrine of the Trinity to the freedom and the mystery or hiddenness of God it comprises the problem of the *ultimacy* or *finality* of the doctrine of the Trinity.

This is the question of the relation of the "economic" to the "immanent" Trinity. Barth is willing to make a distinction between these two, between God-in-himself and God-for-us, *on the ground of God's freedom.*[1] But he is not willing to allow us to

[1] Cf. Ibid., 196f.

stop with a purely "economic" Trinity or Trinity of manifestation (this is essentially what modalism does). God's freedom does not mean his freedom to be other than trinitarian. Barth's fundamental objection to modalistic interpretations of the trinitarian revelation, and therefore his chief argument for the ultimacy of the doctrine, is stated quite simply: "We have to take revelation so utterly seriously that in it as the *act* of God we have to recognize immediately His *being* as well." [2] And again, "revelation is the self-interpretation of this God. If we have to do with His revelation we have to do with Himself and not, as modalists of all periods have thought, with an entity distinct from Himself." [3]

This principle is applied to each of the three "Persons." God is revealed as the Father of Christ, and our Father, because he is so "antecedently in Himself," because "already beforehand, quite apart from the fact that He reveals Himself to us as such, He is what He reveals Himself as being, namely, the Father of Jesus Christ His Son, who as such is Himself God. He can be so, *because He is Himself the Father in Himself, because Fatherhood is an eternal mode of existence of the divine essence*." [4] Similarly Jesus Christ is revealed as the Son, and is able to reveal the Father and to reconcile us to the Father, because he is the eternal Son. He is what he reveals himself to be. Antecedent to the event of revelation and new birth, there is in God the fact that such an event *can happen*, the *possibility* of this event, viz. the Son of God. Revelation "has *eternal* content and *eternal* validity. Throughout all the depths of deity, not as the penultimate but as the ultimate thing to be said about God, God is God the Son just as He is God the Father." [5] Again in the case of the Holy Spirit, what God is in his revelation, he is in himself. The dogma of the Trinity does not *add* anything to the New Testament witness: it only takes that witness seriously in its ascription of the work of the Holy Spirit to God himself. It only makes explicit

[2] Ibid., 490.
[3] Ibid., 358. Cf. 349f., 426f., 437ff., 448, 474, 481, 548.
[4] Ibid., 441, 448.   [5] Ibid., 474.

that the divinity of the Holy Spirit "is true, essential, eternal divinity. The Spirit is holy in *us*, because He is so antecedently *in Himself*." [6] God is the act of communion, impartation, love, gift, in revelation, because as Holy Spirit he eternally exists in a mode of "communityness" of Father and Son.

Barth's argument is summarized in a comment on the *filioque* (which he defends): "We are completely tied to the rule—and regard this rule as fundamental—that pronouncements upon the reality of the divine modes of existence, 'antecedently in themselves' could not in content be any different from those that have to be made about their reality in revelation. The whole of our statements on the so-called immanent Trinity proved very simply for us to be confirmations and underlinings, or, materially, the indispensable major premises of the economic Trinity." [7] Two things are implied here: first, we must proceed to affirm the absolute "immanence" in God of the trinitarian distinctions and relations; and second, in so doing, we must make the doctrine of immanent Trinity conform exactly in content to the economic Trinity. To fail at either of these points is to deny the finality of the revelation by going beyond it for our pronouncements about God. If we take the revelation seriously, there is nothing more ultimate about God than is said by the doctrine of the Trinity.

God's self-revelation does not mean, of course, that his mystery has thereby been abolished. God does not become conceivable so that man is able to grasp and hold him. His grace and loving kindness is ever free from man's possession and comprehension. Even in the form in which he reveals himself (Jesus Christ) he remains free to reveal or not to reveal. He reveals *through* the form, he is not contained by the form. "Inscrutability, . . . hiddenness, belongs to the nature of Him who is called God in the Bible. . . . God is ever and again a mystery." [8] To remove the mystery would be to deny's God's freedom, to deliver him over to man.

It is not within the province of this essay to go into an examina-

---

[6] Ibid., 534. Cf. 533ff.   [7] Ibid., 548.   [8] Ibid., 368, 369.

tion of what Barth means by the mystery or hiddenness of God, but it is important to understand that for him (in contrast to Brunner) the mystery of God is not something that stands behind the revelation, therefore behind his trinitarian nature, so that he in himself might be other than he is in his revelation. "It is the *Deus revelatus* who is the *Deus absconditus*," he is "inscrutable in His *revealed* nature." [9] The Triune God who speaks out is not different from the God who speaks. Although God is hidden and mysterious and remains so because of his essential freedom, there is no dark or terrible God behind the revelation. God who meets man as Father, Son and Holy Spirit is already the God who meets himself and has community in this way.[10]

As already indicated, Barth does make a distinction between God "in himself" and "for us," between essence and operation. On the one hand, he insists that "God's essence and His operation are not twain but one. God's operation or effect is His essence in its relation to the reality distinct from Him, whether about to be or already created. The operation of God is the essence of God, *qua* essence of Him who (*N.B.* with a free decision, grounded in His essence but not constrained by His essence) is the Revealer, Revelation, Revealedness, or the Creator, Reconciler, Redeemer." [11] In other words, God really gives himself to man in revelation. His whole essence is revealed to us in his operation. His operation is his essence. Nevertheless, Barth holds, we must "*distinguish* His essence as such from His operation: in order to remember that this operation is a grace, a free divine decision, also to remember that we can only know about God, because and so far as he gives Himself to our knowledge." [12] The distinction rests on the freedom of God with respect to creation, revelation, redemption. God gives himself entirely to man, "but not in such a way as to give Himself a prisoner to man. He remains *free*, in operating, in giving Himself." [13]

[9] Ibid., 368.
[10] Cf. *Kirchliche Dogmatik*, II/1: 52, 63f., 236, 305, 307, 365, 526; *Doctrine of the Word of God*, 349 and *passim*.
[11] *Doctrine of the Word of God*, 426.
[12] Loc. cit. Cf. also 481.　　　　　　　[13] Ibid., 426.

It is the freedom of God which is the basis of his hiddenness, in the sense of his inconceivability and mystery. His inconceivability means the inadequacy of all our knowledge of him, and this applies to the doctrine of the Trinity as well as to any other aspect of our knowledge of God. Thus distinctions in the operation of God (Creation, Reconciliation, Redemption) are distinctions within the sphere of our conceivability which only "in their utter preliminariness face us with the problem of His *inconceivable* and eternal distinctions." [14] The concepts Father, Son and Spirit, or Revealer, Revelation and Revealedness are only analogous to the eternal, inconceivable distinctions. None of the concepts which we use can be adequate; they can only be useful in pointing beyond themselves to the problem posed by scripture and to the eternal nature of God. We can never get beyond the two unsatisfactory formulations, threeness-in-oneness and oneness-in-threeness; the formula "three-in-oneness" only indicates "that conflation of the two, which we cannot attain to, and for which therefore we have no formula, but of which we can be aware only as of the inconceivable truth of the Object itself." [15] In short, the Trinity remains a mystery, though one over which theology has taken rational trouble, so that we know what is meant when it is said that this is a mystery.

But when all this is said, it must again be emphasized that God's hiddenness is *not* something which stands behind his trinitarian nature, so that he might ultimately be other than triune. With respect to revelation and creation, God is free to will one way or another, i.e. to will it or not to will it. "But He does not possess this freedom in respect of His Godness. God cannot *not* be God. So also—which is the same thing—He cannot *not* be the Father and therefore, can *not* be without the Son. His freedom, His aseity in respect of Himself, consists in the freedom to be God, and that means to be the Father of the Son, determined by nothing but by Himself." [16] God's freedom to be for us does not mean his freedom to be other in himself than he is for us. That he is triune

[14] Ibid., 428.   [15] Ibid., 423.   [16] Ibid., 497.

in his revelation means that he is in himself triune, and there is no higher or more ultimate truth about God than this.

4. *The Nature of the Divine Unity and Variety*

1) We noted earlier that according to the proponents of the social analogy for the Trinity, the New Testament record points primarily to the plurality of the divine Persons, and only secondarily to the unity. Against all such talk, Barth stands in total opposition. For him, the New Testament speaks from beginning to end and unquestionably of the *unity* of God. Barth puts it in terms of the "lordship" of God, which is the activity of God in relation to us, i.e. God's being personally present to us. The New Testament witness may be summarized as a testimony to the one act of God, by which he reveals himself as our Lord, as the One who stands over against us and has come to us in reconciliation and redemption. And it is unquestionably *One* Lord—one Agent, one Thou— who has done this. There is no thought of competition between the lordship of Christ and the lordship of the Father.

The lordship of God, Barth asserts, is to be equated with the *"essence"* of God, the *"deitas* or *divinitas,* the divine οὐσία, *essentia, natura,* or *substantia"*; for God's essence is his being *"qua divine* being . . . the *godhead* of God."[1] It is on the basis of this equation that we are to understand Barth's contention that the "personality" of God is to be associated with his one single essence, rather than with the three "Persons." It is not at all, as Hodgson thinks, simply that Barth is afraid of tritheism. Barth certainly does believe that to speak of three personalities in God "would be the worst and most pointed expression of tritheism, against which we must here guard."[2] But the prime reason for his objection to speaking of three personalities is his understanding of the biblical witness to the unity of God's lordship. The lordship of God is not

[1] Ibid., 401.
[2] *Doctrine of the Word,* 403. Cf. Hodgson, *The Doctrine of the Trinity,* 229.

tripled, it is "triply one," "God is the one God in a threefold repetition." [3] In other words, God meets us, according to scripture, as *one* "Thou" (in threefold repetition), therefore unquestionably as *one person.*

The modern concept of the personality of God is important to the doctrine of the Trinity in preventing the Thou from being made into an It. But this can never mean three "Thou's" or three "I's" if we are to hold to the biblical witness to the unity of the lordship of Christ with the lordship of the Father. And on that unity rests the claim for the equality of essence of the Son with the Father: "from the identity [of the lordship of Christ and the Spirit with the lordship of the Father] *follows* the equality of essence in the 'Persons.' " [4]

The unity of God is further characterized (and emphasized!) by Barth in terms of the doctrine of coinherence and the rule *opera trinitatis ad extra indivisa sunt.* The concept of *perichoresis* or coinherence is for Barth, as for Catholic theology, the completion of the dialectic of unity and trinity. It "signifies at once the *confirmation* of the distinction between the modes of existence (none of them would be what it is—not even the Father!—apart from its co-existence with the others) and the *relativisation* of it (none of them exists as a special individual, all three 'inexist' in one another, they exist only in common as modes of the existence of the one God and Lord who posits Himself from eternity to eternity)." [5]

Barth also agrees with the Catholic theology in associating the concept closely with the doctrine of the identity of essence. This connection is made explicitly only once, where Barth speaks of the *perichoresis* as "a further description of the *homousia* of the Father, Son and Spirit." [6] But the connection is quite definitely implicit in his entire conception of the *perichoresis.* That doctrine means that the Father, Son and Spirit are one *"among themselves."* The "definite" and "complete participation by each mode of

[3] Ibid., 383, 402.
[4] Ibid., 403. (Italics mine.) Cf. 501–503.
[5] Ibid., 425.
[6] Ibid., 555. Cf. Pohle-Preuss, op. cit., 284.

existence in the other modes of existence" follows from the understanding that the one essence of God is truly and indivisibly present in his existence as Father, Son and Spirit. This does not mean
that the modes of existence are identical with each other, but
co-present in each other, just as the knowledge of the Father is
not identical with the knowledge of the Son, but the Father is
knowable only in the Son.[7]

2) The understanding of the doctrine of coinherence as defining the *unity* of God is bound up intimately with Barth's conception of the nature of the trinitarian *distinctions*. It is not "persons"
or "personalities" which are arranged or distinguished in the
essence of God. That is abundantly clear from Barth's discussion
of the ground of the doctrine and in particular the revelation of
the unity of God. There are not three lordships, three Thou's,
three Subjects, which we meet in the New Testament, but only
one. Pointing out that the classical term *persona* was not understood to mean what we mean by "personality," Barth concludes
that the concept of "person"—while important to the doctrine of
God proper and actually deduced from the doctrine of the Trinity, i.e. from the threefold way in which God meets us in revelation—has, as a designation for Father, Son and Spirit, only the
value of giving a sense of continuity with the tradition and of a
"practical abbreviation" in the absence of any adequate term.[1]

---

[7] Barth, op. cit., 424. In the doctrine of coinherence, particularly as it is
stated here in relation to the personality of God, we have the adequate
reply to Brunner's complaint against the *Nebeneinander,* presumably taught
by the orthodox doctrine. Insofar as *Nebeneinander* means "along side of,"
this is not an accurate statement of the meaning of the classical doctrine—
and even less so of Barth's reinterpretation. Together with *Nebeneinander*
(in the sense of coexistence) we must always put *Miteinander* and *Ineinander* if we are to speak correctly of the relation of the divine modes of existence. (Cf. *Doctrine of the Word,* 439, 537, 558.)

[1] Cf. ibid., 408ff. The concept of Person "belongs to another part, namely,
to the doctrine of God proper, and as a *deduction* from the doctrine of the
Trinity. It follows directly from the Trinitarian understanding of the God
revealed in Scripture that this one God is to be regarded not only as an
impersonal lordship, i.e. as a power, but as the Lord, and so not only as absolute Spirit but as a Person, i.e. as an I existing in and for Itself with a thought
and will proper to It. It is thus that He meets us in His revelation. It is thus
that He is God thrice as Father, Son and Spirit." (Ibid., 412.) Cf. also
Dogmatik, II/1, 333f.

Barth does not say that we must necessarily abandon the term, but proposes the designation *"modes of being"* (*Seinsweisen*) as "relatively better." He thinks that this designation not only has a formal precedent in the *tropoi hyparxeos* of the Cappadocian Fathers,[2] but that it actually is the concept which has always been the really fundamental one in the determination of God's threefoldness. The term *hypostasis* "understood in the sense in which it was finally received . . . means *subsistentia* (not *substantia*) i.e. mode of existence of one who exists."[3] St. Thomas' definition really centers around the concept of subsistence, and the same is true of Calvin and later Protestant authors. By "mode of existence" Barth means what the theologians have called *"subsistentia, modus entis*, form or mode of possession," thus he is only putting formally, explicitly and critically at the center of attention the concept which has always been crucial.[4]

It should be perfectly clear that Barth's use of the term "mode" does not carry any of the implications of the term "modalism," as the latter term is commonly used. The "modes of being" are neither temporary nor merely an appearance. They are essential to God's existence. We know God in his revelation in three inseparable yet distinct individual modes of existence, therefore he is so in himself and exists only as such.

In his concern to show the continuity of his view with traditional theology, Barth does not call attention with sufficient force to one very real difference between his thought and the older theology. He is correct, we may agree, in questioning the adequacy of the term "person" as a description of what the classical doctrine meant by the divine distinctions. And he is quite successful in his attempt to show genuine continuity between his concept of "mode of being" and the classical notions of *hypostasis* and *subsistentia* or subsistent relation. But there is a crucial difference. Barth indicates it in commenting on the Augsburg Confession's definition of Person as *quod proprie subsistit*. He says, "we shall . . . have to bracket the '*quod*' in this definition. What *proprie*

[2] Basil of Caesarea, *de Spiritu Sancto*, 43, 44.
[3] Barth, op. cit., 413.   [4] Ibid., 414.

subsistit is not just the Person as such, but *God* in the three Persons: God as *proprie subsistens* in a three-fold way." [5] But in bracketing the *quod*, Barth is making a significant alteration of the definition, and thereby a real divergence from the traditional conception. According to that conception it is the three Persons which subsist. Thus St. Thomas speaks of the *personæ* as *res subsistentes in divina natura*,[6] and Calvin formally defines *persona* as *subsistentia in Dei essentia*.[7]

This way of speaking was possible because these writers did not have to deal with the conception of the personality of God as such. They spoke of God as of a neuter, of *deitas* and of *essentia divina*. Because of this impersonal way of speaking, and the static and almost materialistic conception of substance which it involved, they were able to speak meaningfully of a divine *persona* as that which subsists in the divine nature. This is possible just as long as the meaning of *persona* or person remains vague and uncertain. But when person comes to mean "self-conscious individuality" or a "distinct center of consciousness," and the specific question of the personality of God is raised, the matter is complicated immensely. For if we agree with Barth that personality in this sense is to be assigned to the oneness of God, then in order to keep the Persons or *hypostases* from being parts of God's being we must say that it is he, the Subject, who exists or subsists in these three *hypostases*. Thus Barth speaks of "God in a threefold repetition," "God distinguishing Himself from Himself," God positing himself, God "in another way a second [or third] time," and of the "*repetitio æternitatis in æternitate*." [8] These phrases, indeed Barth's whole conception of the Trinity, require that it be God who

---

[5] Loc. cit. Barth cites Diekamp (*Kath. Dogmatik*, I, 6th ed. (1930), 352f.) as also concluding that "absolute subsistence belongs only to the divine substance as such; to the Persons as such, on the contrary, only a relative subsistence." To this we may add Pohle-Preuss's assertion that the one *summa res* "simultaneously exercises two separate and distinct functions—the functions of one Absolute and three Relatives" (op. cit., 259).

[6] Or of a relation or *hypostasis* subsisting in the divine nature, though St. Thomas qualifies this by saying that "in truth that which subsists in the Divine Nature is the Divine Nature itself"—thus laying a basis for the distinction drawn by Diekamp. Cf. *Summa Theol.* 1, 29, 4.

[7] *Institutes* I, 13, 6.   [8] Op. cit., 402, 363, 421, 498.

proprie subsistit in three modes of being or *hypostases*, not three *hypostases* which *proprie subsistent* in God—though of course God exists only in his three subsistences. God is the One Being eternally determining himself (and therefore eternally determined) in this threefold way.

Of course, it must also be emphasized that this revision of terminology does not indicate a change in basic theological intention. In at least one place St. Thomas himself states that it is properly the one divine nature which subsists (and Diekamp and Pohle-Preuss follow him in this). What is involved here is the clarification of a certain ambiguity in view of the necessity of explicitly affirming the *personality* of God, and the adjustment of our language to the change in the meaning of the term *person* —an adjustment which is directed precisely at preserving continuity of meaning. All of what Barth has to say concerning the designation "modes of being" comes, of course, under the qualification of the inconceivability of God. No term can be adequate, and Barth does not claim that his answer to the question *quid tres?* is more than a *relatively* better answer than is given by the term Person. Any concept we may use here is useful only in pointing "beyond itself to the problem as it is set us by Scripture." [9]

It is important to note, on the negative side, that Barth will have nothing to do with attempts to regard Father, Son and Spirit as distinctions in the content of divine activity, as attributes or "departments of the divine essence and activity." [10] As God is one in his essence, he is one in his activity. All the divine acts, attributes, qualities, functions, must be ascribed in the same way to Father, Son and Spirit. "There is no attribute, no act of God, which would not in like manner be the attribute, the act of the Father, the Son, and the Spirit." [11] Father, Son and Spirit are not names for different (albeit eternal) functions of God (as suggested by numerous authors whom we have discussed earlier under the heading of "monarchianism"). Against all such views, Barth repeatedly insists on the "rule for theologising on the Trin-

[9] Ibid., 422. Cf. 412ff.   [10] Ibid., 415. Cf. 427ff.   [11] Ibid., 415.

ity, *opera trinitatis ad extra sunt indivisa*." [12] The acceptance of this "rule" of course follows directly from his conception of the unity of God's essence and of the *perichoresis*.

Barth does not mean that the distinctions in the divine activity —indicated by the terms Good Friday, Easter and Pentecost, or Creator, Reconciler and Redeemer, or holiness, mercy and love— are unimportant. On the contrary, the threeness which we observe in these phrases may and should indicate and call attention to the problem of the eternal threeness in God. But these distinctions as such are not the distinctions in the divine modes of existence— that would involve a division in the essence of God. We are permitted to recognize that in revelation God meets us "in constantly different action, always in one of His modes of existence, or better put, distinguished or characterized from time to time by one or other of His modes of existence." [13] But we are forbidden to apportion the types of action *ontologically* among Father, Son and Spirit, as if in grasping the distinctions of activity, we had thereby grasped the eternal distinctions. For God is one in his operation—*opera trinitatis ad extra indivisa sunt*—and the distinctions of content in the divine activity are to be made only within the sphere of our conceptions.[14] The "distinctions" of operation may very well be distinguished as attributes, or aspects of God's activity, or qualities or forms, but when these are made into eternal distinctions or modes of existence, then we either divide God into three parts (or truths or even sources of activity) or else we make God at one time Creator, at another Reconciler, and so on, as if these activities were separable.

What Barth is insisting—and this follows from the conception of the unity of the ground of the doctrine—is that God is as much Creator and Redeemer in his mode of existence as Son as he is Reconciler, etc. God is known as Creator and Redeemer only when he is known as Reconciler; Easter is understood only with

---

[12] Ibid., 430. Cf. also esp. 416, 452f., 507; and *Dogmatik*, III/1, p. 52f.
[13] Ibid., 416.
[14] Cf. ibid., 415f., 426ff., 433, 472.

Good Friday and Pentecost. The lordship of God in creation cannot be other than his lordship in reconciliation and redemption. Therefore all the various ways of stating the distinctions of activity, while appropriate to the limits of our conceivability and not to be done away with without violence to the scriptural witness, can only serve to indicate a threeness in God's eternal being which is on the order of a repetition in God, a *repetitio æternitatis in æternitate.*

Though we cannot identify any of the formulations of the triad in revelation, even the concepts Father, Son and Spirit, ontologically with the eternal distinctions, we may properly speak of an analogy between the various triads and the immanent distinctions. Thus creation is *appropriated* to the Father, reconciliation to the Son, and redemption to the Spirit, because the relations between these distinctions in operation are analogous to the relations between Father, Son and Spirit.[15] And similarly for the concepts of Revealer, Revelation and Revealedness, veiling, unveiling and imparting, and holiness, mercy and love. To the rules of Catholic theology regarding appropriation—viz. that it must not be arbitrary but must rest on a real analogy between the terms attributed and the original eternal relations, and that the appropriation must not be exclusive, i.e. must not violate the "rule" that what is appropriated really belongs to all the modes of existence—Barth adds a third principle (for evangelical dogmatics), that "appropriations must not be invented freely," but are genuine when taken from scripture or as an interpretation of appropriations found there.[16]

The doctrine of appropriation represents, then, a positive relation between the threefold distinction in God's operation and the eternal distinction of Father, Son and Spirit in God's essence. We need illustrate this only briefly, in relation to the conception of God the Father as Creator. Properly speaking, the name Father in the trinitarian sense, "signifies God's mode of existence, in which He is the Originator of His other modes of existence."[17]

---

[15] This statement is almost tautological, since (as we shall see in a moment) the knowledge of the eternal relations is itself derived from the formal relations of those elements in revelation.

[16] Ibid., 429.   [17] Ibid., 451.

In this intra-trinitarian relation of origination, we have the "type" of the Creator-creature relation and of all intra-creaturely relations—though in the Trinity without any suggestion of superiority or inferiority. By virtue of this eternal relation we speak of God the Father as the Creator and our Father. This is an "improper" and "derivative" procedure, since actually it is not only the Father, but God as Father, Son and Spirit who is our Creator (and Reconciler and Redeemer); God is one and undivided in his operation as in his essence. Nevertheless, this procedure is not forbidden, nor is it untrue to say that the Father is the Creator. The appropriation is "improper" in the sense that it is one-sided, but the knowledge of God based upon it is true, though relative, knowledge, which is not dissolved and surmounted in any higher knowledge. It is only appropriation because it does not express the *perichoresis*, but it conveys the truth by pointing to the "affinity between the order of God's three modes of existence on the one hand, and that of the three sides of his operation as Creator, Reconciler and Redeemer on the other. Between the relation of the Father to the Son and the relation of the Creator to the creature there exists once for all an affinity: in the one sense as in the other, although in a sense differing *toto coelo*, we are concerned with origination." [18]

5. *Doctrines of Internal Relations*

It will be recalled that in analyzing Barth's understanding of the basis of the doctrine, we passed lightly over the distinctions between God as Creator, God as Reconciler and God as Redeemer—distinctions which occupy a considerable portion of Barth's treatise.[1] The reason for this will now be apparent: those distinctions are to be applied only by appropriation, and that is so because the real ground of the divine threefoldness is found *in the distinctions of "form" or of relationship* which are implicit in the occurrence of revelation and which are manifest in the various triads of the

---

[18] Ibid., 455. Cf. 451ff.; *Dogmatik*, III/1, p. 52ff.
[1] Cf. *Doctrine of the Word of God*, 441–448, 457–474, 513–533.

content of revelation. This understanding is apparent in the first way in which Barth raises the question of the doctrine: the fact of revelation involving the three questions of whence or who, how or what, and result or effect. It is also expressed in the statement of the interdependence of the three moments—the dependence of unveiling upon a veiling and of impartation upon a veiling and an unveiling. Barth puts the matter most directly thus:

If we have rejected the possibility of reading off the distinction between the three modes of existence from the varieties of *content* in the thought of God contained in the concept of revelation, because in the last resort we cannot speak of such things, so now we should and must assert that the *formal* individual characteristics of the three modes of existence can quite well be read off from the concept of revelation—what actually constitutes them *modes* of existence—namely, the characteristics due to their relation to one another. Naturally the why of these characteristics cannot be stated, any more than a why of revelation can be stated. But as we have tried to do, the that of revelation can be stated and described, and that cannot be done—in fact we could not do it—without encountering certain formal characteristics (in and together with the characteristics in content which are not under consideration here) which as characteristics of the one essence of God the Lord prove themselves also to be *inalienable* characteristics.

God's real modes of existence . . . can certainly be read off from the *regularly recurring mutual relations of the three concepts respectively*, as they are most simply to be found between the concepts Father, Son, and Spirit themselves. On these relations is founded God's threeness in oneness. This threeness consists in the fact that in the essence or act in which God is God there is first a pure origin and then two different issues, the first of which is to be attributed solely to the origin, the second, different in kind, to the origin and likewise to the first issue. According to Scripture God is manifest, He is God, in such a way that He is Himself in these relationships to Himself.[2]

This pattern of relationship is exemplified in the concepts Revealer, Revelation and Revealedness; Creator, Reconciler and Redeemer; holiness, mercy and love; and most especially of course

[2] Ibid., 416f., 418.

Father, Son (or Word) and Holy Spirit. In each case there is a relation of dependence of the second on the first, and of the third on the first and the second.

On the basis of this analysis, Barth reaffirms as crucial for the definition of the divine modes of being the classical doctrine of relations. But the way in which Barth comes to affirm this doctrine is highly significant. The relations of origin, or processions, are not here part of a rationalistic or quasi-rationalistic deduction of the doctrine of the Trinity (as in Anselm or Hegel).[3] Nor is the conception of relations here based on the sort of scriptural literalism which thinks that references to the begottenness of the Son and the proceeding or breathing of the Spirit can be taken as unquestionable deliverances about the internal life of the trinitarian Persons (as in traditional Christian thought and in contemporary Roman Catholic theology). Barth grounds the original relations, and thereby the distinction of the divine modes of existence, upon a broader base, the whole order or pattern which is involved in the revelation as attested in the New Testament, and preëminently signified by the terms Father, Son or Word and Spirit.

In other words, Barth is seeking to base the affirmations regarding the internal relations precisely upon the total pattern or form of the divine *oikonomia*, the arrangement of the "elements" or "aspects" of the revelation to which the scriptures bear witness. This appears strikingly in a passage already referred to, in which Barth defends the *filioque*. He notes that the Eastern Church accepts the procession of the Spirit from the Son *ad extra*, in revelation, and counters that if we are to take revelation seriously and not try to go behind it to some other pronouncement on God, we must assuredly affirm the *filioque ad intra* as well.[4] That is, the order of relationship of Father, Son and Spirit, or Revealer, Revelation and Revealedness, etc., is directly and inextricably involved

---

[3] In the case of Anselm, from the nature of God as Spirit. Cf. *Monologium*, chs. 29ff. On Hegel, cf. above, ch. I.

[4] Barth, op. cit., 548. Cf. above, 184.

in God's self-revelation, and that order must be grounded in the immanent Trinity, i.e. in the internal relations of God in his eternal modes of existence.

In accord with the previous analysis of the "economic Trinity" we may, and must, therefore indicate the relations by which Father, Son and Spirit are distinct from one another. God as Father is God in that mode of his existence in which he is the originator or source of his other modes of existence. As Father he is the ground or presupposition of Son and Holy Spirit. This is (at least formally) the traditional doctrine of the *principium* of the Father, according to which the Father is the principle or source from whom the Son and Holy Spirit proceed.

We must be careful in speaking of "processions," however, to see the distinctive way in which Barth interprets this concept. For certain elements of the traditional doctrine suggest the production of one (distinct) essence (or *res subsistentia*) from another, the second being dependent on the first. This idea is reflected (even if guarded) in the orthodox doctrine of *communicatio essentiæ*, according to which the Son receives his essence from the Father, and the Spirit his essence from the Father and the Son, though this takes place within the one essence of God.[5] Barth can accept this doctrine only in a qualified sense, for "the concept of *communicatio essentiæ*, if taken strictly, actually asserts something which cannot be said without denying the unity of the essence of God."[6] The procession of the Second "Person" can only mean the existence of the one essence of God in a second way, God positing himself. It is not, properly speaking, the modes of existence which subsist, but God who subsists in three modes of existence. Thus Barth speaks frequently of the "intra-divine relations" in terms of "movement" (the movement of the One God), or *repetitio æternitatis in æternitate*. The doctrine of *communicatio essentiæ* does serve to indicate the reality of the dependence of God's existence as Son and Spirit upon his existence as Father, but

---

[5] Cf. e.g. Aquinas, *S. Theol.*, I, Q. 27, art. 2; Klein, op. cit., 109, 118; Downey, op. cit., 130f.

[6] Barth, op. cit., 494.

belongs with the older (impersonal) conception of *persona quod proprie subsistit* rather than the notion of the One Lord who subsists in three modes of being.[7]

It follows from what has just been said that for Barth, when we speak of the "generation" of the Son, we are using a very "fragile, disputable figure." The same is true of the concept of the "procession" of the Word. These two figures are indispensable (because grounded in scripture) and complementary. "We may perhaps say that the first figure is nearer the mark, when we regard the action of God in Jesus Christ materially as reconciliation, the second as nearer the mark, when we look at the action formally as revelation."[8] The two metaphors have essentially the same material content. Neither can be reduced to the other (as in the Thomistic tendency to define generation via intellectual procession of the Word). But both figures only point to an object for which they are quite inadequate. Each has its distinctive use.

In saying this, Barth is not saying something altogether novel. The analogical nature of these terms has long been recognized. But it does seem to be true that Barth goes much further in emphasizing the inadequacy and metaphorical nature of the concepts.[9] As the terms Son and Word only point to and indicate the second mode of existence in which God distinguishes himself from himself, the figure of Father and Son (or Father and Word) and the words *generatio* and *processio* only call attention to the inconceivable relation between God in his mode of being as Father and God in his mode of being as Son. The figures do indicate that the kind of relationship or "twoness and oneness in the same existence" which exists finitely between father and son or speaker and word, is the kind of relationship or existence which obtains between the

[7] The same thing may be said concerning the notion *Pater est fons totius trinitatis.* Brunner's use of this phrase (see above, ch. II) suggests the older conception of production of essence, while for Barth the phrase means that the Father is first in-order of the three modes of existence, the *presupposition* of the other two. (Cf. op. cit., 451.)

[8] Barth, op. cit., 497. Cf. 499, 500f.

[9] Similarly, Barth emphasizes the analogical nature of the terms Father, Son and Spirit. This too is recognized in Catholic theology (cf. the citation from Diekamp in Barth, op. cit., 391), but in far less radical fashion.

modes of God's existence. (Thus Barth is able to speak of the mutual love of Father and Son.) But at once we must say that these figures only "summon us to knowledge" by their figurativeness. Negatively, the terms *generatio* and *processio* distinguish the relation in God from any relation of God to creation. Positively, they point to a "reproduction *from* God *in* God . . . the freedom in which God posits His own reality . . . the love in which He is His own object." [10] Neither figure can give us the nature, the "how" of the production, but each can point to the "thatness" and suggest a way of describing the relationship which has analogical validity.

The qualifications concerning our knowledge of the generation or procession of the Son apply also to the procession of the Spirit. The Spirit is distinguished from the Son in the operation in revelation as "the element of God being appropriated by man," whereas the Son "represents the element of God being assigned to man." [11] The Spirit is therefore an eternally distinct mode of the divine being. The phrase of the Creed, "proceeds from the Father and the Son," indicates by the term "proceeds" both the unity of essence with Father and Son and the distinctness from the Son (who is said to be begotten). Barth does not believe that we can specify the difference between *generatio* and *spiratio*. We can only use these terms to signify that God exists in three modes of being.

We can and must, however, affirm that the Spirit proceeds from both Father and Son, on the basis again of the pattern or order of the revelation, the fact that the Spirit in revelation is the Spirit of the Father and of the Son. Moreover, the *filioque* expresses the communion between Father and Son; without it the communion of God and man would lack warranty in the communion of God in himself. On the same ground Barth rejects the phrase "through the Son" as a substitute for "and the Son"; the former does not lead to the "thought of the complete consubstantial communion between Father and Son." [12]

Barth's conception of the Holy Spirit as the communion of

[10] Ibid., 496.   [11] Ibid., 542.   [12] Ibid., 551.

Father and Son deserves further comment because he holds it to be of the greatest importance and yet obviously cannot mean by it what is meant by the proponents of the social theory, viz. the love or fellowship between personal selves or centers of consciousness. In introducing this conception, Barth makes much of the fact that the Greek *pneuma* is neuter and that in the Niceno-Constantinopolitan Creed the term *kyrios* is used adjectivally of the Spirit. This calls attention, Barth says, to the special way in which the Holy Spirit is a divine mode of existence, namely, as the mutual "participation [*Miteinander*] of the Father and the Son . . . the *common factor* between the mode of existence of God the Father and that of God the Son. Not what is common to them, so far as they are the One God, but what is common to them so far as they are the *Father* and the *Son*." [13]

This seems to be a singularly obscure and even misleading way of approaching the matter of the *communion* or *communityness* of Father and Son, for it does not show how the latter is grounded according to the principle of proceeding from the economic to the immanent Trinity, and there seems to be no immediate transition from the notion of "commonness" in the origin of the Spirit to the concept of community—unless Barth were to mean simply that the communityness of Father and Son *is* their common origin of the Spirit.

The affirmation that the Spirit is the act of communion or love between Father and Son could better be reconstructed from the fact that God in his revelation is, as the Spirit, communion, impartation, love, gift. Then, instead of arguing from the commonness in the origin of the Spirit to the notion of communion and thence to the notion of this divine communion as the ground of the communion between God and man, we should be moving directly from the understanding of the Spirit in revelation as communion and love to the eternal basis of that love in the communion of Father and Son. Barth comes close to saying something of this sort when he asserts frequently that the knowledge of the communion of Father and Son "is nothing else than the knowl-

[13] Ibid., 537.

edge of the ground and confirmation of the communion between God and man, as a divine, eternal truth, as created in revelation by the Holy Spirit." [14] The concept of the community of Father and Son may then be grounded directly in the fact that in revelation the communion of God with man means that God is present to man and also that man is present to God. The possibility of this mutual relation, this two-sided communion, is the presence of God to himself in this way as Father and Son. The "complete consubstantial communion between Father and Son as the essence of the Spirit," is "the thing upon which everything seems to us to depend" because it "originally [answers] to the communion between God as the Father and man as His child, the creation of which is the work of the Holy Spirit in revelation." [15]

In this form, the theme of the communityness of God in himself is emphasized also in Barth's discussion of the Doctrine of God (*Dogmatik*, II/1). The God who meets man is already the God who meets himself and has community as Father, Son and Holy Spirit. He wills community for man because he already has community in his trinitarian nature. This means that God's will for community, his desire for fellowship with man, is not based upon a *need* for this fellowship, but upon his will of love (*agape*).[16] So also, the love of Father and Son is here a love of mutual self-giving, not a love of need. It is the ground of that giving, willing, affirming, seeking and finding love which meets us in reconciliation. In this eternal Spirit of love and by bringing forth the Son, God does, of course, negate in himself "existence in loneliness, self-sufficiency, self-dependence," [17] but this does not mean at all that the Son is brought forth out of any "need" for an object of love.

Finally, it must be emphasized that in speaking of the communityness of Father and Son, Barth does not refer to a fellowship

[14] Ibid., 549f. Cf. 538, 551, 553.
[15] Ibid., 551. Along the line of this approach, one might make tentative and qualified use of Hodgson's conception of the Spirit as the bond of fellowship of Jesus and the Father.
[16] Cf. *Dogmatik*, II/1, 63f., 307f., 313; also *Doctrine of the Word*, 553.
[17] *Doctrine of the Word*, 553. Cf. 158.

of selves, but to a communityness of God in himself, God the Son is God bringing himself forth from eternity as the Son, God positing himself a second time, God distinguishing himself from himself—*repetitio æternitatis in æternitate.* The Spirit is the act in which God is the Father of the Son and the Son of the Father. In respect of this fact, the doctrine of the Spirit as the eternal act of communityness may come to have additional importance in guarding against any reduction of the eternal modes of existence to mere functions or acts of God. This conception of the Spirit thus serves to emphasize anew that God not only does distinguish himself from himself in this trinitarian way, but also that he exists *only* in this way. He is himself only in these three modes of being; his Being *is* his being Father, Son and Spirit.

6. *The Significance of Barth's Trinitarianism*

We shall have more to say in the next chapter about the general problem of the doctrine of the Trinity and of Barth's contribution in relation to it. It will be helpful, however, after this rather lengthy statement of his view, to recall one or two of the respects in which Barth makes most significant contributions to trinitarian theology, and then go on to consider the basic question of the relation of these to his view of "general revelation."

1) In the actual elaboration or structure of the doctrine as such Barth is at most points close to the classical and Catholic doctrine —and on the matters of the necessity of the doctrine and the repudiation of the social analogy he is by no means alone. But in the understanding of the ground or basis of the doctrine in revelation Barth does have something distinctive to say and because of this, the classical affirmations take on a new perspective and significance. First, as we showed in detail at the beginning of this chapter, there is the conception of the single basis of the doctrine. The doctrine of the Trinity is seen to arise as an implication or interpretation of the whole witness of scripture, considered in its unity as testimony to the coming of God in Christ. This is a witness both to the divine unity and the distinctions of form or

relationship which are implicit and explicit in the occurrence of revelation. The doctrine is not something pieced together in order to harmonize various other affirmations of faith, not a "combination of utterances"; nor is it the result of an effort to reconcile the revelation and experience of God in Christ with what religious experience or reason teaches about the unity of God. It is rather an explication of the unity and variety of God in his revelation, an analysis which in content is ("indirectly") identical with that revelation as it is described in the New Testament. And from this understanding of the unity of the ground of the doctrine, Barth is able to make intelligible the classical claim for the centrality of this conception of God and to show its importance for the whole of Christian thinking.

Second, and this is directly related to the conception of the unity of the ground of the doctrine, Barth calls attention to a way of reaching back to an understanding of the "internal" or "original" relations of God in his eternal modes of existence which quite avoids the objections usually raised against those conceptions. The objections here, i.e. those which are not simply objections to the doctrine of the Trinity as a whole, are usually directed at the Thomistic scheme, with its elaboration of the analogy from intellectual and volitional processes, and/or at the conception of revelation which is presupposed in the traditional proof-text technique of defending the doctrines of the generation of the Son and the procession of the Spirit.

But Barth does not rest his argument upon either of these bases. The notion of the relations of origin in God, according to which the Son proceeds from the Father and the Spirit from the Father and the Son, rests on the pattern or order of the "elements" of the fact of revelation. This pattern or form, the relation in which Revelation presupposes a Revealer, Reconciliation a Creator, the Son a Father, etc., is as much a part of the revelation and salvation to which the New Testament bears witness as is the distinctness of Revealer and Revelation, Father and Son, Creator and Redeemer. Here Brunner's emphasis on the *Hintereinander* of Father, Son and Spirit may be appealed to. If there is reason to distinguish between God the Father, God the Son and God the Holy Spirit on the basis of the "economy" of revelation, there is equal reason to speak of an order or pattern according to which the Son is the Son of the Father, and the Spirit the Spirit of the Father and the Son.

In suggesting that Barth's view of the basis of the doctrine of original relations is distinctive, we do not mean that this is altogether novel. On the contrary, it would be better to say that Barth has laid bare an essential element (if not *the* essential element) at the root of the historical evolution of the doctrine of the immanent relations. We do a grave injustice to the Fathers when we say that because their understanding of the revelation in the Bible was bound up with a more or less mechanical concept of the manner of revelation, therefore they were altogether misled in this matter of the doctrine of relations. That contemporary Protestantism has not yet returned to an appreciation of the importance of this concept is due to its preoccupation with the problem of the general fact of Trinity and with the problem of the basis of the doctrine.

2) The chief problem which is bound to arise in relation to. Barth's approach to the doctrine of the Trinity is the question of the connection between his view of the basis of the doctrine in revelation and his opposition to all claims for a general revelation or a natural theology. We have already considered Brunner's charge that Barth's estimate of the importance of the doctrine and his placing it at the head of the dogmatics is to be explained finally in terms of the polemic against natural theology. But the question may still be raised whether the conception of the single ground of the doctrine is dependent on, or necessitates the judgment that there is no knowledge of God whatsoever apart from his self-revelation in Christ. This question has a certain pertinence because the assertion of the single ground of the doctrine involves the assertion that *this doctrine is rooted solely in revelation*. Does, then, the knowledge of God which is expressed in the doctrine of the Trinity stand in opposition to all "other" knowledge of God?

This question can be answered in the negative. To be sure, we must insist that the knowledge of God as Father, Son and Holy Spirit is rooted entirely in the revelation to which the scriptures bear witness. But this does not in itself exclude the possibility of an apprehension or revelation of God which is in a sense other than, but not altogether discontinuous with the trinitarian conception. That is, the trinitarian understanding of God is not necessarily, by virtue of its being based exclusively in the revelation in Christ, utterly discontinuous with (e.g.) the monotheism of other religious traditions or philosophical monotheism.

There is a sort of continuity—and this is a sort which is frequently held to exist—which must be denied. That is the continuity which would exist if we were to say that the doctrine of the Trinity arises from the addition of faith in the Son and Spirit to the prior acknowledgment of God as Father. If we were to say that God is known as Father in the trinitarian sense apart from Christ, we should be faced with the problem of adjusting belief in Christ to the prior belief in the Father and making the doctrine of the Trinity into a synthesis. We are contending that this is not the way in which the New Testament speaks of the relation of the Father and the Son. The New Testament reference to God the Father is always to God the Father of the Son. *The Father, in the trinitarian sense of the term, is not known except as the Father of the Son.* But this need not mean that God is not known at all except in this way or that he cannot be called Father. It does mean that to speak of God as Father in the trinitarian sense is to signify that he is the Father and our Father in a way and with a meaning which is clearly to be distinguished from all other conceptions of God as Father.

In other words, the Father who is known to us as the Father of the Son cannot be described in any other way than as he who is known to us as the Father of the Son. This is not merely tautology. It is a way of saying that in the conception of God as the Father of our Lord Jesus Christ we have a conception of God which cannot be said to be simply equivalent to any other notion of the "Fatherhood" of God—even that in the Old Testament, and here we must dissent from Barth and Calvin on the uniformity of the biblical witness—and that this new understanding of God the Father cannot be stated without reference to the act of God in Jesus Christ.

This does not give us the right, however, to go on to say that this understanding of the Fatherhood of God has "*nothing* to do" with all other conceptions of God as Creator or Father, if such phrases are to be taken at simple face value. Nor does Barth's own understanding of the Father as Creator bear out such assertions of discontinuity. Barth holds that God is revealed as our Creator only in Christ, because only in Christ does the event of the new birth occur by which God's lordship over our existence is revealed and is a fact. God's lordship over our existence, however, does not mean simply his power over our physical existence. In this context it refers to his lordship over our existence *as his children*. By our reconciliation to him in Christ we are made aware that he is our Lord, our Creator, in a fellowship which has been lost and (apart from Christ) hidden from us. Only as Reconciler does God reveal himself as our Creator in this sense.

So far, we can follow Barth. The understanding of God as the One who creates us as his children, who is Lord of our existence in this way, in such a radical way that the Redemption in which this creation is restored is described as new birth and resurrection— this is truly a revelation of the Father which is completely bound to the revealer Jesus Christ. There is a real tension between *this* conception of creation and "the familiar truth, that the world must have and really has a Creator"; but the fact that these two conceptions are not equivalent does not mean that they have "nothing to do" with each other.

The same sort of argument may be developed in respect of the unity of God. We have argued that the unity of the Triune God is not something imposed from without but given in and with the revelation of variety. The revelation is not something which has to be reconciled with an already accepted monotheism. But this does not mean that all other apprehension of the unity of God is wholly false or that Christian monotheism has nothing to do with the monotheism of philosophy or Islam. The unity of God which is affirmed by the doctrine of the Trinity is not any sort of unity, and this means that God's revelation of his unity in the variety of his existence as Father, Son and Spirit is not equivalent to or simply continuous with any other apprehension of his unity. But this again does not imply total opposition, unless we hold that the only two alternatives are identity and complete dissimilarity.

In short, it is difficult to see how the conception of the unity of the ground of the trinitarian doctrine, or the contention that this doctrine is based solely on the revelation to which the New Testament bears witness, stands or falls with either the acceptance or rejection of the possibility or actuality of "general revelation" or natural theology. I am not here arguing either for or against the latter notions. I am only suggesting that the understanding of the basis of the trinitarian conception which is indicated by Barth's approach, and which I believe to be necessary, is not inseparable from his reputed opposition to natural theology. The crucial point is that the doctrine of the Trinity is not dependent upon the affirmations of a natural theology or a general revelation, but springs directly out of the self-disclosure of God in Christ. If we wish, therefore, we may say (without any retreat from our basic position) that the unity of God here revealed is precisely revealed as confirming—though in a way which also enriches, corrects, converts and complicates—the monotheism of an *analogia entis* or of Judaism. And so, if on the basis of our understanding of the content of revelation we ask of Barth this concession, we need not at all thereby detract from the significance of his understanding of the unity of the ground of trinitarian thought.

7. *The Trinity and the Paradox of Grace*

The conception of the basis and the role of the doctrine of the Trinity which we have taken as the key to the understanding of Barth's treatise finds significant reflection and confirmation in D. M. Baillie's essay, *God Was in Christ*. Baillie has little to add to the formal statement of the doctrine of the Trinity as such. Though he disavows any attempt of his own to reconcile the wide divergence in recent thought between Barth's view of the divine *personæ* as modes of existence and the Anglican development of the social analogy, there is little question but that his sympathies lie with the former.

The historic doctrine of the Trinity, Baillie contends, has even in the Cappadocian Fathers, been "very different from the idea of God consisting of three distinct persons in the modern sense." [1] The latter idea is reminiscent of the crude literalism and over-simplification of the Arian common-sense theology. Nevertheless, Baillie does think it important to retain the "personalistic mode of speech" in order to emphasize "this truth that God is always and wholly and in ever respect *personal*. Nothing in God is impersonal. His Word is personal, His Spirit is personal." [2] God's personality is obviously different from our personality, because he alone is perfect personality. Therefore, in speaking of the *personæ*, we say He and Him, not It, but also He (instead of They or Them) in referring to the Triune God—"God is three 'Persons,' but He is also the infinite and universal Person in three 'modes of existence.' " [3]

The important aspect of Baillie's discussion of the Trinity, for our present purpose at least, is the way in which he develops the relation of the doctrine of the Trinity to the "paradox of grace," which is the central motif of his study. In this we have an illuminating illustration of what is meant by Barth's insistence on the comprehensive significance of the trinitarian dogma. The central paradox of the gospel, Baillie finds, is summed up in the phrase "I, yet not I, but the grace of God," i.e. in the understanding of the Christian man "that every good thing in him, every good thing he does, is somehow not wrought by himself but by God." [4] Everything is to be ascribed to God, yet without compromising our freedom. From the paradox of grace, there follows a conception of God which is similarly paradoxical. God, in the New Testament sense, is "the One who at the same time makes absolute demands upon us and offers freely to *give* us all that

[1] Baillie, op. cit., 142.
[2] Ibid., 143.
[3] Ibid., 144.
[4] Ibid., 114. Cf. 106 sq.

He demands. . . . The One who calls us to work out our own salvation on the ground that 'it is He Himself who works both the willing and the working' in our hearts and lives." This is what is meant by the proper name "God." It is His nature "to dwell in man in such a manner that man, by his own will choosing to do God's will . . . nevertheless is constrained to confess that it was 'all of God.' " [5]

This, Baillie says, is the Christian conception of God. And this assertion does not conflict at all with the affirmation that the doctrine of the Trinity is the distinctively Christian conception of God, for the two are really identical. What is said in the language of devotion about the paradox of grace is nothing else than what is said in doctrinal terms in the trinitarian dogma:

What the doctrine of the Trinity really asserts is that it is God's very nature not only to create finite persons whom He could love, and to reveal and impart Himself to them, even to the point of incarnation (through His eternal Word) but also to extend this indwelling to those men who fail to obey Him, doing in them what they could not do themselves, supplying to them the obedience which He requires them to render (through His Holy Spirit). All of this, says the dogma of the Trinity, is of the eternal nature and essence of God. He is Father, Son and Holy Spirit, and the Son and Spirit are consubstantial with the Father. And this outgoing love of God, His self-giving, is not new nor occasional nor transient, but 'as it was in the beginning, is now and ever shall be, world without end.' Surely this doctrine is the objective expression of the same great paradox which finds its subjective expression in the confession: 'Not I, but the grace of God.' [6]

In other words the conception of God which emphasizes the "character" of God as holy and loving beyond all measure, as

---

[5] Ibid., 121, 122.
[6] Ibid., 122f. The relation suggested in this paragraph, and indeed the whole conception of the paradox of grace which it presupposes, has a profound affinity with Barth's argument that the doctrine of grace presupposes and is dependent upon the completion of the doctrine of the Trinity in the affirmation of the full deity of the Holy Spirit, i.e. by the recognition that the Spirit at work in the Christian community is unconditionally the *Holy* Spirit. Cf. *Doctrine of the Word of God*, 535f.

taking the initiative in merciful seeking and redeeming—the conception which is grounded first in Jesus' teaching about God, e.g. the parables of the lost sheep, coin and son, and his declaration of his own mission to save sinners—this conception and the trinitarian conception of Father, Son and Holy Spirit in one God are "not really divergent but convergent and ultimately identical. The first needs to be crystallized into the second, and the second needs to absorb the first." [7] Our knowledge of God as merciful and loving in this way, in the way which is expressed in the paradox of grace, is dependent on and comes through the One in whom that paradox was perfectly and fully realized, whose life was the life of God incarnate. What happened in Christ and through him did not end with his crucifixion but continued among his followers in an experience that was different and yet the same; it was "independent of His actual presence in the flesh, though not independent of His *having* lived on earth in the flesh." [8] It is this paradoxical Christian knowledge of God which comes to (necessary) expression in the doctrine of the Trinity. The latter doctrine only states formally that the God of the paradox of grace, who is known in the Incarnation and Pentecost, is *eternally* the same. The doctrine of the Trinity is of all-embracing importance because it is the objective expression of the paradox of grace, the "crystallization" of the gospel itself.

In this description of the role of the doctrine of the Trinity there is clearly presupposed the unity of the ground of the doctrine. Baillie insists that the Christian idea of God is not to be separated from the Incarnation; it is not "theism" plus Christology, for if we leave out the Incarnation we do not know what is meant by "God" in the Christian sense.[9] Similarly, he argues for the unity of Christian experience. The gospel does not speak of different experiences which might be attributed to Persons having separate functions, as if God the Father were eternally transcendent, the Son incarnate in Christ, and the Spirit present in us.

[7] Ibid., 144.
[8] Ibid., 145. (This is the ground of the affirmation of the *filioque*.)
[9] Ibid., 65f.

No, "the New Testament can also speak of God the Father dwelling in Christ, and of the Holy Spirit being given to Christ; and it can speak of God the Father dwelling in us and we in Him, and of Christ dwelling in us, and we in Him. . . . the New Testament makes no clear distinction . . . between having God's presence with us, having Christ dwelling in us, and being filled with Holy Spirit." [10] Here Baillie is rejecting the sort of monarchianism which bases the doctrine of the Trinity in three distinct experiences and refers these back to Father, Son and Spirit as different functions of God. The reason for this is that "all three come at every point into the full Christian experience of God. It is not a case of three separate experiences: it is all one." [11]

At the same time the content of the knowledge of God (as holy and merciful, as seeking and giving, as requiring and providing the means of fulfillment) is inseparable from the distinct form of God's self-giving in Jesus Christ the Son and the illumination of our minds to the significance of Christ, which is God dwelling in us through the Holy Spirit. The paradox of grace is therefore seen to require an affirmation both of the unity and threefoldness of God.

In short, the doctrine of the Trinity is a summary of the conception of God which is implied in the paradox of grace. For this reason the doctrine is of prime importance in Christian life and worship, and Baillie aligns himself with Hodgson and Lowry and against Brunner in maintaining that while the doctrine is of course a theological doctrine, it is "an indispensable summing-up of the Christian Gospel for the life of worship." Without this doctrine, our whole conception of God is perverted and impoverished, therefore "its constant use in our worship helps to secure that we are drawing near to God as He really is—the God who was incarnate in Jesus Christ." [12] Baillie does not develop further the way in which he thinks the doctrine might be used in worship, though his criticism of the social theory makes it apparent that he could not endorse much of what Hodgson and Lowry have to say on this matter.

---

[10] Ibid., 146f., 153.   [11] Ibid., 153f.   [12] Ibid., 156.

In spite of the brevity and incompleteness of Baillie's treatment of the Trinity, his work has profound significance in illuminating further the basis of the doctrine and its role in theology. The notion is this time put in terms of the unity of Christian experience and thus is complementary to Barth's analysis in terms of revelation. Whether we speak (from the objective side) of God's act of self-revelation or (from the subjective side of the event) of our experience of the paradox of grace, the point is the same, that the doctrine of the Trinity arises directly and necessarily (and solely) out of the event which these phrases describe. It is because of this understanding of the nature of the biblical root of the doctrine that Barth and Baillie are able consistently to affirm the immediate and comprehensive importance of the trinitarian doctrine.[13]

[13] I.e. they are able to affirm this in terms consonant with contemporary theological discourse. Catholic theology of course makes equally forthright claims for the centrality of the doctrine of the Trinity, but as we have indicated, on grounds which are quite incompatible with at least one of the inescapable presuppositions of contemporary Protestant thought, the historico-critical understanding of the Bible.

PART IV

A CONSTRUCTIVE STATEMENT

CHAPTER VII

The Foundation of an Adequate Trinitarianism

1. *The Necessity of the Doctrine of the Trinity*

In preceding chapters of this study we have commonly spoken of the Trinity as a "problem" for contemporary thought. This means simply that the focal point of current thought with regard to the Trinity is the question of the role, the theological place or significance of this doctrine. In other words, it is the question of how contemporary theology is to orient itself with regard to what has traditionally been called the distinctively Christian conception of God.

This question, as we remarked earlier, is one which must inevitably have come to the fore in the present revival of Protestant theology. This is true, we said, because the current of contemporary thought has been fed on the one side by the tradition of Schleiermacher and Ritschl and all the radical questionings of the nineteenth century, and on the other by a renewed appreciation of the Christian theological heritage. It is true because the trend of interest has seemed to be moving from the problem of man to soteriology and Christology and thence necessarily to the nature of the God who is known in Christ. And this is true because the revival of the category of revelation as the foundation of Christian affirmation makes logically necessary a reconsideration of the classical Christian view of the revealed nature of God.

Moreover, the whole pattern of contemporary concern with the doctrine of the Trinity reveals with unmistakable clarity a growing awareness of the positive significance of this doctrine.

Both the number and variety of explicit efforts to reinstate the doctrine of the Trinity in a central place in the theological scheme serve to emphasize the inadequacy of the "reductionistic" attitude toward the notion of the Trinity and to point to the necessity of some positive reconstruction of the doctrine. While the conception of the doctrine of the Trinity as irrelevant or of secondary importance only is still a major factor in contemporary Protestant theology, this viewpoint has become vastly more difficult to maintain. It is no longer possible to accept the easy attitude that the doctrine of the Trinity is of only antiquarian or historical interest, or that it is simply the product of a speculative philosophy foreign alike to the modern mind and the central interests of the gospel. The direction of contemporary theological discussion is (at the very least) toward a far more sympathetic and constructive treatment of the doctrine of the Trinity than prevailed at the beginning of the twentieth century or at the close of World War I. Not only in the "neo-Reformation" theology, but also in Anglican and "ecumenical" thought, and to a lesser extent in contemporary "liberalism" we can see a widely influential recognition and appreciation of the essentially trinitarian character of Christian revelation and experience.

As a result of our analysis of the various ways in which this problem has been dealt with in recent theology, we must now make the further assertion that *where* (and insofar as) *the conception of God's self-revelation* (or his act of reconciliation or salvation) *in Christ is taken seriously, the doctrine of the Trinity comes inevitably into a central place in the Christian understanding of God.* By the doctrine of the Trinity, we mean at this point the conception of God as in his very Being (i.e. ontologically or essentially) Triune—one God, the Father, the Son and the Holy Spirit. We are not at the moment speaking of the exact *nature* of the trinitarian distinctions, or of the doctrine of relations, but only stating the proposition that if we intend to affirm seriously (and this is surely the intention of most contemporary theologians) that God has truly revealed himself and reconciled us to himself in Jesus Christ, then we must inevitably say that the terms Father,

Son and Holy Spirit refer to eternal and co-equal "distinctions" in the One Being or Essence of God.

We have rejected the approach to the doctrine which is characteristic of Roman Catholic and Conservative Protestant theology, insofar as this theology rests on an uncritical view of the biblical revelation. In relation to this defense of trinitarianism, the criticisms of nineteenth- and twentieth-century liberalism are relevant and valid. But when the work of biblical criticism is done, we still find ourselves confronted in the divine act by the God who reveals himself in a certain threefold way. The contemporary theological enterprise is committed to the affirmation that God has indeed *revealed* himself in Christ. And it is especially significant that even those theologians who consider the *doctrine* of the Trinity as of relatively minor importance are ready to confess that this revelation (or the Christian experience of God) is threefold, that the terms Father, Son and Holy Spirit designate a certain variety or manifoldness in our relation to God which must be taken into account in any explication of the encounter with God which Christian faith attests.[1] This admission means that the real question for us is not whether there is a threefoldness of revelation, but rather what is the nature of that threefoldness and what it signifies with respect to our knowledge of God himself.

In the sphere of this basic question, we have seen reason to reject those views which hold that the conception of Trinity is to be applied only to God in his revelation and not to God in himself, i.e. which stop short of what in traditional terms would be called a doctrine of the "essential" or "ontological" Trinity. Under this category we must include the conception of the Trinity as a dramatic symbol (Knudson), contemporary modalism, and Brunner's notion of the Trinity as a defensive doctrine. All of these views, insofar as they speak only of a Trinity of revelation or activity or experience, call into question the reality and ultimacy of revelation, for they suggest that God in himself might be other than God in his revelation. We therefore must re-affirm the judgment that God in himself cannot be other than God in

[1] Cf. above, ch. II, §§ 2, 3, 4.

his revelation. If we have to do with God's revelation in Jesus Christ, then it is God himself with whom we have to do; and if God is come to us in his Holy Spirit, then it can be no less than God who is so come to us.

This assertion is the reply to both modalism and subordination-ism. God is himself in his revelation as Son and Holy Spirit no less than as Father; and since he reveals himself as Father, Son and Holy Spirit he must be so eternally and be God precisely as Father, Son and Spirit. The doctrine that God is in himself three "Persons" or modes of existence is a necessary consequence of the assertion that God has truly revealed himself in Christ. The denial of this leaves us either with the conception of a hidden divine essence (or *monas*) which stands behind the revelation (as in modalism) and which might conceivably be other than the revelation, or with a view like that of Brunner, in which the revelation in Christ turns out to be only a partial revelation of the divine reality.

Similar to the modalistic doctrine of a Trinity only of revelation is what we have called the *monarchian* conception that the terms Father, Son and Spirit refer to distinctions in the "content" of divine activity (e.g. God's sovereignty, redemptive love and presence). The latter view has a strong appeal in that it permits us to speak of eternal divine functions or fundamental aspects of divine activity, thus of a sort of "essential" Trinity, without being involved in the difficulties of the traditional effort to define the divine "Persons." If one rejects the societal conception of the Trinity, the monarchian view is without any question one of the livelier options at hand. It is important therefore that the relation of our conception to it be stated with considerable care.

We have already pointed to a serious ambiguity which is present in the statement of the monarchian position itself. That notion may mean that Father, Son and Spirit only stand for qualities or attributes of God. But if pressed far enough, then this conception leads to an intolerable division of the ethical nature of God, because it is not guarded by a doctrine of coinherence of activities and violates the Augustinian rule, *opera trinitatis ad extra indivisa sunt*. Moreover, the attempt to equate the Father, Son and Spirit with Creator, Reconciler and Redeemer, or Sovereign, Redeemer and Sanctifier, has the effect of making the doctrine of the Trinity into simply a difficult way of saying something which can be said more easily in quite another way. If the doctrine of the Trinity means only this, then it is in itself of only secondary importance—and we have seen that contemporary monarchianism is, in fact, associated with the relegation of the doctrine to a subordinate place.

We may now add to this estimate of monarchianism a further and more decisive comment, viz. that the Christian conception of God as redeeming love or of God as Creator, Reconciler and Redeemer, cannot really be stated except with reference to the doctrine of an "ontological" or "essential" Trinity. That God is the Reconciler does not mean for Christian faith simply that he is the sort of God who loves men and seeks to reconcile them to himself—it does mean this, and also that God is eternally our Creator and Redeemer (or Sanctifier)—but Christianity comes to this assertion *only by way of* the confession that God has reconciled us to himself in his only Son our Lord, who is himself God. That God is the Father and our Father can be said in the Christian sense only by saying that he is the Father of the Son. In other words, *we cannot separate the "form" and the "content" of revelation*: the conception of God as Reconciler gets its Christian meaning from the fact that he was in Christ reconciling the world to himself, i.e. that he is the Son of the Father.

It is correct to say that the doctrine of the Trinity is identical in content with the conception of God as redeeming love (or with the paradox of grace), and this is most important in estimating the significance of the doctrine; but we must see (and D. M. Baillie does see this clearly) that the conception of God as redeeming love gets its meaning from the confession of God's coming as the Son of the Father and the Spirit of the Father and the Son. Whereas Aulén has said that the trinitarian conception does not add anything to a previously discussed notion of divine love, but only "defines more accurately certain affirmations about the mode of God's revelation . . . ," [2] we should have to say that the notion of divine love gets its specific meaning precisely from what Aulén terms the "mode of revelation." There is no other standpoint from which the Christian idea of God as love can be explicated and the truth of the trinitarian conception judged in relation thereto. The meaning of God's love is not to be understood apart from the revelation of that love in Christ; the content of revelation is not known apart from the form of revelation. The act of God in Christ *is* his love. The revelation of his redeeming love is for Christians inseparable from his revelation of himself as Father, Son and Holy Spirit.

Correlatively, we must also say with respect to monarchianism that the distinctions in the content of divine activity indicated by such triads as Creator, Reconciler and Redeemer, are not in the first instance the ground of the doctrine of the Trinity. The affirmation that God is in his being three *personæ* or *hypostases* does not arise indirectly out of the effort to ground each of these activities or functions in the being of God. It stems instead directly out of what may better be called the *mode* or *form* of revelation, the distinction in the act of revelation or redemption between *him* who stands above and apart as the one to whom Jesus points and to whom everything is referred, who is the presupposition of the work in Christ; *him* who confronts man in Jesus Christ as the objective content of revelation; and *him* who seizes and possesses man so that he is able to receive and participate in revelation, new life, salvation.[3] This distinction the New Testament indicates by the words Father, Son and Holy Spirit.

These terms cannot be equated with the terms Creator, Reconciler and Redeemer, or Sovereign, Redeemer and Sanctifier, for the Father is not only Creator, but also Reconciler, Redeemer, Sanctifier, etc.; and there is no activity of the Father which is not

[2] G. Aulén, op. cit., 255.
[3] Cf. below; also above, ch. VI, §§ 2, 3, 7.

also an activity of the Son and the Holy Spirit.[4] The terms Father, Son and Spirit refer to a different sort of threefoldness than is indicated by these other triads; the primary threefoldness which the New Testament attests is better indicated in the phrase "from whom, in whom and through whom." It is true, to be sure, that in this phrase, as in the distinction between the Son as the objective side and the Spirit as the subjective side of revelation, we are speaking of a certain "variety" in the divine activity. But this is not a variety in the "content" of activity, i.e. of departments of activity or functions; it is rather a variety of form or pattern or structure. *The threefoldness indicated by the terms Father, Son and Spirit is a threefoldness in the structure or pattern of the one act of God in Christ and therefore the structure of all divine activity and of the Being of God* (this is true whether we proceed from the divine act to his being, or define being in terms of act).

The difficulty of identifying the doctrine of the Trinity with types of divine activity or divine functions can also be clearly seen in the problem of distinguishing (on this line of thought) between Christ and the Holy Spirit. K. E. Kirk has shown that in St. Paul's thought no clear distinction can be drawn between the results predicated of being "in Christ" and the results of being "in the Spirit." We are justified, sanctified, sealed, circumcised, have joy, faith, love, communion in both; "the same results are predicated of both conditions." Furthermore, the distinction between Christ as the source of the ethical aspect of the Christian life, and the Spirit as the source of the ecstatic cannot be maintained.[5] In other words, the distinction between Christ and the Spirit which is presupposed by the doctrine of the Trinity is not a distinction in the content of divine activity or Christian experience. It is the sort of distinction which Kirk speaks of as the difference between communion (with God in Christ) and possession (by God in the

[4] Cp. Oscar Cullman, *Christ and Time*, 25f., 113. Cullman interprets correctly the NT witness to the unity of the work of the Son and the Father in creation and redemption, but quite misunderstands the intention of the later trinitarian formulations.

[5] K. E. Kirk, in Rawlinson, ed., op. cit., 205f.

Spirit), or which is indicated in Thornton's distinction between Christ as the content of the new life and the Spirit as the agent of the new life, or (better) Barth's distinction between Christ as the objective content of revelation and the Spirit as the subjective side of revelation.[6] This is the sort of distinction which required the Church to speak of *personæ* and *hypostases*, and which prevents us from equating Father, Son and Spirit simply with divine functions or varieties in the content of God's action. *It refers to the "structure" of God in his Being and Act rather than to types of action.*

There is, to be sure, real value and truth in associating the threefoldness of Creator, Redeemer and Sanctifier (or however it may be formulated) with Father, Son and Holy Spirit. But we must recall that in so doing we are really interpreting the meaning of the former terms to conform with the latter conception. That is, when we speak of God the Son as Redeemer, we understand redemption or reconciliation by reference to God's giving of his only Son; and when we speak of God as sanctifier (as distinguished here from creator and redeemer) we refer to his presence in us, completing the work of reconciliation and redemption; thus we may properly speak of the work of the Holy Spirit as sanctification (or in Barth's terms, redemption). In other words, the "economy" upon which the doctrine of the Trinity rests is immediately the economy designated by the terms Father, Son and Spirit, the economy according to which God confronts us (in the one event of reconciliation and revelation in Christ) as the One who is the Father of Jesus Christ and therefore our Father, the One who is also our Lord as the Son of the Father, and the One who is our Lord as the Spirit enabling us to participate in the event. We may associate creation with the Father, redemption with the Son, and sanctification with the Spirit, because we see a certain correspondence between these aspects of the divine activity and what we *already* understand to be the distinction (and the relations) between Father, Son and Spirit.

---

[6] Cf. Kirk, op. cit., 227ff.; Thornton, *The Incarnate Lord*, 322ff.; Barth, *The Doctrine of the Word of God*, 512ff.

We must rigorously reaffirm, then, with the Catholic theology and with Barth, the rule *opera trinitatis ad extra indivisa sunt* and also the possibility only of *appropriation* of the varieties of content of divine action to the divine *personæ* or modes of existence. The "rule" does not mean that there is no distinction between creation and redemption, etc., but rather that these divine "functions" are inseparable and that God is one divine agent. The doctrine of appropriation means that there is a certain analogy between these distinctions of divine activity and the threefold distinctions of the divine *personæ*, or better between the relations of the elements in the content of divine activity and the relations of Father, Son and Spirit. But again, we must recall that we have already understood the meaning of the distinctions of content by way of the threefoldness of Father, Son and Spirit. Thus we may speak indifferently of Creator, Reconciler and Redeemer (Barth), or Creator, Redeemer and Sanctifier (Edwards, Fulton), or holiness, mercy and love (Barth), or sovereignty, love and presence (Thomas), or power, wisdom and love (Abelard, Rashdall). If we were to take these statements of threeness as definitive, we should have to be seriously concerned about the question whether "redeemer" and "love" should be applied to the Son or to the Holy Spirit, and also about the question whether there are not other aspects of divine activity which are equally important but cannot be identified with any one of our chosen three.[7] The fact that we can use such various statements of the threefoldness of the content of divine activity is, I suggest, due precisely to the fact that in each formulation we have assimilated the meaning of each of the terms to a prior conception of the distinction between Father, Son and Holy Spirit in revelation. When the terms "love" and "redeemer" are applied to the Son, they have reference to the objective side of revelation and reconciliation which is God come to us in Christ as love and redeemer. When these terms are appropriated to the Spirit, they refer to the subjective side, to God as

---

[7] Cf. D. M. Edwards' comment that he sees no final reason why other divine functions should not also be hypostatized. Above, ch. II. The activity of Judgment would be an example of such a function.

love in the sense that he is not only come to us but in us opening us up for himself, God as redeemer in the sense of completing the act of reconciliation and revelation.

2. *The Single Ground of the Doctrine*

Thus far, we have been defending the general proposition that if contemporary theology is to take seriously the confession that God has revealed himself in Jesus Christ, and the New Testament witness to the threefoldness of God in this revelation (indicated by the terms Father, Son and Spirit), then it must reaffirm the doctrine that God is in his being triune. The distinction between Father, Son and Spirit is not simply one of manifestation, nor one which can be equated with eternal functions or aspects of divine activity. The terms Father, Son and Holy Spirit designate eternal distinctions (which we tentatively call *personæ*, or *hypostases* or modes of being) which refer to the very existence of God.

Now, however, we must reckon with the distinction we have drawn between two quite different ways of understanding the ground and necessity of such a trinitarian conception. The first of these ways, which is widely characteristic of contemporary thinking, views the doctrine of the Trinity as a "synthesis" or harmonization of various elements of revelation and Christian experience. The doctrine is said to result from the reconciliation of the Christian affirmation regarding Christ and the Holy Spirit with the received faith in God the Father, or to be the synthesis of the plurality involved in the Christian revelation with the unity of God.[1]

We had occasion, in calling attention to the prevalence of this view, to ask whether, in its terms, the doctrine of the Trinity could ever be maintained to be a really primary element of the faith. Now, of course, if this conception of the basis of the doctrine is correct, then no objection can be made on such a score. But I think it can be shown that this conception, in fact, rests on a serious misunderstanding of the New Testament witness to

[1] Cf. above, ch. V, esp. § 4.

Christ. The doctrine of the Trinity is *not* to be understood as an attempt to reconcile the deity of Christ with the deity of God the Father, or the threefoldness of revelation with the monotheistic requirements of reason or general religious experience. For according to the New Testament, and therefore according to the doctrine of the Trinity, insofar as Christ is thought of as God, his deity is not thought of as in competition with or other than the deity of the Father, but *one* with the Godhood or the lordship of the Father. The confession of the deity of the Son and the Holy Spirit does not for a moment call into question the unity of God, but affirms that unity in the most vigorous terms.

An oblique corroboration of this assertion may be seen in H. Richard Niebuhr's article on "The Doctrine of the Trinity and the Unity of the Church." [2] Niebuhr distinguishes three "religions" in Christianity, each of which may and at times has become a practical unitarianism: the religion of the Father, which is the worship of the Creator God of nature and natural theology (this becomes unitarian in what is commonly called Unitarianism, in Monarchianism and Arianism); the religion of the Son, which is the worship of God in Jesus Christ (this tends to become exclusive in Marcion, the Jesus-cult of pietism, Swedenborg and Ritschlianism); and the religion of the Spirit, in which God is found in the direct awareness of personal religious experience (and which tends toward unitarianism in the Spiritual Franciscans, the doctrines of the inner light, and modern immanentism).

Each of these tendencies rests upon convictions which are legitimate within Christianity, Niebuhr suggests, but are faulty in their exclusiveness. The three are really logically and historically interdependent. Unitarianism and trinitarianism depend on each other in the sense that "Unitarianism asserts the monotheism of Christian faith against all polytheism; Trinitarianism protests against the identification of the one God with the author of nature, with Jesus Christ, with the Spirit, but is dependent on the assertion of unity by the Unitarians." [3] Each of the three uni-

. [2] *Theology Today*, III, 3 (October, 1946), 371–384.
[3] Ibid., 379.

tarianisms is a protest against the others and yet shows its logical interdependence by tending to pass over into one or both of the others. The doctrine of the Trinity is therefore the statement of the inclusive faith of the whole church. It is "a synthesized formula in which all the partial insights and convictions are combined." [4]

Niebuhr's analysis of the interrelatedness and interdependence of these three unitarianisms points clearly to the fundamental defect of the synthetic approach to the doctrine of the Trinity. Each of these "religions" rests on the supposition that one or other of the elements of the experience of God can be taken alone, as if separate and independent of the others (or that they can be reduced to one). The doctrine of the Trinity is a denial of this possibility. Instead of calling it a "synthesized formula" which *combines* these elements, however, it would be better to say that the doctrine of the Trinity expresses the inseparability and essential unity of these "elements." These unitarianisms are not simply partial insights, but distortions insofar as they assume the divisibility or separateness of the religious convictions on which they rest. The doctrine of the Trinity calls attention to the fact that each of them involves a denial or corruption of the Christian revelation.

The religion of the Father assumes the possibility of the worship of God the Father apart from the coming of God in Christ and the Spirit. But for Christianity, to say that God is Father means in the first instance that he is the Father of our Lord Jesus Christ, and from this fact meaning is given to the notion that he is our Father. The religion of the Son fails to see that Christ is the center of the New Testament witness only as the revelation of One who is beyond and has come in him, and that only in the Spirit do we "through him . . . have access . . . to the Father." The religion of the Spirit becomes only a deification of the human spirit, of one who is possessed rather than the One who possesses,

---

[4] Ibid., 383. Niebuhr's suggestion that the doctrine of the Trinity is an inclusive doctrine, which guards against exclusive stress on any one of the tendencies in Christianity, is very helpful. But we must be quite careful not to suggest that these tendencies are quasi-independent convictions only loosely united in the doctrine of the Trinity.

unless the Spirit be recognized as the Spirit of Christ and of God the Father of Christ—i.e. unless it be the Holy Spirit who proceeds from the Father and the Son.

My point is that it is not adequate to speak of the convictions about the Father, about Christ the Son, and about the Holy Spirit as more or less independent "elements" or parts of the Christian faith which are combined in a whole. For they are so interrelated that the absence or subordination of one not only makes the picture incomplete, but alters the nature of the others so that they are no longer the same convictions. We may speak of a "coinherence" of Christian witness, such that the acknowledgment of God the Father and God the Spirit is immediately present in the acceptance of Jesus Christ; the acknowledgment of Jesus Christ as Son and the Holy Spirit as the Spirit of the Father and the Son is necessarily present in the worship of God the Father; and the recognition of God the Father and of his Son our Lord Jesus Christ is directly involved in the presence of the Holy Spirit. Brunner's summary of the New Testament witness is quite correct in this respect: "Only through the Son have we the Father, only through the Son have we the Spirit, only through the Spirit have we the Son. In all, however, the one God reveals himself and gives himself to us." [5] The three "elements" or "experiences" are immanent in one another. (Here, incidentally, is the basis for the doctrine of coinherence.)

The chief point of criticism of the "synthetic" approach to the doctrine of the Trinity, then, is not that it is unable to escape the charge that the Trinity is only a secondary affirmation of faith, or only an ultimate intellectual formulation or a corollary of Christology. If we were to stop with this objection, we should only be begging the question of the role of the doctrine of the Trinity. The ultimate objection is that this approach to the doctrine rests on a false and misleading separation of the "elements" of the Christian revelation. From our previous analysis we can

---

[5] Brunner, *Dogmatik*, I, 229. Thus Brunner starts very much in the right direction, but he also speaks of the necessity of reconciling the lordship of Christ with the lordship of the Father. (Cf. ibid., 221f.)

see that this takes two main forms. One is the separation of the
basis of the affirmation of the unity of God from the root of the
affirmation of trinity—this is particularly evident in the elaborations of the social theory. The other is that line of interpretation
which seeks to understand the Christian view of God as a result
of the addition of faith in Christ (and the Spirit) to monotheism,
as if faith in the divinity of Christ and the Holy Spirit were somehow in competition with faith in the unity of God.[6]

This must be judged untrue to the spirit and the language of
the New Testament. It is undeniable of course that the monotheism
of Judaism is a source of Christian monotheism, but it does not
follow from this that the New Testament witness to Christ is
to be thought of as something to be reconciled with monotheism
(as suggested e.g. by Lowry and Whale). On the contrary,
monotheism is most explicitly reaffirmed by the New Testament
gospel of Christ and the Holy Spirit. As Barth puts it, the lordship
or divinity of the Son and the Spirit is one with the lordship or
Godhood of the Father.

J. M. Creed has called attention to the point in his Hulsean
lectures on *The Divinity of Jesus Christ*.[7] Commenting on Water-
land's contention that only the orthodox doctrine of the Trinity
"can prevent the confession of Christ's Divinity from imperilling
the truth of monotheism," he writes that this carries us "too
easily and too quickly to our goal. The argument derives such
cogency as it possesses from a logical and quasi-mathematical
procedure, which leaves out of account all the actual considerations which have led men to affirm the unity of God and the
Divinity of Jesus Christ his Son. We have assuredly left behind
not only the language but the deeper motive of the New Testament faith when the confession of the Divinity of Jesus Christ can

---

[6] A possible third form of the "synthetic" view might be seen in the
notion that the doctrine of the Trinity stems from the three experiences
which make up the event of revelation (e.g. Pittenger). This view comes
closer to the conception we are suggesting, but it needs to be emphasized
that this is really a "threefoldness" of experience and that there are not
separate "ways of knowledge" of God, but inseparable and coinherent
"aspects" of the one revelation of God.
[7] Cambridge (1938).

be felt to constitute some kind of threat to the faith in one God, and when to circumvent this threat it is proved to be necessary to forge the highly technical concepts of *ousia* and *hypostasis*." The apprehension of the divinity of Christ in the New Testament, Creed argues, is precisely an apprehension of him as "the Revelation of God beyond." [8] The divinity of Christ (and the Spirit) is therefore not a problem to be reconciled with an accepted monotheism, but an affirmation and explication of monotheism through God's revelation of himself.

D. M. Baillie's discussion of the relation of Christology and theology also sets the matter in the right perspective. He asks, "Is it easy to believe in God? In the kind of God that Jesus gives us? Not a 'deistic' God, or even a 'theistic' God (*for Christianity is not theism plus Christology*), waiting for men to discover His existence and then pass round the idea with its proofs; but the kind of God whom we find in the New Testament? Is it easy to believe in such a God? Is it easier than to believe in the Incarnation? Surely *the Incarnation is not an added difficulty*, but is rather the sole way in which the Christian conception of God becomes credible or even expressible." [9] If we leave out the paradox of the Incarnation, then we do not know what we mean by "God" in the Christian sense. Baillie goes on to argue from this that all Christian theology must be Christologically determined, but for our purposes the converse of this relation is the point to be emphasized. The Christological question does not stand alongside the theological question (in the specific sense of the term theology); *the Christological question is a question about the nature of God*. Thus a true Christology does not tell us just that God is like Christ, but that God was *in* Christ; it tells us about the Activity and Being of God. The Christological question is at once a question about God.

If we are to be true to the gospel of God's act in Christ, we may even say that the specifically theological question has a certain logical priority over the specifically Christological question. It

[8] Op. cit., 124, 129.
[9] Baillie, op. cit., 65 (italics mine). See also above, ch. VII.

was not simply an historical accident, but it was a logical consequence of the nature of the revelation to which the New Testament bears witness, that Nicea and Constantinople preceded Chalcedon. This last comment is somewhat ancillary to our central line of argument, but it is important as indicating that we do not know the triunity of God by the separate apprehension of the divinity of Christ and the Spirit and adding this to our acknowledgment of God the Father. We rather apprehend God the Father in the Son through the Spirit. "No one who denies the Son has the Father. He who confesses the Son has the Father also" (I Jn. 2:23). "By this you know the Spirit of God: every spirit which confesses that Jesus Christ has come in the flesh is of God, and every spirit which does not confess Jesus is not of God" (I Jn. 4:2f).

Our thesis here finds a corollary in the familiar observation that the logic of Arianism is the logic of polytheism. The demand for the subordination of the Son stems from the conception of the Son as "another" God, of his deity as in competition with the deity of the Father. The declaration of Nicea, ὁμοούσιον τῷ πατρί, is precisely an insistence that there is no such conflict. This is not an artificial, external or forced reconciliation of the divinity of the Son with the divinity of the Father. It is an affirmation springing out of the New Testament witness to the unity of the work of the Son with the work of the Father. In Christ dwells not another divinity, but "the whole fullness of deity bodily" (Col. 2:9). There is "one Spirit . . . one Lord, one faith, one baptism, one God and Father of us all, who is above all and through all and in all" (Eph. 4:4f.). The "subordinationist" passages of the New Testament do not speak of another deity in Christ, but point to the oneness of the work of Christ with the work of the Father, and therefore to the unity (and equality) of Father and Son.

We can conclude, then, the understanding of the doctrine of the Trinity as an effort to reconcile or combine faith in the divinity of Christ and the Spirit with the unity of God or the received tradition of the Creator or Father God, rests on a mis-construction of the New Testament witness. And we join with Karl Barth and D. M. Baillie in affirming the essential unity of the basis of this doctrine. We are to see the doctrine of the Trinity as grounded simply and directly in the self-revelation of God in Jesus Christ. It is arrived at, not by the relating of this revelation to other revelations, but as an immediate consequence of this revelation and reconciliation taken in and by itself. It is the most signal feature of Barth's treatise on the Trinity that he brings this to light, at least by implication, in the whole of his elaboration, and more directly in the preliminary analysis of the statement "God reveals Himself as the Lord." Whatever else one may say about this formula, it does serve to denote in a most striking way the real unity of the root of the doctrine of the Trinity. And this notion finds impressive confirmation in the entire structure of Barth's exposition.[10]

The doctrine of the Trinity is thus not an answer to the question, what is the relation of the deity of Christ to monotheism or a prior conception of the Fatherhood of God?—it is an answer to the question, what is the nature of God as he reveals himself in Christ? The doctrine is an *analysis* of what is directly involved in the revelation which the New Testament attests. The content of the affirmation that God is triune is not different from the content of the confession that Jesus is the Lord, or that God has revealed himself in Christ, or the acknowledgment of the paradox of grace, or the assertion that "God so loved the world . . .," or any other summary statement of the gospel, for the affirmation of the tri-unity of God is an explication, "a necessary and relevant analysis," of what is involved in any of these statements. It is necessary because only in the trinitarian conception does the full meaning of these statements come to light. Both the unity and the variety which the doctrine of the Trinity seeks to express are given in the New Testament witness to the one divine act. The threefoldness of Father, Son and Spirit does not contradict but expresses the

[10] Cf. above, ch. VI, esp. § 2.

oneness of God's essence or lordship, and the unity of the Subject of the event does not negate but is constituted by the distinction or order of Father, Son and Spirit.

This conclusion regarding the basis of the trinitarian doctrine is of decisive significance both for the question of the importance of this doctrine in Christian faith and for the problem of reconstruction of the doctrine itself. These questions will concern us in the following chapter. But before turning to them, I want to make two further observations regarding the immediate scope of our present contention. First, it is important to remember that in this discussion we are concerned chiefly with the *systematic* rather than the *historical* development of the doctrine. It is not necessary to the argument to work out a reconstruction of the historical evolution of the doctrine of the Trinity, even if the limits of this essay permitted such an endeavor. We can be quite willing to allow that in some strains of early Christian thought there was definitely a sense of conflict between the deity of Christ and the unity of God, though we should want to recall that this was the line of thought which issued in Arianism and was judged untrue to the New Testament witness. The repudiation of subordinationism and the affirmation of *homoousios* was a repudiation of the possibility that the convictions about Christ could be thought to be in conflict with convictions about the unity of God, just as the rejection of modalism was a denial of all attempts to reduce the revelation to a theophany.

Similarily, it is undeniable that (*ordo cognoscendi*) the *doctrine* of the Trinity arose in the struggle against heresy. But it is quite consistent with this fact to say that the resultant doctrine is seen to be (*ordo essendi*) a necessary and immediate explication of the New Testament revelation. The doctrine of the Trinity expresses the distinctiveness of the revelation in Christ without dividing the deity. Monarchianism and modalism failed in the former respect, Arianism in the latter. Whether it was fully realized from the first or not, the New Testament witness to the revelation and redemption in Christ involves the affirmation of the triunity of God as Father, Son and Holy Spirit. What we are saying about the nature of the trinitarian doctrine finally arrived at in the church is in no way in conflict with the observation that in the actual genetic development of the doctrine its immediacy and centrality were only gradually realized. We are saying, rather, that in its conclusions the church was truly bearing witness to the revelation attested in the New Testament.

Second, in asserting that the whole of the doctrine of the Trinity is grounded solely in the revelation of God in Jesus Christ, we are not excluding the possibility of "general revelation," or asserting the complete discontinuity of Christian monotheism with all other monotheism. We are saying, first, that the trinitarian understanding of the unity of God cannot be simply identified with any sort of unity; it is not a unity of mere singularity or isolation, but a unity in which there is variety, in which God lives in three *personæ* or *hypostases*. Hodgson is formally quite correct in saying that the trinitarian conception of God involves a new conception of the unity of God. And it is hardly necessary to argue the point that the Christian view is here radically different from the conception of a Maimonides or a Mohammed. But whatever is to be said about the inner complexity or variety of the being of God on the basis of the doctrine of the Trinity, the fact is not altered that Christianity does stand on the side of (e.g.) Judaism and Islam in denying that there can be more than one God and Lord, in negating all plurality or multiplicity in or of God. While affirming the ultimacy and self-validating character of God's self-revelation in Christ, we may very well say that the unity of the innertrinitarian life of God is a confirmation and validation of other explicit or even vague notions of the unity of God, though of course this confirmation comes in a way which also judges, measures, transforms and converts all other conceptions of the unity of God.[11] As Christians, we can look at the unity of God only in

[11] On this see also ch. VI, § 6. I differ here with Barth, who seems to feel that because Christian monotheism is not identical with the monotheism of Judaism and Islam, or the sort of vague monotheism which is found in almost every religion, therefore Christianity has "nothing to do" with this other "sort" of monotheism. (Cf. *Doctrine of the Word of God*, 406.) Barth is correct in insisting that the Christian conception of the unity of God is

terms of his revelation of himself in Christ, but we can also recognize that God has indeed not left himself without a witness in
any place.

In defending the single ground of the doctrine of the Trinity,
we are also saying that the knowledge of any one of the *personae*
is inseparable from the knowledge of the others. We have the
Father only with (or in) the Son and the Spirit, the Son only with
the Father and the Spirit, and the Spirit only with the Father and
the Son. This assertion has particular reference to the knowledge
of the Father and the Son. The doctrine of the Trinity is not properly to be understood as a result of the addition of faith in Christ
as the Son to prior faith in God the Father, rather God is
known as Father in the trinitarian sense only in his self-revelation
in Christ, i.e. in the Son and in the Holy Spirit. God the Father
means the Father of the Son. The whole knowledge of the triunity
of God, of Father, Son and Spirit, arises out of the revelation
which the New Testament attests.

Again, it need not be said that the trinitarian conception of God
as Father—i.e. of God in the *hypostasis* or mode of existence which
is the presupposition of his other modes of existence, God as the
Father of the Son and our Father—is *altogether* in opposition to
every other conception of the "Fatherhood of God." Even in
Barth's terms, one might see an analogy between the new conception of God's lordship over our existence by virtue of his being
Father of the Son, and the general notion of the Father-Creator
who is the author of creaturely existence. But what must be
asserted vigorously is that the trinitarian conception of God as
the Father is neither to be identified with nor determined by any
prior conception of God's "Fatherhood," but arises from and is
grounded simply in the acknowledgment of the Father of our

---

not to be *measured* by just any sort of monotheism, but in the passage cited
he fails to distinguish between "confirming" a sort of monotheism and
"being measured by a sort of monotheism." These two are quite different.
The trinitarian concept may be said to *confirm*, or to *orient* itself positively
toward, a general conception of the unity of God (at least in the negative
sense that oneness means no plurality of gods), without being measured or
judged by another sort of monotheism.

Lord Jesus Christ. From this new and self-sufficient vantage point, we may conceivably give an affirmative answer to the question whether any other idea of God as Father bears an analogy to the one defined by the doctrine of the Trinity.

In this second comment, then, I am suggesting simply that the judgment that the doctrine of the Trinity is grounded wholly in the revelation in Christ does not prevent us from affirming the possibility or actuality of "general" revelation. While at every point (the unity of God, or his being as Father, Son and Holy Spirit) the doctrine of the Trinity proceeds simply from the confession of Jesus Christ as Lord, it does not follow that we must speak of complete absence of analogy between the Christian and non-Christian conceptions of God. I have put the matter in largely Augustinian terms, which seem to me most adequate, but it need not be held that this is the only possibility. One might develop similar arguments along Thomistic or other lines. From the point of view of the conception of the unity of the ground of the doctrine of the Trinity, the important thing is that we should understand this doctrine to proceed simply and immediately as an "analytic" explication of what is involved in the event of revelation and reconciliation in Jesus Christ. This explication is therefore inevitably *confessional* in nature. We may, if we wish, stop here and say nothing regarding the relation of this Christian conception of God to "other" notions of God, or we may speak of radical discontinuity, or radical congruity,[12] or some sort of relative congruity between this revelation with its consequences and other "revelations." Whichever of these alternatives we take is a matter of relative indifference for our present contention, as long as we understand what is the basis of our trinitarian affirmation; from this vantage point we may or may not see the truth of this affirmation exhibited in other ways.

[12] I.e., it might be argued that from the point of view of the revelation in Christ, we discover all conceptions of revelation to be implicitly trinitarian.

CHAPTER VIII

The Direction of Trinitarian Reconstruction

1. *The Significance of the Trinitarian Conception*

The view that the doctrine of the Trinity is a necessary analysis of the revelation which the New Testament attests has far-reaching consequences for our estimate of the significance of that doctrine and its role in Christian theology. We discovered earlier (Ch. V) that on the "synthetic" interpretation of the doctrine, there is great difficulty in seeing how the notion of Trinity can really be an *arché* of Christian thought. The understanding of the doctrine at which we have now arrived, however, means that this doctrine is precisely in itself a primary affirmation of faith, a doctrine which follows directly from and is an immediate explication of the confession that God has revealed himself to us in Jesus Christ. This view makes intelligible and necessary the claim that the Trinity is the final and all-inclusive doctrine, the "supreme principle, the very center of the whole faith" (Garrigou-Lagrange). It is this because it is an immediate consequence of the gospel, because the revelation on which everything depends cannot be stated except in trinitarian terms. The doctrine of the Trinity is of all-embracing importance because it is the objective expression, the "crystallization" of the gospel itself. It is not just one part of the doctrine of God, but is integral to every aspect of the doctrine of God and to every other doctrine as well.

The full implications of this conception of the role of the doctrine of the Trinity could be adequately elaborated only in a complete systematic theology. But we can at least sketch some outlines of what is involved. We have to reaffirm, of course, the usual contention (*vs.* modalism and subordinationism) that the trinitarian doctrine secures the truth of the revelation and redemption in Christ, by declaring that it is no less than God himself who meets us in every aspect of this event, and that God is really in himself what he has shown himself to be, viz. God the Father, Son and Holy Spirit.

In addition to this, certain consequences follow for the doctrine of God as such. The Christian understanding of God as Creator, as Redeemer and as Sanctifier (or however we may wish to label these characteristics of God's activity) is directly informed by the conception of the Trinity. To say that God is Creator does not mean simply that he is the ground and origin of creaturely existence, but that he is the author and lord of our existence in a particular way, namely, as the One who is the Father of Jesus Christ and therefore our Father, who calls us to be his children in this way. To say that God is Redeemer means that he is the One who has given himself to us as the Son of the Father. To say that he is Sanctifier means that God not only has come to men but gives himself to men and is present in them as the Holy Spirit. We assert then the precise contrary of the notion that the trinitarian concept is a mold into which the distinctively Christian idea of God (e.g. as holy or redemptive love) is fitted. We have to say instead that the idea of God as holy or redemptive love gets its meaning from God's self-differentiation as Father, Son and Spirit.

On the side of the more "metaphysical" attributes of God, we have to say that the doctrine of the Trinity is of importance in regard to everything that is to be said about the divine unity. The unity of God is not the bare undifferentiated unity of utter simplicity; it is a unity of variety or manifoldness, in which there is distinction and order or arrangement, an inner richness and complexity (though not the sort of complexity which would mean divisibility—the trinitarian "persons" are not *parts* of God, and in guarding against such misinterpretation the notion of the divine simplicity has its significance; the simplicity of God refers to the unimpaired unity of his essence or Godhood). Moreover, if we are able to say, on the basis of the doctrine of relations (see below), that God's inner distinguishing of himself as Father, Son and Spirit implies a communion or communityness of Father and Son in the Spirit, then we must say that this innertrinitarian love and self-giving is the ground and possibility of God's love and self-giving to man. His will for community with and among men, his *agape* for men, proceeds freely from the community which God has in his trinitarian nature.

The importance of the doctrine of the Trinity for Christology and pneumatology derives immediately from the testimony of the doctrine to the unity of Christian experience. The trinitarian doctrine not only prevents us from identifying God simply with a Creator-God of nature and natural theology, thus falling into a "unitarianism of the Father," but it also makes impossible a Christology which is not wholly theocentric or a pneumatology which is not genuinely Christocentric and theocentric. The doctrine of the Trinity means that our affirmations about God as Father, Son and Spirit are inseparable and interdependent. All of the "unitarianisms" which H. R. Niebuhr describes are inadequate not only because they are incomplete but because they distort the conception of the object of worship.[1] No Christology can be adequate which does not recognize that Christ is at the center of the faith because he is the Son of the Father and because the Spirit which works in the Church is his Spirit. That is, no Christology can be adequate which is not explicitly trinitarian. The Christological question *is* a *theological* question. It is a question about the presupposition of the Incarnation, about him who is the Father of the Son, to whom Christ points as the One who has sent him; and this question is no less a question about the effect of God's act in Christ upon men, i.e. about that Spirit of the Father and of the Son which possesses men and completes in them the act of reconciliation. The Christological question and the theological question

---

[1] Similarly, Aulén declares that "as long as Christian faith in God preserves this threefold viewpoint, it also maintains its unified and organic character." Op. cit., 258.

are not really two questions, but two aspects of the same question. The question "who is Christ?" cannot be answered apart from the question "what is the nature of the God who is revealed in Christ?"—that is, the question of the Trinity.

Similarly, we must say that the Christian understanding of the Spirit is defined by its explicitly trinitarian character. The Holy Spirit, the "life-giver," is not to be identified with the human spirit, or any creaturely principle of spirituality, or anything less than the being of God himself. It is God himself who is the agent as well as the content of his revelation, who possesses us and enables us to receive and participate in his revelation and reconciliation. As Barth sees, this aspect of the doctrine of the Trinity has profound consequences for the doctrine of grace. It means that God is not only Subject of revelation in coming to man in Jesus Christ, but also ultimately Subject of man's response to revelation. It is the affirmation of the deity of the Holy Spirit which is the presupposition of the confession "not I, but the grace of God." [2] Furthermore, the doctrine of the Trinity requires us always to understand the Spirit which is the life-giver, the Spirit of the community, as the Spirit of the Son as well as of the Father. The Spirit is not just any spirit, not some vague immanence of God, but the Spirit of Jesus Christ. Christian language about the religion of the spirit, or the immanence of God, or religious experience, is inseparable from the historic revelation in Jesus Christ. The Spirit of which the Christian speaks is the *Holy* Spirit, the Spirit of *agape*, which is the Spirit of Christ.[3]

In short, the two affirmations, that the Trinity is truly rooted in revelation and that it is rooted simply and directly in revelation, determine the significance of the doctrine. It can be referred to as the "supreme principle of the faith" because it arises as an imme-

[2] It is significant that the emphasis of both Barth and Baillie on the centrality of the doctrine of the Trinity is closely associated with an insistence on the critical importance of the Holy Spirit and the doctrine of grace. There is real need for both systematic and historical exploration of the relation between the latter doctrines.

[3] Thus Paul insists that the works of the Spirit be judged by the love which is the love of Christ (I Cor. 12–14; Gal. 5). Cf. also my article, "The Holy Spirit and the Trinity," *Theology Today*, VIII. 1 (April, 1951), 29–40.

diate consequence of revelation. The Christian understanding of revelation, of reconciliation and redemption, of God, of Christ, of the presence of God in the Spirit, of grace—indeed the whole of Christian doctrine—can be stated only in trinitarian terms. The doctrine of the Trinity is not simply a mystery which, if we possessed the beatific vision, would be seen to illuminate all the other mysteries (Garrigou-Lagrange), but is a conception which we can now see to illuminate the whole of the faith because it is expressed in the whole faith. The doctrine is, we may say, a dogma in the sense in which Micklem defines that term, namely a doctrine which cannot be denied (provided one understands the consequences of his denial) without denying the Christian revelation itself. Or better, since the language of the doctrine is our language and therefore fallible, we cannot deny the meaning which this doctrine intends without denying the revelation. For Christian faith, this doctrine is an absolute, truly an *arché*, a first principle of thought.

2. The Trinity and Philosophy

The relevance of the doctrine of the Trinity to philosophy and natural theology—or better, to certain conceptions of philosophical import (e.g. creation, the nature of being, the personality of God, the meaning of history)—follows directly from the conclusion that the trinitarian doctrine is an immediate consequence of the Christian revelation, and therefore an *arché* of Christian thought. The central problem of contemporary theology, in respect of the doctrine of the Trinity, is the reëstablishment and reconstruction of the doctrine in terms of revelation. We are here concerned primarily with indicating the essential lines which such an undertaking must follow. The possibility of a "trinitarian philosophy" depends in part upon the successful accomplishment of this primary task. But given a proper understanding of the ground and role of the doctrine, no *a priori* limits can be drawn as to the use or significance of the trinitarian conception in the understanding of the whole of experience. Trinitarianism may become the starting point from which all finite existence is viewed and the context within which all finite experience is to be placed.

This does not mean that the doctrine of the Trinity is a truth derived from universal philosophical premises. We must vigorously reaffirm the classical judgment that this doctrine is a "revealed doctrine," not, of course, in the sense that propositions about the Trinity are revealed, but in the sense that this doctrine gives expression to the experience of those who stand in the situation of revelation. This judgment is implicit in the almost universal contemporary rejection of the Hegelian interpretation of the Trinity as a pictorial expression of a profound philosophical truth, and in the fact that almost all of the major contemporary efforts to reinstate and restate the doctrine of the Trinity are uniformly willing to rest the case for the doctrine simply on the basis of revelation and Christian experience. Our analysis of the basis of the trinitarian conception has led us to affirm the validity of this procedure. Whatever may be concluded about other doctrines, the doctrine of the Trinity has rightly been considered to be wholly a doctrine of revelation, as regards both its historical basis and its role in systematic theology.[1]

This being said, however, the trinitarian conception must be recognized to be of philosophical significance in two closely related ways. First, the notion of the Trinity as such directly involves metaphysical doctrine of the highest order. As soon as we have rejected modalism and monarchianism, we have committed ourselves to a trinitarian doctrine which purports to describe the nature of ultimate reality. The concrete development of the doctrine of the Trinity, to which we shall turn presently, is itself partly to be understood as an analysis of being—and more specifically, as an analysis which requires the development of a category of being described in traditional formulations as "relational being," or "subsistent relation." This is a new understanding of ultimate being, one necessitated by revelation. All consideration of the being of God must be related to this new understanding. It follows that given the doctrine of the Trinity, we

[1] Cf. esp. ch. VII, above.

cannot properly speak of being except in terms which reflect the trinitarian insight. The philosophical import of this judgment is obvious. We are saying that in the doctrine of the Trinity, the metaphysician learns something about God and being which must be taken into account in his metaphysic. This knowledge materially affects both his direction and his resources as a philosopher.[2]

In this assertion, we are already involved in the other aspect of the philosophical significance of trinitarian doctrine. This is the use of the trinitarian conception in Christian philosophizing and criticism of philosophy. This is possible and appropriate both because this notion is a Christian *arché* and because it is an inherently metaphysical doctrine. Our suggestion, then, is that reflection undertaken from the specific standpoint of the trinitarian understanding of God may show that conception to provide illumination of the nature of the created world in general as well as of the divine Being. That is, the proper exploitation of the trinitarian principle may produce a philosophical system more comprehensive and coherent than would otherwise be possible. It is not possible in this present study to undertake a thorough analysis of where such reflection might lead us. We can do no more than lay the groundwork upon which such further explication may rest, and suggest what the formal character of this enterprise would be.

The sort of "trinitarian philosophizing" which seems called for, if we are to consider the Trinity as truly a first principle of Christian thought, may be illustrated by reference to Charles N. Cochrane's analysis of the conflict between Christian and classical thought, especially as seen in Athanasius and Augustine.[3] Cochrane describes the task of fourth-century theology as the work of developing the implications of the Nicene theology, in which the fundamentals of trinitarianism were precisely formulated. The Trinity was understood as a first principle of thought, by which

---

[2] This suggests that the true philosophical significance of Christianity is not to be found in the approach of the so-called "philosophy of religion," but rather in the metaphysical import of Christian doctrine itself. With the argument above, cp. E. Gilson, *God and Philosophy*.

[3] *Christianity and Classical Culture*, chs. X–XII.

Christian faith was able to take up into itself all truth, i.e. a principle which might be applied to the problems with which classical thought had wrestled unsuccessfully and which would prove able to surmount the difficulties in which the classical views were inextricably involved.[4]

This process involved the translation of the trinitarian religious language into cosmic or metaphysical categories—not with the aim of discerning finite analogies which would serve as grounds for the demonstration of the truth of the Trinity, for the Trinity was unhesitatingly accepted on the basis of the revelation in Christ as defined in the Nicene theology—but with the intent of exhibiting the significance of the trinitarian principle as the basis for "a new physics, a new ethic and, above all, a new logic, the logic of human progress." [5] Trinitarianism is not an inductive conclusion from *scientia*, but an *arché*, a presupposition of thought which is given to men in the new *logos* in Christ. It is the light which is seen in revelation and thus becomes the light *by which* we see ourselves in relation to the universe. The trinitarian principle is therefore seen as useful "negatively . . . as the basis for a radical criticism of classical error; positively, as the point of departure for a fresh attack on old problems, exempt from the defects which had vitiated the thought of classical antiquity." [6]

For Athanasius, trinitarianism meant especially the doctrine of the consubstantiality of Son and Spirit with the Father, and the wholly spiritual conception of God which is necessitated in the account of the divine generation and procession. This insight, Cochrane suggests, opened the way to "a revolutionary view of the *operatio Dei* on the universe." [7] The affirmation that the

---

[4] Cf. ibid., 359ff., 385, 410f. To be sure, it was argued, on the basis of application to concrete problems, that the trinitarian principle was superior to any of the classical principles of understanding, and that trinitarianism meets the requirements for a first principle or precondition of thought (so Augustine, cf. ibid., 412f.); but it must be remembered that these contentions always rest on a prior commitment to the Nicene theology, and that it is *out of* the acceptance of trinitarianism that the relevance of this principle as a presupposition for an adequate cosmology and ethic is seen.

[5] Ibid., vi.

[6] Ibid., 419. (The reference here is particularly to Augustine.)

[7] Ibid., 366.

Word, who is the agent of creation, is of the whole being, life and power of the Father, meant that creation is to be understood as a free act of God, not a necessary emanation from the divine Monad.[8]

For Augustine, the acceptance of trinitarianism further involved the apprehension of the creative principle as a single essence whose nature is expressed and known in three *hypostases*, or in metaphysical categories, three principles—of being, of order and of activity or motion (or being, intelligence and life). The latter are not independent and exclusive *archai* (as in classical philosophy), but principles which, though distinct and not to be confused or resolved into one another, exist as a substantial unity and are mutually coinherent.[9] Thus in the Trinity, Christianity claimed to have discerned "the *logos* or explanation of being and motion, in other words, a metaphysic of ordered process," according to which nature is transfigured by being seen as "the theatre of divine activity."[10]

What is said about creation must also be said about human history, which is understood by trinitarianism as the "record of the divine economy."[11] History centers in the redemption of mankind through the incarnation of the Word, but now manifests the working of the Spirit in and through mankind from the beginning. Thus "trinitarian Christianity . . . pointed to an interpretation of history purely and simply in terms of the will of God.

---

[8] Cf. ibid., 367. Hodgson perceives something of this same connection in his contention that Nicea meant the end of the notion of the *logos* as the intermediary between God and creation. But instead of saying that the affirmation of *homoousios* forbids the use of the doctrine of the Trinity in relation to creation, we ought to say that the decision of Nicea involved a radical revision of the concept of creation and that therefore the trinitarian concept is a fundamental ground of the understanding of creation as the free activity of God. Cf. Hodgson, *Towards a Christian Philosophy*, 157f.

[9] Cf. Cochrane, op. cit., 409f., 423. This conception in Augustine's thought is probably to be related to the development of the psychological analogy (the trinity in the self of being or memory, intelligence or understanding, and will or love as the moving principle), though Cochrane does not make this relationship clear. The connection is not, so far as I can see, a necessary one. Mascall's suggestion (see below) is evidently similar to what Augustine is here saying.

[10] Ibid., 437, 436.   [11] Ibid., 368.

Such an interpretation, already foreshadowed in *De Incarnatione* of Athanasius, received fulfillment with Augustine's *De Civitate Dei*," in which the Trinity is explicitly understood as the principle of order and motion, the creative and moving principle of history.[12]

The task for contemporary theology is obviously not that of simple repetition of the ancient pattern of application of the trinitarian standpoint. The problems of modern thought and interpretation of experience are not identical with those which confronted the classical world. But in relation to these the work of contemporary theology may be said to be *formally* identical with the ancient endeavor, viz. the setting of the whole of experience and thought in the context of the trinitarian principle, and in this effort we cannot but be guided by the work of previous generations. This is especially true with regard to those persistent problems of creation, the personality of God, the meaning of history, etc. Contemporary Christian concern with the problem of history, for example, reveals a reappropriation of Augustinian insights. But not nearly enough account has been taken of the critical relation of Augustine's view of history to his trinitarianism. This needs to be made explicit, together with the relation of contemporary views of history to the trinitarian *arché*.

If the propriety and possibility of such a trinitarian philosophizing and criticism of philosophy be granted, we must say at once that we stand here at the threshold of an endeavor whose implications are almost entirely unexplored in the contemporary theological scene. It might be said, of course, that Leonard Hodgson's argument for a "revision" of the concept of unity fits the pattern suggested. But, while we have no objection to this argument in principle, Hodgson offers very little indication of the significance which he thinks this revision has for problems other than the specifically trinitarian one.

Similarly, E. L. Mascall seems to be taking a step in the direction of this kind of philosophizing in his notion of a strictly *ex post facto* philosophical use of the doctrine of the Trinity, specifically

[12] Ibid., 456. Cf. 480, 482.

in his tentative suggestion that the three fundamental facts of experience—the "infinite realm of abstract possibility," the "limited realm of actual concrete occurrence," and the "process of change" in the latter realm—may be correlated or appropriated to the Father, Son and Holy Spirit, respectively. The understanding of the distinction of the divine Persons, and the mutual coinherence by which "they all concur in the unity of the creative act," provides a point of view for understanding the interrelation of these facts (and thus of the contrasts between the actual and the possible, and between permanence and change, from which contrasts the three irreducible facts of experience are presented).[13]

A truly striking illustration of trinitarian philosophizing can be found in Miss Dorothy Sayers' analysis of the trinitarian structure of literary creativity—*provided* we make certain major adjustments in the theological method which is bound up with this analysis.[14] For, while on one side, her conception of the structure of finite creative activity might be understood as an insight drawn specifically from the trinitarian understanding of the Creator, we have seen that she does not consistently maintain that perspective and explicitly seeks to use this insight into the working of the human maker as a proof or corroboration of the doctrine of the Trinity itself. It is this latter aspect of Miss Sayers' thought which requires us to think of her work, like that of Lionel Thornton, as a reflection of a "philosophical trinitarianism" about which serious questions must be raised.

The difference between "trinitarian philosophizing," which we have here accepted, and "philosophical trinitarianism," which is to be questioned, may be clarified by distinguishing between four possible methods of procedure. 1) We may try simply to work out analogies to the Trinity for the sake of interpreting or illustrating the meaning of the notion. This I take to be the primary significance which Augustine attached to the analogies developed in *De Trinitate* IX–XV. 2) Or, we may begin with the trinitarian conception as grounded wholly in revelation and see in the doc-

---

[13] E. L. Mascall, *He Who Is*, 187–190.
[14] Cf. *The Mind of the Maker*, and the detailed analysis above, ch. III.

trine a principle or notion which illuminates a variety of aspects of finite existence. This is what we have called trinitarian philosophizing and criticism of philosophy. 3) We take a step further, however, when we see in the philosophical usefulness of the trinitarian concept, or in finite analogies, a confirmation or validation and determination of the doctrine itself. 4) And finally, we may go all the way and seek to establish the truth of the doctrine independently of the claims of revelation and Christian experience.

It is only the last two of these viewpoints which can properly be called "philosophical trinitarianism" in the sense of being in any way a continuation of the pattern of nineteenth-century thought associated with the name of Hegel. Obviously, neither Miss Sayers nor Father Thornton would wish to be placed in the fourth category, but would rather affirm the third of these points of view, viz. that the analogies from finite individuality and creative activity serve to confirm and corroborate the truth of the trinitarian doctrine. These writers both begin with the assumption that the Trinity is a doctrine of revelation. Yet in the light of the way in which their arguments are worked out, we found it necessary at least to raise the question whether these attempts to find corroborative *validation* of the doctrine in the nature of finite individuality, or the experience of the creative artist (or any other general characteristics of finite existence), do not inevitably lead in the direction of an independent derivation of the doctrine and thus to the abandonment of the basis in revelation. This query is given special point by the fact that (especially in Thornton's argument) this modified form of philosophical trinitarianism seems always to involve a tendency to make the conception of the Trinity conform to some kind of threefoldness which is discovered in the created order in general, and thereby in effect to *derive* the doctrine from some other ground than that of revelation.[15]

It should be clear from this that the immediate objection to philosophical trinitarianism arises from our conception of the single basis of the doctrine of the Trinity. But at the same time the arguments of both Miss Sayers and Father Thornton involve

[15] Cf. above, ch. III.

another question, which bears closely on the problem of the Trinity and philosophy, but which is essentially distinct from the question of the basis of the doctrine. This is the general question of the corroboration of revelation on philosophical or other grounds—in other words, the question of general revelation. It will be appropriate, therefore, to conclude this section with a brief comment on the issue of general revelation and its relation to the kind of trinitarian philosophizing outlined above.

Revelation, I should hold, must be considered to be essentially self-validating. As the act of self-unveiling and self-imparting of God, as (existentially) the creation and exhibition of a new relationship between man and God, revelation is itself a *center* of new understanding and interpretation. It means the establishment of a new point of view, *from which* we seek to understand our existence. The revelatory moment is "that part of our inner history which illuminates the rest of it and which is itself intelligible"; revelation gives "to the mind the impulsion and the first principles it requires . . . to do its proper work." [16] Therefore, while the truth of revelation may be *exhibited* in the explication and application of the rational pattern which the revelation offers, the truth of revelation cannot finally be *established* by any human activity. We cannot somehow take leave of our presuppositions and consider all viewpoints objectively, i.e. test the validity of revelation on the basis of other principles. Christian theology can know nothing of such other or prior principles. Its final norm is always the revelation of God in Jesus Christ.

This conception of revelation is not incompatible with a belief in "general revelation" or "natural theology," if it be understood that the insights of the latter are confirmed, judged and converted by the revelation in Christ, but it does require us to suspect any attempt to confirm or test (and therefore to correct?) the revelation in Christ by reference to "more general" or "universal" principles of religion or philosophy. If we wish to speak of a

---

[16] H. R. Niebuhr, *The Meaning of Revelation*, 93, 109. Cp. Hodgson's conception of revelation as providing the "key feature" which Christian theology explicates and Christian philosophy takes as its basic principle of explanation for the whole of experience (*The Doctrine of the Trinity*, 25ff.).

philosophical significance of the trinitarian conception as "confirming" its truth, then we must recognize that such "confirmation" is at least partially circular, i.e. we must take with utmost seriousness Thornton's comment that the "rational justification" for accepting the doctrine of the Trinity "can only appear in its full force within the order of experience which the biblical revelation itself created, that is to say within the New Order of the Spirit." If we do not recognize this, then we are on the way toward the substitution of some more ultimate criterion for the revelation.

Given such a qualification, however, we may properly speak of a trinitarian philosophizing as *exhibiting* the truth of this conception precisely by the illumination which it brings to the problems of human existence and its ability to lead to other truths.[17] We have argued earlier that while the unity of the triune God is by no means identical with the monotheism of Maimonides or Mohammed, still Christian monotheism could be said to confirm (by judging, correcting, converting, complicating and enriching) other conceptions of the oneness of God. Similarly, the Christian knowledge of God as eternal Father is never to be confused with other conceptions of the fatherhood of God, because the former always means "the Father of the Son"; yet from the starting point of our acknowledgment of the Father of our Lord Jesus Christ, we may be led to find in other speech about divine fatherhood something which must be said to have positive relation to the Christian notion. [18] The same kind of argument applies to the general problem of the Trinity and philosophy. We may adhere strictly to the self-authenticating nature of revelation, and thus to the essentially confessional nature of our theological explication, yet—precisely as a result of viewing the whole of experience from the trinitarian standpoint—discover that in truth God has nowhere left himself without witness. In these terms, the notion of trinitarian philosophizing and criticism of philosophy

[17] On such a basis, Miss Sayers' analysis of the threefold nature of all creative art can become a legitimate and fructifying theological endeavor.
[18] Cf. above, ch. VI, § 6; ch. VII, § 2.

can make positive connection with a conception of general revelation.

3. *Personality and the Trinity*

It was our fundamental contention in the previous chapter that the revelation which is attested by the scriptures and proclaimed by the Church requires us to confess immediately and as a central principle of faith that there is a certain variety or threefoldness in the very being or essence of the God who has revealed himself in Christ Jesus, a threefoldness designated by the terms Father, Son and Holy Spirit. God is one God, yet he is one in whom there are these distinctions, or who distinguishes himself eternally and in this way. In the first portions of this chapter we have sought to indicate something of the significance of this confession for the whole of Christian theology and philosophy. We must now raise the question of the further definition of this unity and threefoldness, i.e. of a more precise statement of the *content* of the trinitarian conception of God.

In approaching this problem, it will be helpful to recall briefly certain characteristics of the revelation which is the ground of the trinitarian affirmation, for these comprise the conditions which an acceptable statement must meet. In the first place, the revelation is uncompromisingly a revelation of one God. Christianity is irrevocably committed to monotheism, and this precisely on the basis of the revelation attested by the New Testament. There is nothing there which calls into question the unity of God, i.e. which suggests that Father, Son and Spirit are three gods, and the Church has consistently repudiated all formulations of the doctrine of the Trinity which might suggest a *plurality* of or in God. The name "God" is a proper name, not a generic term. The name of the Father, Son and Holy Spirit, into which we are baptized, is one name. In other words, in the statement of the doctrine of the Trinity we do not for a moment deny or even question, but precisely affirm the oneness of God.

Given the unity of the essence or being of God, what sort of distinctions or differentiations do the words Father, Son and Spirit refer to? Obviously, these are not such as to divide God, either in the sense that Father, Son and Spirit constitute a plurality of gods, or are parts of God. The former view is excluded by the witness of revelation to the unity of God, the latter by the testimony to the fullness of the presence of God in each of the three. On the other hand, the distinctions are "essential" distinctions, i.e. they belong to the very being of God. The terms Father, Son and Spirit do not refer simply to God in his revelation, but to God in himself. Otherwise we have only a pseudo-revelation. Moreover, our analysis has led us to reject the view that the trinitarian distinctions can be equated with distinctions in the content of divine activity, or with divine aspects or qualities (or, in the older terminology, attributes).

Now a further step may be taken with respect to the divergence between what have been called the psychological and the social interpretations of the Trinity. In its modern form, this question has become basically one of the relations between the trinitarian conception and contemporary understandings of the meaning of "personality" (as applied both to man and to God). This way of putting the matter raises at once the problem of the recent interpretations of the doctrine of the Trinity as meaning that Father, Son and Holy Spirit are each "persons" or "personalities" in the modern sense of the word. Thus the attempt to carry further the statement of the content of the trinitarian affirmation requires us now to take up a definite position with regard to these proposals. There are at least two major areas in which the modern claims for the social analogy must be tested: 1) does this analogy, as now stated, truly indicate the sort of threefoldness which is suggested by the New Testament witness? and 2) does it succeed in properly maintaining the unity of God? [1] In a word, I believe that the answer to both questions must be in the negative, and we are now in position to spell out this judgment in some detail (though we

---

[1] A third question is that of the relation of this development to traditional interpretations of the dogma of the Trinity, but this is a far less debatable question. Cf. below, 269ff.; also Appendix B.

run the risk here of a certain amount of repetition of our earlier analysis of these views).

1) With regard first to the unity of God. It will be recalled that the defenders of the social theory of the Trinity consider the witness of the New Testament to point almost exclusively to the divine distinctions rather than to the unity. Thornton expresses the general attitude when he says·that the interest of religious experience is primarily in the distinction of Persons, whereas the unity of God is the interest of reason. Now, of course, these writers do indeed hold that the New Testament teaches the unity of God, and a much more real unity than that of a harmony of individual wills, though they find the unity in the background of the New Testament witness rather than in the foreground. The important fact is that from their point of view the *problem* of the doctrine of the Trinity is the problem of conceiving the unity of God. The essential doctrine of the Trinity means that the object of Christian worship is Three and "in some ultimate sense One." [2] According to Hodgson, the faith which the doctrine of the Trinity requires is faith in the unity of God. We know God directly in his several Persons, but not in his unity; we therefore begin with the threefoldness and make the unity a matter of mystery [3]

At the same time, the unity of God is held to be not less real but more real than finite unities. The question is, then, how are we to conceive this unity which comprehends distinct persons, centers of consciousness and activity, so as to keep this doctrine from being simply an ethicized tritheism? Two sorts of answers are offered to this question—Hodgson's conception of organic or intensive unity (together with his appeal to certain idealistic arguments), and the notion of the permeability and interpenetration of personality (Thornton). We may take these up in order.

First, we must ask whether Hodgson's conception, especially as seen in the illustrations he offers, really takes us in the direction

[2] Lowry, op. cit., 67. Cf. 54.
[3] Cf. Hodgson, op. cit., 95, 102, 106f., 140, 180. Cf. Thornton, *The Incarnate Lord*, 407-413

of understanding how *personal selves* can be organically united. Hodgson is quite correct in asserting that the doctrine of the Trinity requires that the unity of God be conceived in terms other than those of static and bare inner simplicity. But there is nothing new in this. From the beginning, trinitarian theology has understood that the divine unity is not merely simple, but rather manifold and rich. Moreover, there is certainly nothing repugnant to reason in the notion of an *organic* unity. But the unity of an organism would seem to be a type of unity in which certain elements (or unities) are combined in a higher, more complex unity, a type of unity which Hodgson specifically rejects. This would appear to exclude all physical analogies, either from organic or inorganic nature.

Indeed, the only actual finite unity which Hodgson can cite as an example of "internally constitutive unity," in which the unity is found neither in one of the elements nor in a further element, is the unity of thinking, willing and feeling in the self. But even assuming the validity of this conception of the self, it is difficult to see how it would help us to conceive the unity of three distinct persons. This is still a psychological analogy, not an analogy for the unity of a society of persons. That is, the illustration of the unity of the self shows that the idea of an internally constitutive unity is not unreasonable *when the constituents are thinking, willing, and feeling*. Its usefulness to Hodgson's case depends upon some further demonstration that *personalities* are of such a nature as to be capable of being comprehended into, or of comprising a unity of intensity.

It is in order to satisfy this need that Hodgson introduces the idealistic argument for the inclusiveness of (Absolute) personality. This conception, however, appears to have the same basic defect as the illustration of the unity of an organism: these idealistic arguments refer to the inclusion of finite personalities in the higher unifying life of the Absolute. This is not an example of unity of intensity, but of unity by inclusion. Even if this is not intended —if Hodgson wishes to eliminate from this conception the suggestion that the unifying life *includes* the constitutive personalities, and to affirm instead that the constitutive personalities *are* the unifying personal life—we are still left with a most serious difficulty which pertains not only to this idealistic argument but to the definition of internally constitutive unity as such. The constituent elements are held to be fully distinct persons. But to say that they are constituents and that they complement one another is to say that they are *parts* of God (and ought we not to say *incomplete* and interdependent parts?—this is surely the case in the "internally constitutive unity" of the self). These fully distinct persons must therefore coexist with and be limited by one another, i.e. be *finite* persons.[4] This leaves us with serious difficulties concerning the infinity of God and raises the question of the relative status of the divine and human persons in relation to the life of the Godhead, the more so when taken in conjunction with the view that the Christian life is adoption *into* the life of the Trinity.

Finally, it appears that when we pass from the realm of the unity of less-than-personal elements (thinking, willing, feeling) in the self to the "unity" by intensity of distinct selves or personal beings, without their being comprehended in any higher unity or interpenetrating one another, the only sort of unification of which we have any direct knowledge whatsoever is the unity of a social group or a harmony of wills. This would indeed seem to be suggested by the notion of "love" as the "unifying power" of the Persons.

Lowry, though he makes use of Hodgson's concept of unity of intensity, really departs from that notion and tends to posit a unity in an ultimate essence or being which is "beyond" the Persons. Yet he does not clearly indicate what sort of essential unity he intends. He speaks of three centers of a "common consciousness," but this is a very difficult notion which, if it is not to be simply a name for something quite unknown, needs to be carefully investigated, or at least some relevant analogies adduced. Lionel Thornton, it should be noted, rejects the concept of three centers of one consciousness (which had earlier been suggested by

[4] Cp. D. M. Baillie, op. cit., 141.

William Temple in *Christus Veritas*) precisely because we do not know enough about what consciousness is.[5]

The chief alternative, then, to Hodgson's conception of intensive unity is the notion of the "permeability" or "interpenetrability" of personality, which was so much a part of the late nineteenth-century development of the social analogy. This concept seems to have been given up by Hodgson and Lowry, but Thornton utilizes it extensively.[6] If such a conception of personality could be successfully defended, it would certainly go far toward overcoming the problem of conceiving the unity of God on the social analogy. That conception involves the assertion that the exclusiveness of human personality is to be accounted for (as Thornton puts it) by its finiteness, its attachment to a physical organism, and its moral imperfection. Perfect, wholly spiritual, infinite personality (or as the earlier exponents of this theory said, essential personality) is defined by its inclusiveness, its capacity for interpenetration.

But, we may ask, if personality is essentially and ideally inclusive rather than exclusive, would not the lines of distinction between perfect (and identical?) personalities be altogether eliminated? Or, if interpenetration of personality means less than merging of personal identity but more than mutual love and communion, what is the nature of this middle ground? More important, we may ask what grounds there are for asserting that personality is essentially of this sort. The nineteenth-century defenders of the social analogy developed this conception in response to the contention of some idealists that, since personality could exist only in relation to other personalities, the Absolute could not be a person. But neither the fact that human personality develops and exists in society, nor the notion that finite personality is essentially dependent on relations with other personalities, nor

[5] Cf. Thornton's chapter in *Essays Catholic and Critical*, 139ff.
[6] It should be recalled that Thornton has doubts about the application of the term "personality" as such to either the unity or the plurality of God, and prefers to say three "Persons." But his argument centers on the *fellowship* of divine Persons and in this connection makes much use of the notion of interpenetration. Cf. above, 137f.

the conception of the unity of the Christian fellowship, can lead us logically to the conclusion that these interdependent personalities are essentially or ideally "permeable." Interdependent personalities could be conceived as mutually exclusive as well as mutually "interpenetrable."

It is curious that none of the recent proponents of the social analogy has appealed to contemporary analyses of sociology and social psychology. The whole movement symbolized by the work of G. H. Mead has led to the recognition that personality is inescapably and essentially "social." The self comes into being and continues to exist by interaction with the social matrix. Self-realization is not opposed to, but is a positive aspect of the socialization of the self. While for certain purposes a personality may be treated as an independent entity, it must, as Gardner Murphy insists, "be understood as an aspect of a social process; it cannot, in most cases, be considered as a self-contained unit." "Man is . . . a nodal region, an organized field within a larger field, a region of perpetual interaction, a reciprocity of outgoing and incoming energies." [7] Here might seem to be a useful base for the social analogy. We can, in these terms, speak of a permeation of personality, and certainly of personality as "open" rather than a closed, discrete, independent entity. But the philosophical implications of this analysis are by no means clear. If we take the line of those interpreters who would make individual personal existence merely a mode of the social whole, then we have a possible way of speaking of personalities being united in one (social) being. But this is certainly not the sort of unity which Hodgson and Lowry have in mind (though it might more readily be accepted by Thornton). Moreover, the emphasis on the social nature of personality must not be so interpreted as to overlook the individuality and uniqueness which are also, on this analysis, a part of the very definition of personality. The socialization of personality does not mean the loss of individuality, but precisely the realization and unification of the self. The development of personality is a development in the direction of individuality and

[7] Gardner Murphy, *Personality*, 767, 7.

self-awareness, of organization into unity "and awareness of such organization and individuality, the sense of personal identity, continuity, distinctiveness, responsibility." [8]

It is precisely this latter aspect of contemporary understanding of personality which makes the argument for the social analogy so tenuous. For we should have to say that, according to this socio-psychological analysis and contrary to Thornton's view, "perfect" personality would be more, not less, distinct and individual than finite, imperfect personality. Moreover, in other areas of thought the trend is strongly in the direction of emphasizing the "discreteness" or distinctness of individual personality. This is true of the general philosophical development since Descartes, as self-consciousness has come to be accepted as a defining characteristic of personality. And in contemporary Christian anthropology, we need only think of the pervasive influence of Kierkegaard's notion of the existential situation of the individual; or perhaps of the "I—Thou" conception, which for all the intimacy of the relation presupposes clearly the separateness and distinctness of the persons involved; or of Reinhold Niebuhr's contention that self-transcendence is constitutive of personality.

In view of modern understandings of personality, then, we have to say that the theory of "permeability of personality" as so far presented does not really provide us with a satisfactory way of saving the recent interpretations of the social analogy from tritheistic implications. Even the kind of interpenetration of personality suggested by sociological analyses does not take us far enough in the direction desired by these theologians. If we begin with the analogy from a society of persons as our *primary* analogy, we can get no further than the conception of a Trinity of three ultimate personalities, agents, perceivers, centers of consciousness—hence three beings (though interdependent and in some sense interpenetrating beings). I do not think that we need to exclude entirely the use of the social analogy from the interpretation of the doctrine of the Trinity (see below, § 5). But certainly the use of the analogy by Hodgson, Lowry and Thorn-

[8] Ibid., 2f. Cf. 487ff.

ton fails to make clear how such a conception can be made consistent with the unity of God. Thornton is less subject to this stricture than either Lowry or Hodgson because he does not rely exclusively on the social analogy, but seeks to make use also of the psychological analogy. Yet Thornton does not escape the problem for two reasons. First, he has no clear conception of the nature of analogy. This is even more true of Hodgson and Lowry, who seem to feel that the word "person" can be applied literally or univocally to Father, Son and Spirit, without any real difficulty. Thornton recognizes the problem which a doctrine of analogy might help to solve, viz. by his assertion that "person" and "personality" are different and his refusal to apply the latter term either to the threeness or the unity of God. But Thornton does not explain this difference and nowhere indicates clearly the analogical nature of the term "person." Second, he makes the social analogy primary, and while it may be possible to find use for this analogy in the context of a primary appeal to the psychological analogy (and perhaps by way of recent social conceptions of personality), it does not seem to me that we can successfully invert this process. Thus Thornton himself is hesitant about the ability of reason to apply an analogy from finite individuality, though he has no doubts about the application of the analogy from finite plurality. As in the case of Hodgson and Lowry, we must say that the "unity" of God which comprehends the "personal centers of activity" is either a social unity of three personal beings or is some ultimate sort of unity for which we have neither analogy nor language.

When all this is said, however, it must be agreed that if Hodgson, Lowry and Thornton are correct in their understanding of the revelation, then this is perhaps the only sort of unity which we can attribute to God. If it is the case that revelation clearly teaches the existence of three fully personal selves in God, then Hodgson is right that this is a part of the empirical "data" which must be taken into account and not explained away in speaking of the unity of God. Though we may not think he succeeds in showing how concrete unities really exemplify the precise sort of "intensive" unity he has in mind, yet if the data of revelation will permit no other type of divine unity, we must indeed be content with this, or with some theory of the permeability of personality. The prior point of judgment on the social theory must be the interpretation of the biblical materials.

2) The place to begin is doubtless with the use which is made in the social theory of the notion of Christ's sonship to the Father, for this appears to be the real root of the argument. From one point of view, the conception refers to our "adoption" into the sonship of Christ, which Hodgson takes as the primary (and even exclusive) characteristic of the Christian experience of redemption, and as the basis of the conception of a divine society. (This point of view is reflected also in Thornton's stress on the experience of *koinonia* as the essential element in Christian experience, though Thornton does not so strongly suggest that the fellowship of Christians is internal to the divine life.) Without denying the importance of this Pauline metaphor and the reality of the experience, we may ask first whether Hodgson's view does not involve the suppression of other equally important metaphors—the synoptic conception of new life in the Kingdom, or the Johannine notion of new life, neither of which implies that the Christian life is a life *in* God, or the Pauline conception of slavery to Christ, or of our access *through* Christ to the Father, or of the Church as the body of Christ.

But even the metaphor of adoptive sonship does not imply that the Christian is taken into the divine life in the sense in which Hodgson means this. It is Christ as the second Adam, the firstborn of the new creation, who is the archetype of the Christian's life and into whose sonship we are adopted. It is difficult to see anything in Paul's language about the adoption of sons (Rom. 8:15; Gal. 4:4–6) which "suggests that there is a social life *in* the godhead." [9] To be sure, there are numerous passages in which Paul seems to speak of the redeemed community as participating in or partaking of the divine life—or better, of the Christian community as characterized and constituted by the presence in it of the divine

[9] Hodgson, op. cit., 49. (Italics mine.)

(i.e. as the Spirit, grace, love, etc.). This is also suggested by the Johannine conception of new birth and eternal life. But to understand this life in the new community—in the body of Christ—as internal to the divine life, so that as adopted sons we look out upon the world from within the life of the Trinity, involves the introduction of a further assumption which begs precisely the point at issue.

What the metaphor of adoptive sonship asserts is that by the work (possession) of the Holy Spirit, Christians are inspired to a relation of dependence on God and fellowship with him like that which Jesus Christ, the *incarnate* Lord, sustained. This can readily be interpreted as a mystical union with and participation in the life of Christ. But in order to make the transition from the fellowship of Christians with one another and with Christ to the notion of adoption into the life of the Trinity and the conception of a divine fellowship of persons itself, we must assume the identity of the experience of Christ incarnate with that of the eternal Son (i.e. as regards the relationship to the Father). Thus Webb, Thornton and Hodgson all speak of transferring the relation of loving sonship in which Jesus stood to God directly into the divine life itself. It is in this assumption, together with the correlative notion that the New Testament bears witness chiefly to the plurality of God, that the chief difficulty is to be found.

We do not mean to suggest that the New Testament, at least in its "practical" Christology, does not imply the deity of Christ. It does that. The work of Christ is the work of God, the love of Christ is the love of God. God was truly in him. What is true in the adoptive sonship concept is that in being related to Christ we are truly related to God. But when Hodgson summarizes the historical records as giving us a conception of God in which "the Son is eternally giving Himself to the Father through the Spirit," [10] he omits the pervasive and crucial New Testament emphasis on the *act* of God, which is suggested by the word "incarnation." There is little in his conception which preserves the theme of the *sending* of the Son, of the Word *made* flesh, of the

[10] Op. cit., 142 *et passim*.

Cross as God's act, of God reconciling the world to himself in Christ. This is important, because in the conception of the divine act is to be found the center of the New Testament witness to the unity of God, such that the coming of God in Christ is not at all thought of as calling into question the oneness of God. The New Testament does not speak of the Son as a divine source of activity alongside (and equal to) the Father. Even in the Johannine conception (or perhaps especially here) the Son's work is not his own, it is the work of the Father. Insofar as the Son works, he does what has been delegated to him by the Father; he does nothing of himself, he is the agent of the Father. The Father works in him.[11] He is the *word* of God.

In this connection we may refer to the failure of the proponents of the social theory of the Trinity to recognize that the term *Son* denotes primarily a relation of origin from one who is a Father. Surely this is the intended reference when Paul speaks of "Jesus Christ his only son" and John calls him the "only begotten." The Son is not only loved by the Father, he is *born* of the Father. Similarly, Hodgson ignores that line of New Testament thought which identifies Christ as the Word of God. He seems to think that because the *homoousios* doctrine won out over the subordinationism which was implied by the original Greek *logos* conception, the *logos* doctrine has no further usefulness for trinitarian theology. But this rests on the assumption that the only significance the *logos* ever had for Christian thought was that of an intermediary between Creator and creation.

As a corollary of the New Testament witness to the *sending* of the Son, the *act* of incarnation, we must say that when the New Testament speaks of Christ as the head of the new community, and ourselves in fellowship with him (as distinct from our fellowship with the Father), it refers to Christ *incarnate*. We need not therefore close our eyes to that motif of the New Testament in which Jesus appears quite subordinate as compared with the Father. The presence of this strain of thought in the Johannine passages describing the "mutual relations of Father and Son"

---

[11] Cf. esp. Jn. 5 and 14ff.

(so Thornton, cf. Jn. 14-17) indicates that even the fellowship there referred to is not to be taken simply as a description of fellowship *in* the Godhead, but as an indication of the fellowship between the incarnate Christ and him who is called Father, a fellowship into which the disciples may be taken. These so-called subordinationist passages may thus be interpreted, not as statements of the metaphysical status of the eternal Son, but as testimony to the unity of the work and lordship of Christ with the work and lordship of the Father, therefore (indirectly) to the deity of Christ and the unity of God.

Here we may recall Brunner's emphasis on the definite order in which the New Testament always speaks of Father, Son and Spirit. He is wrong, we have suggested, in the way in which he uses this concept to exclude the notion of co-existence, but right in seeing that the New Testament testifies always to the *movement* from God to man. God comes to us in Christ and the Spirit. Through the Spirit we see the Son as the Son of the Father, and through the Son, the Father as the Father of the Son. "In all, however, the one God reveals himself and gives himself to us." [12] In Christ, the holy and merciful God meets us in revelation, reconciliation and redemption, while in the Holy Spirit he makes the historical givenness into internal experience.

It is not correct, then, to say that the New Testament bears primary witness to the divine plurality. On the contrary, it speaks continually of the *one* God and Father of us all. In the New Testament there is no interest in Jesus (as man or as God) apart from the action of God the Father. Jesus Christ is glorified just because his work is the work of the one God and Father. "Whatever Jesus was or did, in His life, in His teaching, in His cross and passion, in His resurrection and ascension and exaltation, it is really God that did it in Jesus; that is how the New Testament speaks." [13] It is necessary that from the fact of his revelation in

[12] Brunner, *Dogmatik*, I, 229.
[13] D. M. Baillie, op. cit., 67. I have taken this sentence out of its context, in which Baillie is speaking of the deity of Christ. But this makes the statement all the more useful, for it indicates that the deity of Christ is not in any sense to be understood as in competition with or other than the deity of the Father.

Christ and his enabling us to receive that revelation by the Holy Spirit, we should affirm the triunity of God. But we do not affirm this on the basis of the belief that the source of the activity of God in Christ is another source (or center of activity, or personal life) different from him whom the Bible calls God and Father. Insofar as the New Testament speaks of Christ as God, it speaks of his lordship as one with the lordship of the Father.[14] The unity of God, in other words, is not only not questioned in the New Testament; *it is most radically reaffirmed.* There is but a single source of the activity of revelation, of reconciliation—one agent, one "Thou" by whom men are confronted. The name of the Father, Son and Holy Spirit, into which men are baptized, is *one name*.

Finally, the assumption that the personal relations between Christ and the Father may be directly read off as personal relations within the Godhead seems to be inextricably involved with a defective Christology. Baillie has put his finger on the difficulty here. He points out, in commenting on the doctrine of *anhypostasia*, that modern theology with its historical understanding of the New Testament is irrevocably committed to the position that Jesus was not simply Man, but *a* man, a human person. If we are to take seriously the historical nature of God's act in Christ, then we must affirm that that act took place in the life of a concrete, particular human being. We may add that this does not necessarily require the abandonment of a doctrine of *enhypostasia*, for it might be possible to affirm both that Christ was Man and *a* man. And there were important considerations which led to the insistence on the universal manhood of Christ.

But would Hodgson really be satisfied with this, or even with the doctrine of generic manhood? He compares the Incarnation to the absence of a son from his family, and speaks of the limita-

---

[14] Conversely, when the New Testament speaks of Christ as another distinct personal life or center of activity from God the Father, it speaks of him who is a servant, whose work is not his own—i.e. of Christ after the fashion of his humanity, or sometimes as a preëxistent heavenly being. It is not a coincidence that in Christian thought, subordinationism and polytheism have tended to go together.

tions which are to be stripped away from the life of Christ in order to reach a conception of the divine life. The Son "retains on earth those relationships to the Father and the Spirit which are His eternally, but He exercises them under the conditions of human life on earth." He is "in mind, both passively and actively, the subject of experiences mediated through a physical body at a particular time and place in the history and geography of this world." [15]

Baillie's judgment on the implications of this conception appears to be well-founded. This is a form of Apollinarianism. The subject of the experiences of Jesus Christ was not a human subject (not even generically human), but a divine subject, the mind of the *logos*, the eternal Son, operating under the conditions of body and of time and place. Hodgson takes seriously these conditions and gives a more human account of this life, whereas Apollinarius gave a docetic account of it. Hodgson asserts that the incarnate Son knows in a human manner, and he is willing to attribute "a distinctively human consciousness" to Christ.[16] But he cannot mean by this that the Son was transformed into a man—this would violate his whole notion of the continuance of the essential personal relations between Father and Son. Nor does he mean that in Christ there are two centers of consciousness, two persons. He can only mean that the "human consciousness" is one of those conditions through which the experience of our Lord is mediated, while the *subject* of that experience, the *center* of consciousness, the spiritual essence, the *nous*, remains that of a divine subject, the eternal Son of God. This seems to deprive of meaning the New Testament witness to one who *as man* had "experience of God in faith and prayer." [17] It raises serious doubt as to the sense in which the life of Christ can be a pattern for our lives, and as to the validity of the affirmation that Christ is a redeemer for us because he took upon himself our life and genuinely shared in it.

It seems that Lionel Thornton's Christology shares something

---

[15] *The Doctrine of the Trinity*, 68, 69. Cf. Hodgson, "The Incarnation," in Rawlinson, ed., *Essays on the Trinity and the Incarnation*, 379, 387.

[16] Hodgson, "The Incarnation," op. cit., 392.

[17] Baillie, op. cit., 88.

of the same difficulty. Jesus for him is not a man on the level with other men. He represents a new and higher stage in the series. He is a new species. Thornton says that "Our Lord stands on the level of the eternal order, . . . He does not belong to the organic series. It belongs to Him; and He is organic to it through His human organism. . . . He supplies the super-organic principle of individuality to His organism. . . ." Again, *"although He became finitely individual in His human organism, He is not in Himself a finite individual.* For He is not an organism but the Creator, who has taken organic creation into union with Himself." [18] If I understand Thornton in these passages, he is saying that in certain respects, viz. in respect of his human organism, Jesus Christ is finitely individual but in other respects and essentially his individuality is divine. This is qualified, of course, by Thornton's view of the continuity between the human and the divine. Christ is not less individual, but more truly individual than we: "the principle of unity proper to His human organism in respect of its organic character is subsumed under the principle of absolute individuality proper to His Godhead." [19] If Thornton here does not mean simply that the physical organism is associated with a divine mind or center of activity, if he wishes to exclude all notions of part God and part man, his view still seems to imply that the human in Christ is not quite truly human. His humanity is not essentially the same as ours; he is not *homoousios* with us. Here again, the Christology appears to "exclude the possibility of recognizing the Jesus of the Gospel story as a real man." [20]

[18] *The Incarnate Lord,* 292, 420.   [19] Ibid., 363.

[20] Baillie, op. cit., 91f. The same sort of criticism would have also to be applied to the Christology of E. L. Mascall (cf. *Christ, the Christian and the Church*), though Mascall distinguishes much more sharply than Hodgson or Thornton between the metaphysical *person* and the psychological *personality*. Christ was a divine person (i.e. a metaphysical self or subject) with a divine and a human nature (presumably, human nature = personality). This could be interpreted so as to avoid the kind of social analogy offered by Hodgson and Thornton, though Mascall does not tell us what the implications of his view for trinitarian theology are. Actually, he appears to take advantage of all the psychological connotations of considering the divine Persons as selves or subjects; though how he can do this consistently is difficult to see. On the Christological side we are still left with the question how human nature can be complete without a human subject or self. To say that

The importance of this Christological excursion for us is that it brings clearly to light the easy assumption of identity between the experience of the incarnate Christ and the eternal Son which is characteristic of the defense of the social analogy. The divinity of Christ is not as transparent a matter as these men would have it. God in Christ is God incognito—God manifest but God hidden except to the eyes of faith. When we affirm the deity of Christ we cannot simply transfer his personality into the Godhead. To do so is to call into question the reality of the Incarnation. The process of stripping away limitations from the personality of the incarnate One in order to arrive at a conception of the personality of the eternal Son presupposes that we already know the distinct personal existence of the Son from the Father. But this is one of the things about which we ought to be inquiring. We have no right to assume it. Such an assumption, I have tried to show, rests upon a view of Christ which does not do justice to the gospel witness to his real humanity. This, together with the almost complete disregard of the New Testament witness to the unity of God, especially as seen in the oneness of the divine activity in Christ, cannot but raise the most serious doubts regarding the contemporary defense of the social analogy for the Trinity.

In saying this, we are not merely making a negative judgment. For the whole argument has a positive implication for the problem of personality and the Trinity. In denying that the notion of three divine "persons" or "personalities" is an accurate explication of the New Testament witness, we have also been contending that the unity of the God who has revealed Himself in Christ is a *personal* unity. The biblical God is One Subject, One Thou, One personal Being. It is for this reason that the language of the social analogy seems incompatible with the conception of the unity of God which is a primary condition of any formulation of the doctrine of the Trinity. This condition is not an *a priori* concep-

---

it is only metaphysical self-hood which is lacking, not psychological, is simply to run away from the crucial problem of the metaphysic of personality and to have a Christology which is neither metaphysically nor psychologically adequate.

tion of unity, to which the doctrine is arbitrarily made to conform, but is directly involved in the nature of the revelation which is the ground of the doctrine. In Father, in Son and in Holy Spirit, it is the one Lord and Savior who meets us. In view of everything that has been said above, we must affirm that the "personality" of God belongs to his unity, to his essence (though God is of course not *a* personality in the sense of being one person alongside others).

In this judgment, we find ourselves in agreement not only with the main current of Protestant thought in the last century and a half, but also with such modern Roman Catholic interpretations of the doctrine of the Trinity as those of Penido and Pohle-Preuss.[21] But the question may be asked where this puts us with respect to traditional formulations, which certainly spoke of three *personæ*. Thus C. C. J. Webb has contended that traditional Christianity spoke of personality *in* God rather than the personality *of* God.[22] Now, of course, it is true that Christianity has historically referred to *personæ* in God, but the further assertion of Webb depends on the assumption of an essential identity between the meaning of *persona* and "personality" or "person." A brief look at the history of the word *persona* in trinitarian theology will help us to see whether this assumption is valid.

The first thing to be noted is that when the word first appears, in Tertullian's formula *una substantia tres personæ*, its meaning is highly ambiguous. It might indicate something on the order of what we would call "personal relations," if we take as normative Tertullian's references to scriptural colloquies. But it could also mean—and this I think a more likely supposition—"role" or "function," if we emphasize the dramatic and legal associations of the term, or its translation into Greek as *prosopon*.[23]

[21] Cf. above, 109ff.

[22] *God and Personality*, 47ff. Cf. above, 133f.

[23] Cf. Bethune-Baker's assertion that *persona* never meant what person means in popular usage. "It always designates status, or character, or part, or function"—not in the sense of separation from a living subject, but "attention is always fixed on the character or function rather than the subject or agent. It is always a person looked at from a particular point of view, a person in particular circumstances; that is, it conveys the notion more of the environment than of the subject." *Introduction to the Early History of Christian Doctrine*, 234.

When we come to the definition of Boethius, *persona est naturæ rationabilis individua substantia*, we find a concept which does point more definitely in the direction of the modern term "person." The fact that Boethius was seeking to define the *persona* of Christ would suggest this. But we noted earlier that this definition, although almost universally referred to, did not fit well when theologians spoke of the divine *personæ*. This is most clearly indicated in St. Thomas, who defines the *personæ* primarily as subsistent relations and only secondarily in Boethius' language.[24] In the definition itself, the two essential notes are individuality, (*individua substantia*) and rationality (*naturæ rationabilis*). But rationality was commonly considered as a universal which might attach to many individuals. Thus what Boethius meant was not that a *persona* is an individual substance with an individual rational nature, but that a *persona* is an individual substance *of*, or (according to philosophical realism) participating (with other *personæ*) *in* rational nature. Insofar as the idea of self-consciousness was contained in this definition, that idea was clearly to be associated with rationality.

Thus the medieval theologians could accept Boethius' definition, and when they spoke of *tres personæ* in *una substantia*, could mean three subsistents in one divine mind or consciousness or self-consciousness. That they did mean the latter is to be seen in the almost universal acceptance of the psychological analogy for the Trinity. In short, while God was spoken of as *tres personæ*, just because *persona* did *not* mean what is meant by the modern term "personality," Christianity (at least as represented by the Augustinian-Thomistic tradition) cannot be said to have been committed to a doctrine of personalities *in* God, but rather to a doctrine of the personality *of* God.[25]

So far as the English word person is concerned, it is important to remember that since the time of Descartes and Locke, self-consciousness has come to be viewed as of the essence of per-

[24] *S. Theol.*, I, xxviii, xxix. Cf. above, 113.
[25] Cf. also Appendix B.

sonality; and it is shortly after this development that orthodox theologians begin to use the term person to refer to the unity of God rather than to the distinctions. The conclusion to be drawn from this is that only as long as the meaning of the term person remained ambiguous could it be used to refer to the divine "Persons." But when a person, or personality, came to be defined as a self-conscious center of individuality or activity, or a distinct center of consciousness, the term became a source of profound embarrassment to trinitarian theology, since both the element of rationality or consciousness and the divine activity had traditionally been referred to the unity of God. The *meaning* designated by the concept of the personality of God has always been implicit in the Christian conception, and finds classic expression in St. Augustine, but the actual use of the term dates from the struggle against the explicit assertion of the impersonality of God in modern naturalism and certain forms of idealism.

In conclusion, it should be made quite clear that in describing God as one personality, not three, we do not imply that the concept of finite personality can be applied univocally to God. Certainly personality in the human mode is characterized by a dependence on other persons, a lack of complete self-determination, which cannot be affirmed of divine personality. We are saying rather that, insofar as the notion can analogically be referred to God, it must be referred to him in his unity. We must also insist that God is, in every respect, personal. The *hypostases* are not less personal than the essence. God is always to be spoken of as *He* rather than *It*; thus in referring to the Father as distinct from the Son and the Holy Spirit, we must say *He* and not *It* (and so also for the Son and for the Spirit). In saying this, we of course do not mean that God the Father is another person from God the Son or God the Spirit, but that the God who confronts us as the eternal and infinite Thou is He who is the Father, He who is the Son and He who is the Holy Spirit. It may perhaps be possible thus to speak of God as *threefold* (not three) *as He* and *one as Thou—*by which we mean that as present to us God is one Lord, one essence, one Thou, and therefore one in personality, but he is present to us as Father, Son and Holy Spirit and therefore "He" in a threefold sense.

4. *The Language of the Doctrine of the Trinity*

The analysis of the problem of personality and the Trinity indicates that in very important respects, the explication of the content of the trinitarian confession is a question of language, of communication. In the phraseology of Catholic theology, it is the question of the "grammar" of the doctrine of the Trinity. When we say God is Trinity, we must give some answer to the query three what? one what? or, three in what sense? and one in what sense? And we must give an answer which expresses as nearly as possible what we really mean to affirm and which will serve to communicate something of the meaning to others.

On the side of the unity of God, this problem is obviously not so acute. Except among those who object to the use of all "philosophical" terms, there is general agreement that we must and can intelligibly speak of God's unity in terms of one *being*, or *essence*, or *substance* (as equivalent to *mia ousia, una substantia*, and *homoousios* in the classical formulæ). And in view of our discussion in the preceding section, we may add to these designations the term *personality* (or person).

To this proposal, it may be objected that since the word Person has so long been used, it ought to be retained as a technical designation for Father, Son and Holy Spirit, for the sake of continuity with tradition or because of the precise meanings which this word (or rather the term *persona*) has acquired in theological usage. There is always the possibility (a necessity for Catholic theology) of continuing to use the phraseology "three Persons" but with an explicit indication of the radical divergence between the meaning of "person" in ordinary speech and its meaning in the trinitarian formula, i.e. the possibility of continuing to use the word in its archaic sense and distinguishing it sharply from the modern "personality." But this alternative seems unsatisfactory for three reasons. First, there is the question whether even in its traditional sense the term is really clear enough to be useful to us. We may recall the original ambiguity of *persona*, the suspicion of Augustine regarding the word, the difficulties which the definition of Boethius involves, and the prevailing medieval (and modern Catholic) explication of *persona* in terms of the doctrine of relations. In other words, while the term Person may stand as a convenient abbreviation or symbol for a very complex pattern of definition, it is in itself of uncertain value in symbolizing that definition. But this is not a fatal difficulty, for any term that we might use would have a similar defect.

More important is the problem of communication. It is suggested that the use of the term Person serves to maintain continuity with the tradition. But does it? It provides a *verbal* continuity, in the sense that "person" is the customary translation of *persona*. But in view of what has been said, can we really believe that continuity of *meaning* is preserved? We may take the attitude of Moses Stuart, that if in using the word "person" we explain to our hearers that we do not use it *more humano*, but in a distinctive sense, then we are not to blame if they abuse it and accuse us of polytheism. This is similar to the line taken by Catholic theology. Penido, for example, distinguishes two quite different senses in which the term personality is applied to God—the philosophical and the theological. The former is applied to God as essentially distinct from creation, existing in and for himself, sovereign in intelligence and freedom. To say that God is three persons in this sense would be tritheism. The trinitarian analogy is of another, complementary sort. The philosopher speaks of a personal God to maintain the divine attributes of life, intelligence and will against the agnostics, and the distinctness of God from the world against patheism. The theologian speaks of a different sort of incommunicability when he speaks of three Persons.[1]

But even this careful sort of distinction, in which the word "person" in one usage turns out to mean something radically differ-

[1] Penido, op. cit., 337. Cf. above, 110.

ent from all ordinary meanings of the word, involves an unrealistic attitude toward the problem of communication. The danger of misunderstanding is shown both by certain tendencies toward tritheism in conservative Christianity and the fact the word "person" has been a fundamental factor in the widespread suspicion of the doctrine. Unless the doctrine of the Trinity is to be definitely misleading except to the theologians, it must be questioned whether even the need for maintaining continuity with the tradition can justify the use of this term. Properly, it can be said that if we really wish to maintain historical continuity with what the doctrine of the Trinity has meant, we ought *not* to speak of God as "three Persons."

Finally, we cannot escape the question of the sense in which the modern conception of personality is to be applied to God. We can no longer, as could the ancient and medieval fathers, speak of God as a neuter. The course of modern theology has committed us irrevocably to the explicit affirmation that God is personal. And that he is *one* in personality! This explicit affirmation is a peculiarly modern one; however, the meaning which it expresses was at least implicit both in the Bible and in the theological tradition. What is new in the contemporary situation, as a result on the one hand of the development of the concept of personality and on the other hand of modern denials of the personality of God, is the necessity of saying explicitly that we believe God to be a personal Being, a Thou, and thereby rendering the designation "three Persons" gravely misleading.

What we have just said means that in using the terms person and personality to specify the unity of God rather than his three-foldness, we are not departing from the real import of the classical formulæ. This is not a change in theological intention, but an adjustment of our language to the change in the meaning of the term person. Real continuity of meaning in Christian witness may require, as in this instance, very radical adjustment in the language of doctrinal formulations.[2]

[2] Cf. Aulén's statement that tendencies toward tritheism "become stronger as the concept of personality becomes more definite and elaborate. To repeat

The ascription of the concept of personality to the unity of God means that we have another term to place along with essence or substance in the one half of the trinitarian formula, but leaves us still with the problem of finding a relatively suitable term for the threefoldness (unless, of course, we are satisfied simply to use the Latin or Greek term). For the vocabulary of worship, it may not be necessary to go beyond the designations Father, Son and Spirit or the notion previously mentioned of God's threefoldness as He and oneness as Thou. But for the theological enterprise, which requires us to state as explicitly as possible what the presuppositions and implications of our worship and our faith are, something more must be said. In Augustine's words, "we wish some one word to serve for that meaning whereby the Trinity is understood, that we might not be altogether silent, when asked what three, while we confessed that they are three." [3] Our situation is complicated by the fact that we have a word which has the sanction of tradition and which is not likely to be given up by large segments of Christendom, yet which seems quite unsatisfactory in crucial respects. Even among those who perceive the wide disparity between the meaning which the term person has come to have, and the sort of divine threefoldness which we believe to be involved in the affirmation that God is Trinity, there is evident reluctance to abandon the older terminology simply because no acceptable alternative is at hand.

Yet it seems to me that this must not be put in too pessimistic a way. For it may properly be asked why the "something more" which theology gives to faith has to take the form of a *single* term or phrase. And to this query, there is no ultimate rejoinder. The drive for neatness and simplicity can very easily carry us too far, and cause us to forget that we are speaking of him who tran-

---

verbatim the trinitarian confession of the ancient church, 'three persons in one Godhead,' is under such circumstances contrary to the original intention of maintaining the unity of faith in God, and leads to conclusions which the trinitarian formula was intended to guard against. Faithfulness to the letter in that case becomes faithlessness toward the spirit and purpose of the ancient confession." Op. cit., 257.

[3] *De Trin.*, VII, 11.

scends all our knowing and speaking. There is no final reason at all why the trinitarian understanding of God must be reducible to a simple formula. Our concern here, therefore, must be seen in proper perspective, as the desirability of having a relatively exact term which can serve both the negative function of excluding false meanings and the positive function of pointing to the kind of distinctions we apprehend in Father, Son and Holy Spirit.

The negative function of theological formulations ought never to be discounted. This should be evident from the fact that many of the terms of traditional trinitarian formulations were first introduced and justified as a means of combatting error. *Persona* was chosen by Tertullian to indicate the "depth" of the distinctions between Father, Son and Spirit in such a way as to rule out the monarchianism of Noëtus and Praxeas. In the Greek formula, *hypostasis* was maintained in preference to *prosopon* (the normal translation of *persona*) in order to avoid Sabellian implications which arose from the combination of *prosopon* with *homoousios*.

Of course, the affirmation of the triune nature of God is not to be understood in purely negative terms. The statement that there is in God a threeness does not mean simply that he is not a bare unity; nor does the confession of the unity of God involve simply a denial of plurality. The evolution of the doctrine of the Trinity is also a search for language which can express positively the character of the unity and the distinction. Thus we too wish to speak in a way which both distinguishes our affirmation from modern forms of modalism and monarchianism on the one side and from the societal view on the other, and also indicates an eternal and "ontological" threefoldness of the one being and personality of God.

I am increasingly persuaded that the most useful term for our purpose is "modes of being" (or "modes of existence," the two terms being taken here as interchangeable). In contemporary Protestant thought, this phrase appears most prominently in the thought of Karl Barth. But Barth is by no means alone in this. The term is employed in a comparable sense in the nineteenth century by the mediating Hegelian, I. A. Dorner,[4] and in the contemporary scene by the careful and precise Roman Catholic theologian, Abbé Penido.[5] Barth's term, *Seinsweisen*, can, of course, also be translated "ways of being," as in the *Dogmatics in Outline*, but "modes of being" seems a more accurate expression of his meaning and less suggestive of distinctions of function or manifestation. Barth means to stress, and in this we agree, that these are not merely ways of God's being in relation to man, but *God's ways of being God*.[6]

As a designation for the divine distinctions, "modes of being" has the initial advantage of at least some formal precedent in earlier formulations—in the *tropoi hyparxeos* of the Cappadocian Fathers,[7] and in the *modus entis* of the medieval Latin theologians. What is more important, however, this term says what we really want to say—or better, it is a reasonably adequate summary of what we want to say about the threefoldness of Father, Son and Holy Spirit—and preserves genuine continuity of *meaning* with the traditional formulations. It indicates (and this is what *tropoi hyparxeos* was meant to assert in opposition to *tropoi apokalyp-seos*) that the distinction between the "modes" is one which pertains to the very being or existence of God and is therefore eternal. It means the same sort of inner determination of being which was intended by *persona* and *hypostasis*. This can be seen in Tertullian's classic statement that God is three "not in condition (*status*) but in relation (*gradus*), and not in substance but in mode of existence (*forma*), and not in power but in special characteris-

---

[4] Cf. above, 16.   [5] Cf. above, 110.

[6] Indeed, the phrase "God's ways of being God" has much to be said for it as a term for the *personae*. It is a more vivid term than "modes of being" and it indicates what the latter also intends. So far as meaning is concerned, I see no reason why these two designations cannot be used interchangeably. However, while "God's ways of being God" is perhaps more susceptible of use in worship and preaching, "modes of being" seems to me preferable in theological analysis, because it is much less awkward than repeated use of the longer phrase and more precise than such manageable abbreviations as "ways of being."

[7] Cf. Basil of Caesarea, *Ep.* 189.7; *De Spiritu Sancto*, 43, 44; also John of Damascus, *De Fide Orthodoxa*, 1.8.

tic (*species*)" [8]—and also in the fact that *persona* and *hypostasis* in medieval theology were primarily defined by the notion of subsistent relations.

Furthermore, this term has the special value of suggesting that it is not so much the "modes" which subsist in the being of God, but the one God who subsists in these three modes, Father, Son and Holy Spirit. This is important because of the necessity of ascribing personality explicitly to the unity of God. In view of the latter, we may speak not only of three eternal distinctions "in" God but also of God as distinguishing himself eternally in this way or determining himself in a threefold way and therefore being so determined (as for example in Barth's concept of *repetitio æternitatis in æternitate*). To speak of divine modes "of" being—rather than elements "in" the being of God—emphasizes also the identity of the divine essence and guards against any suggestion that Father, Son and Spirit are parts of God (i.e. it expresses the meaning of the doctrine of coinherence).

But in emphasizing that, properly speaking, it is the one divine essence which subsists in three modes of being,[9] we must at once insist that only in this way does God exist. "Modes of being" does not refer to distinctions in the content of God's activity or to God only in relation to the world, but to his inmost being, the "structure" of his existence. Therefore there is a real value in speaking of distinctions *in* the divine essence, or of the *modes* as subsisting. This excludes any interpretation which would make the *personæ* either simply modes of activity in relation to the world or phenomenal forms of an undifferentiated noumenon. When we speak of God—the One Being, Essence, Personality—subsisting in three modes of being, or of threefold self-determination, we do not refer merely to a Personality which expresses itself in a threefold manner. We mean that God's being is constituted in and by this threeness; this is the "structure" of his being; he is personal in this way, i.e. his triunity constitutes his person-

[8] *Adv. Praxeas*, 2. Bethune-Baker's translation, op. cit., 140.
[9] Our divergence from the tradition is at this point really one of emphasis, for St. Thomas notes that it is properly the Divine Nature which subsists. Cf. *Summa Theol.* I, Q. 29, 4. Cf. above, 191.

ality (hence Trinity may well be a more fundamental category than personality in the doctrine of God; and certainly we must think of divine personality as comprised in this threefold way). The balance of affirmations cannot here be abandoned: God determines himself in this way and he is so determined.

The chief apparent difficulty with the phrase "modes of being" lies in the fact that the term "mode" has often in philosophical discourse denoted a quality or aspect or accidental characteristic. This objection, however, is not so serious if we emphasize that we are speaking of modes *of being* or modes *of existence*, or of God as *existing* in these modes. *Mode of being* here means God's way or manner of existing *as God*—as God for us and as God in himself. It is perhaps inevitable, since the basis of our affirmation of an eternal divine threefoldness is the triunity of God in his revelation, that a proper doctrine of Trinity should be in danger of a "modalistic" misinterpretation, which would make of Father, Son and Holy Spirit only modes of God's relation to the world. This temptation is the more acute when the one personality of God is explicitly affirmed and we emphasize that it is the one being of God which *proprie subsistit*. In view of this, the term mode of being, taken as a whole, has the advantage of indicating both the nearness and the distance of the doctrine of the Trinity from "modalism"—nearness in that we begin with the manner of God's self-revelation and affirm that it is as one being (personality) that God determines himself in a threefold way; distance in that we unequivocally affirm that these three modes are of the very existence of God, that he is in himself and eternally thus.

A word of caution must be added in relation to this or any other designation which is proposed as an interpretation of the classical terms. We must not expect too much. The term "modes of being" is only a useful and relatively satisfactory designation. All our language about God is at best analogical. No more in speaking of the unity of God than in speaking of his threefoldness, do we mean that our statements are adequate to his being. In affirming the personality of God, we are at the same time affirming that his personality is threefold in a way in which human personality is not. It is obviously important to emphasize the positive nature of the trinitarian affirmation. The Church has always insisted that the concept of Trinity has more than a simply metaphorical significance. We do have a reason for affirming the doctrine of the Trinity and we believe that we know what we mean when we do so. Nevertheless, our trinitarian formulæ are not claimed to be unqualifiedly or univocally veridical descriptions of God's being.

Furthermore, it must always be remembered that the classical terms *hypostasis* and *persona* were themselves deemed acceptable only after a long and careful process of definition, in the course of which they came to be understood to mean a great deal which was by no means evident in the terms themselves. The word Person has seemed relatively so simple and clear only when not properly understood, and taken in the popular rather than the technical sense. There were not at the time of the development of the doctrine of the Trinity and there are not now available any terms which can simply be taken over as clearly and obviously indicative of what we wish to say about the Father, Son and Holy Spirit. Thus, in its early use, the Latin *tres personæ* tended to emphasize the unity of God, while the Greek *treis hypostaseis* tended to place the emphasis on the distinctness of Father, Son and Spirit. Each needed the corrective of the other. Similarly, the concept of threefold self-distinguishing or self-positing may need to be balanced by the concept of distinction *in* God. The latter guards against any suggestion of a tripling of the divine being which might arise from the former, while the former guards against the suggestion of parts of the divine being which might arise from the latter.

The traditional formulæ and any modern equivalents are useful thus as technical terms which stand for the whole complex of statements by which we seek to state what is intended by the confession of the divine triunity, and which will be relatively adequate to symbolize and to communicate what we are bound to affirm. Further than this we cannot go, except by reference to our entire systematic construction. It is in the construction as a whole that we can make clear the essential meaning of the metaphysical category which we designate as *persona, hypostasis*, relational being, or mode of being. This task we must now bring to a conclusion in terms of the doctrine of internal or inner-trinitarian relations.

5. The "Immanent" Trinity: the Doctrine of Inner-trinitarian Relations

One of the most striking features of contemporary Protestant discussion of the doctrine of the Trinity is the almost total neglect of the doctrine of relations, particularly the notions of the *principium* and the processions. This aspect of the orthodox doctrine of the Trinity received the sharpest criticism from those nineteenth- and twentieth-century theologians who inclined to consider the Trinity as a doctrine of doubtful or at best only peripheral significance. And where, as among some neo-Ritschlians and in contemporary monarchianism, it was allowed that Father, Son and Spirit may stand for some sort of ultimate distinctions in God, the notion of internal relations was almost invariably looked upon with the gravest suspicion, generally as a presumptuous claim to knowledge which had no foundation other than that of an outworn biblical literalism. Among contemporary reconstructions of the doctrine of the Trinity, we have found that only Barth makes any important use of the concept of relations. Of the others, only Thornton, Micklem and Lowry make even incidental or indirect use of the concept, and Hodgson (for his own reasons) opposes it.[1]

This lack of interest in the doctrine of relations, even among those who are concerned to emphasize the importance of the trinitarian concept, is presumably to be accounted for on the grounds that contemporary theology is preoccupied with the discussion of the basis and the general notions of Trinity, and that a profitable analysis of the internal Trinity awaits the outcome of the present discussion. But can one really be satisfied with such an explana-

[1] Cf. Thornton, *The Incarnate Lord*, 416f., 419; Micklem, op. cit., 118; Lowry, op. cit., 103f. The conception of the communion of Father and Son, which may properly be considered part of the doctrine of relations, is of course fundamental to the social analogy.

tion? On the contrary, while for the sake of discussion we can distinguish between and consider separately these two aspects of trinitarian doctrine, in reality these two aspects are so interrelated that neither can be properly conceived apart from the other. The question of the "original relations" is not one which is simply subsequent or additional to the problem of indicating the distinctness of Father, Son and Spirit. Rather, the notion of the relations is as directly rooted in revelation as is the distinction between the three eternal modes of existence. In fact, if our understanding of the ground of the doctrine of the Trinity is correct, the basis of the doctrine of original relations of Father, Son and Holy Spirit is the same as the basis of the affirmation that Father, Son and Holy Spirit are eternally distinguished.

We have asserted that the ground of the confession that God is in his essence three *hypostases* or modes of existence is an irreducible distinction in the act of revelation and reconciliation (as it is attested by the New Testament). God is present to us in a threefold self-differentiation. He makes himself known as the One who stands above and apart, the One to whom Jesus points as his Father and therefore our Father. At the same time, he is the One who confronts man in Jesus Christ as the objective content of revelation, i.e. the Son. And he is the One who seizes and possesses man so that he is able to receive and participate in revelation, new life, salvation, viz. the Holy Spirit. Plainly, there is a certain order or pattern here which is inseparable from the fact of revelation itself.[2] And this is an order which, as Barth rightly suggests, is indicated by all the various ways of designating the threefoldness (Father, Son and Holy Spirit; revealer, revelation and revealedness; creator, redeemer and sanctifier). It is an order in which the first term is the presupposition of the second, and the first and the second the presupposition of the third. In the New Testament, the Son (as Lord) is distinguished from the Father by being the Son *of* the Father, i.e. by being *from* and having his origin in the Father; and the Holy Spirit is Lord by being the Spirit *of* the Father and *of* Jesus Christ.

[2] Cf. above, ch. VI, §§ 5, 6; ch. VII.

Therefore, if it is right to move from the threefoldness of God in his revelation to an eternal divine threefoldness, it is equally right and necessary to refer the pattern or form of the threefoldness to the eternal being of God. What is more, if our analysis of the threefoldness of revelation is correct, *the fact of the divine triunity is itself to be understood only in connection with the pattern or order of the divine modes of existence.* This is expressed most clearly by Barth, who holds, in accordance with the tradition of Augustine, Aquinas and the Council of Florence, that in the concept of original relations lies the real distinction of the divine modes of existence. But this contention finds corroboration also in Brunner's emphasis on the "order" in which the New Testament always refers to Father, Son and Spirit—the *Hintereinander*.[3]

The doctrine of relations must therefore be an immediate concern of contemporary trinitarian discussion. In this doctrine, the classical theology (and modern Roman Catholic theology as well) expresses a crucial aspect of the New Testament witness to the revelation in Jesus Christ and therefore of the doctrine of the Trinity. We cannot, of course, share the conception of revelation which is presupposed by much of the traditional analysis of the modes of procession and the distinction between generation and spiration. Nor can we share the confidence of Catholic theology in the adequacy of the "Thomistic analogy" as a means for the development of the doctrine of relations. But we must recognize at least that the affirmation that Father, Son and Holy Spirit are three *hypostases* or modes of being of God involves also the assertion that these modes of being stand in a certain order, a certain inalienable structure or arrangement. This we must affirm in accordance with the principle, as it is formulated by Barth, that "pronouncements upon the reality of the divine modes of existence, 'antecedently in themselves' could not in content be any different from those that have to be made about their reality in

[3] We must reject, of course, the conclusions which Brunner draws from this, viz. that the *Hintereinander* precludes our speaking of a *Nebeneinander*, or at least of a *Miteinander* and *Ineinander*.

revelation." According to the biblical witness, the Son is the Son *of the Father*, the only-begotten, and the Spirit is no less the Spirit of Jesus Christ than of the Father of Jesus Christ. What we say about the "immanent" Trinity must reflect these relations.

In the structure of divine existence, then, God's being the Father is the presupposition of his being the Son and the Holy Spirit. The Son is "of" or "from" the Father, and the Spirit is "of" or "from" the Father and the Son. Whether we ought properly to speak of "relations of origin" depends upon what we mean by this phrase. Since we incline to say that it is properly God, the one divine being, who subsists in three modes of existence, we cannot speak of origin in the literal sense of *communicatio essentiæ* (or of the dictum *Pater est fons totius trinitatis*, which has the same connotation of an origination and transmitting of essence). But we can speak of original relations in the sense that God's mode of existence as the Father is the *ground* of his mode of existence as the Son, and these two are the ground of his mode of being as the Holy Spirit.[4]

If, however, by the divine relations or processions we do not mean literally production and communication of essence, neither do we mean simply logical order or progression, as the word "presupposition," taken alone, might suggest. We mean what was intended by the notion that the Father is the *principle* of the Trinity, *provided* that this is understood clearly in terms of the subsistence of the one divine being in three modes of existence. That is, interpreting the problem of relations by recourse to the analogy of personal existence, we say that in the eternal divine self-differentiation, God's being the Father is ontologically the possibility and ground of his being the Son and the Holy Spirit. This does not mean, of course, that there is any temporal priority, or that the Son and Holy Spirit are in any sense *less* than the Father. There can be no thought of diminution of deity here, for God is wholly existent in each of the modes of being. In the lan-

---

[4] Cf. Calvin's assertion that "the name of God is . . . used of the Father only insofar as He is the *principium* of Godhead, not by being the source of the essence, as the fanatics pretend, but in respect of order." *Inst.* I, xiii, 26. Cf. 24, 25.

guage of the traditional formulations, the divine modes of being are *coinherent*; none is a *part* of God.

With reference to the Holy Spirit, the primary question of internal relations has historically been the question of the *filioque*. Strictly speaking, when we have said that the "order" of the divine modes of being means presupposition or ground rather than literal communication of essence, and that it is properly the one divine essence which subsists, we have made it unnecessary (and perhaps not even meaningful) finally to settle the question whether the Spirit proceeds from the Father *and* the Son or from the Father *through* the Son. We must say certainly that God's being Holy Spirit depends upon his being Son as well as Father. For the Christian experience of the Holy Spirit, while now independent of Christ's physical presence, is not independent of his having lived in the flesh. And the test of the presence of the Holy Spirit, as distinguished from other spirits, lies in the fact that this Spirit is the Spirit of Christ, gives the mind of Christ, works through love, and testifies to Christ. Otherwise the conception of the Holy Spirit degenerates into only a vague notion of divine immanentism or spiritism. This relationship *ad extra* must be grounded in the relationship of Father, Son and Spirit *ad intra*. The conception of the *filioque* has a certain advantage in indicating unequivocally that God's being the Father and the Son is the presupposition of his being the Holy Spirit, but any ultimate distinction between "from the Father and the Son" and "from the Father through the Son" is made unnecessary by the notion that it is the One being of God which subsists in three modes. We are able to take with full seriousness the Catholic dictum that the "processions" are as from a single principle.[5]

So far, in the consideration of the relations of Father, Son and Holy Spirit, we have been, as it were, working backward, thinking in terms of presupposition and ground. The full significance of the notion of relations, however, can be seen only when we look at the "order" of the divine modes of existence from the

[5] Cf. also my article, "The Holy Spirit and the Trinity," *Theology Today*, VIII, 1 (April, 1951), 29ff.

other direction. God is Father, Son and Holy Spirit, in that order, though without any suggestion of diminution or subordination. The meaning of this can be seen when we recall the nature of the self-differentiation of God in his revelation. The Son is God come to us in revelation and reconciliation; the Holy Spirit is God come in possession, opening us up to receive revelation, making effectual the reconciliation in Christ Jesus. Therefore, to say that in God's eternal existence in three modes of being there is an order or movement from Father to Son to Spirit, is to say that he is *ultimately*, in his *being*, a *being-for*, a going forth. There is nothing more ultimate in God's being than this three-foldness of his life.

This, then, is the ontological foundation for God's love as it comes to us in Christ.[6] We affirm that God *is* love, and this we define by reference to his gracious presence to us in Christ and the Holy Spirit. To say that God *is* love is to deny that his being can be different from his action and to affirm that he is in himself a "being-for." It is precisely in the doctrine of processions that such an assertion becomes intelligible. This doctrine enables us to see how God's love is not merely his temper in relation to the world, but is his very being. The Triune God is in his own life a being-for another, an eternal and internal self-impartation which is the ground of his gracious, free self-impartation to man.[7] That is, the self-reflexiveness of the divine being, the internal being-for, is the possibility of the divine love for that which is other than God. The latter is of course a free act.

As soon as we have said this, however, we have to ask in what sense, if any, this conception of internal relations requires us to speak of an eternal communion or "communityness" or love between Father, Son and Holy Spirit. This is the final, and in some ways the most difficult, question of trinitarian doctrine.

---

[6] At this point, we are able to speak of the freedom of God's love and personality from dependence upon the world. Note that we are not saying that God must be triune in order that he may be free from dependence on the world; rather that he is Trinity, therefore we may speak of him as love and personality in himself, and this independently of created existence.

[7] Cf. what was said above (§ 1) regarding the significance of the trinitarian conception for every aspect of the doctrine of God.

This notion has, of course, obvious significance if the Trinity be understood as a society of persons, but the sort of communion there implied presupposes a near-tritheistic conception of the distinctness of Father, Son and Spirit. Barth also makes much of the idea of "communityness," both in the *Doctrine of the Word* and in the *Doctrine of God*, where God's "inner-trinitarian life," his "community in himself," is identified as the presupposition of his community with men. But Barth is not altogether clear as to the basis of this conception.[8]

The difficulty thus lies both in the warrant for and the meaning of this concept. In accordance with what we have hitherto concluded regarding the Trinity, it is clear that whatever is to be said about the communion or community of Father and Son must be said in recognition of the fact that this is a communion of God in himself. It is a community, not between selves, but "between" the divine modes of existence, between God's ways of being God. The question is, then, whether we are to conceive the distinction between Father and Son to be of such a nature that we can properly use the terms communion and love to refer to the relation between them. At this point we seem to be beyond the help of immediate analogy, for we are ascribing to the personality or being of God a threefoldness which is different from anything we know in finite personality. Nevertheless, there are two complementary aspects of our understanding of the revelation in Jesus Christ which seem to indicate the necessity of speaking of a "communion" in the inner-trinitarian life of God, and thus of specifying further 1) the depth of the distinction between the divine modes of existence, and 2) the difference between God's mode of existence as the Son and his mode of existence as the Holy Spirit.

The first of these aspects is the notion of inner self-giving which we found essential to the doctrine of processions. The second is the acknowledgment of the Spirit in revelation as impartation, as love, as gift, as God working in us communion with himself. From this we can go on to affirm that the Spirit in his eternal

[8] Cf. above, 200f.

being is an act of "community" of Father and Son, "proceeding" from both and designating the relation between these two modes of existence as one which may be described analogically as "communion." That is, the communion of Father and Son, the eternal community of God in himself, is to be affirmed as the ground of the communion between God as our Father and ourselves as his children.[9] We should then be able to say that the distinction between Father and Son involves a certain confrontation and mutuality. It would not be the case, however, that the Spirit "confronts" Father and Son, the Spirit being the communion or act or *agape* which is the relation of the first two modes of existence.

On the basis of these two lines of thought, then, we can see both the relevance and the intended meaning of the traditional affirmations regarding the mutuality of Father and Son and regarding the Spirit as the "bond of love." And the trinitarian conception becomes increasingly important as a statement of the ground or foundation in God's own life of his self-disclosure as the Lord, his self-giving in Jesus Christ, his establishment of community between himself and men. Moreover, there is a point of contact between this conception of God's determining himself (as the Son) in such a way as to have community in himself, and the traditional conception of the Son or Word as the complete and consubstantial image of the Father. We cannot accept, however, the argument that the Son is the necessary object of the Father's love. If we are permitted at all to speak of an eternal love of Father and Son, it can only be in terms of *agape*, of complete self-giving. The love of Father and Son is thus an inner procession of self-giving love, which is the ground of God's outward *agape* and therefore of creation and redemption. The notion that the Son is "needed" as an object of love or fellowship is ultimately compatible only with the social analogy for the Trinity.

The question remains, however, how the conception of an inner-trinitarian love or community can be related to our judgment that God is one in personality rather than three. As we have

---

[9] Cf. the suggested revision of Barth, above, 201f.

said before, the community of Father and Son in the Holy Spirit must be a community of God in himself, not between personal selves. Though we do not say that personality is an adequate term for God's being, we do say that insofar as this word can be applied to him at all (and it is necessary to do so), our primary analogy must be from the individual finite personality. Yet we are now attributing to divine personality something which is not characteristic of the single human personality.

Can this be shown to be an intelligible procedure? I believe that it can, when we recall that while finite personality is essentially discrete, it is also incomplete by virtue of its dependence on relations with other personalities. That is, man as a social being, one who becomes personal by relation to other selves, is not a wholly self-determining being. Now, what we are affirming about God is that he is perfect, self-sufficient personality precisely by virtue of his inner, trinitarian self-determination. He is not self-sufficient personality by being a society of selves, for no amount of addition of incomplete, dependent selves will total an independent self. It is true, rather, that each finite self finds its own completion and determination in mutuality with other selves. Thus the analogy cannot be drawn from the society of persons. Instead we must say that God is complete personality by being eternally related with himself as Father, Son and Holy Spirit. That is, in drawing the analogy from finite personality, we recognize that the insufficiency and dependence there observed is a function of creatureliness, and that perfect or infinite personality contains within itself the relatedness or mutuality which is external in the case of the finite person. This is a relatedness which is analogous to the relation of love and communion which exists between finite selves, but now understood as a relation between the self-determinations or modes of existence of the one personal God.[10]

---

[10] Here use might be made of the notion of the Word as the perfect, thus consubstantial image of the Father, or of Augustine's analogy of memory, understanding and will. However, these analogies, while clearly preferable to social analogies, are still metaphorical analogies rather than analogies of proportion or proportionality, to use the technical distinctions of Catholic theology.

If this interpretation be sound, then the conception of an eternal communión in the being of God may indeed be an essential element of the doctrine of the Trinity, and the ultimate distinction between the divine modes of being can be understood in terms both of the order (the processions) and of the mutual relations of Father, Son and Spirit. Moreover, we see that not only is the trinitarian being of God the ground and presupposition of his gracious self-giving in creation, revelation, reconciliation and fulfillment, but his triunity is also the nature of his personality.

6. *The Trinity and Christian Worship*

It is only proper that we should conclude this study of the doctrine of the Trinity with a comment on the role of the doctrine in Christian worship and preaching. We reserve this for the last because it permits us to return to the basis and ground of all our trinitarian conceptions. Everything that we have said has grown out of worship in the broad sense, and in that sense the crucial importance of trinitarianism is its importance for worship. We come to affirm the trinitarian nature of God because he whom we meet in Jesus Christ, whom we acknowledge as our Lord, and therefore whom we adore, is he who is known to us as the Father, the Son and the Holy Spirit. He whom we acknowledge and confess as the eternal Thou confronts us as the One who is in himself threefold in this way.

Thus the conclusions which we have reached regarding the centrality of the doctrine of the Trinity in the understanding of revelation and therefore in Christian thinking are themselves an expression of the significance of this concept for Christian worship and preaching. *The doctrine of the Trinity is the immediate implication and therefore the presupposition of the worship of the God who has revealed himself to us in Christ. The gospel can neither be truly stated, nor the Word truly proclaimed, nor God truly worshipped, without our affirming what is made explicit in the doctrine of the Trinity.* The God whom we confess and proclaim is the trinitarian God, therefore, as D. M. Baillie writes, "the constant use [of this doctrine] in our worship helps to secure that we are drawing near to God as He really is—the God who was incarnate in Jesus Christ."[1]

The question to be raised is what is meant by "use" of the doctrine of the Trinity in worship. At least two negative comments are called for. First, while we agree formally with Hodgson and Lowry that the trinitarian conception of God has important consequences for Christian worship, we cannot concur in their suggestion (or that of Roman Catholic thought) that we ought in our worship to recognize "clearly and consciously" our "distinct relationship" to each of the Divine Persons. The God whom we confess and adore is not three persons, with each of whom we might have communion severally. Such a notion is inescapably tritheistic in its implications. The God whom we confront and worship is the *one* Thou, therefore when we address him we do not address now the Father, now the Son and now the Spirit, but the One who is eternally a Thou to us, who is not known in one of his modes of existence except as he is known in his other modes of existence and therefore in his indissoluble unity.

Second, we must beware of the notion that the significance of the doctrine of the Trinity for worship depends upon the availability of some simple and nontechnical trinitarian formula and the use of that formula in devotional literature. Such formulæ have never been available. The phrases *una substantia tres personæ* and *mia ousia treis hypostaseis* cannot be said to lend themselves very obviously to devotional use (except possibly in contemplation). And the apparent simplicity of the phrase "God in three Persons" rests almost entirely on the misleading character of the term "Persons."

This observation suggests that the question of the relevance of the doctrine of the Trinity to Christian worship is not a question of the explicit use of some precise trinitarian statement in devotional activity. For the terminology of worship, we may not need to go beyond the biblical language, of the one God, who is Father, Son and Holy Spirit, or of the one Thou, who may be spoken

[1] Op. cit., 156.

of as He in a threefold sense. Or, we might find the phrase "God's ways of being God" a sufficiently vivid equivalent of "modes of being" to make it useful in certain forms of liturgy. *The crucial question, however, is whether our worship be in fact the worship of the triune God, and if it is truly centered in the confession of Jesus Christ it cannot help but be so.* Here we may agree with Lowry's (indirect) suggestion that all proper Christian worship is implicitly trinitarian. It is not simply self-surrender and dedication to one who is called God. It is acknowledgment of the One who is known to us in Jesus Christ, the One whom we call our Father because he is the Father of Jesus Christ, the One with whom we have communion in the Holy Spirit. This is what needs to be made explicit in our worship. In affirming that God is our Father, we are saying that he is eternally Father; in confessing Christ as our Lord, we are confessing that his lordship is one with the lordship of the Father (i.e. the deity of the Son, *homoousion to Patri*); and in acknowledging that it is through the Holy Spirit that we are able to confess Christ as Lord and have God as our Father, we are affirming the lordship of God in a third way. And in all this, the one God is present to us.

The doctrine of the Trinity, *qua* doctrine, is not the center of Christian worship. That center is the God who is described by the doctrine of the Trinity. The doctrine has its importance in determining the pattern of worship so that it shall be truly directed to him who is known to us in Christ. *It is thus at once the ground and consequence of Christian worship, "the foundation of all our communion with God, and comfortable dependence upon him."* [2]

[2] *Declaration of the Faith and Order owned and practised in the Congregational Churches in England* (1658).

Appendix A

The Terms "Economic" and "Immanent" Trinity

It has become customary in the discussion of trinitarian theology to distinguish between the "economic Trinity" and the "immanent Trinity." The former term is taken from Tertullian's distinction between the divine *substantia* or *monarchia*, which is one, and the divine *oikonomia*, i.e. dispensation, activity or administration, according to which Father, Son and Holy Spirit are distinguished. The term "immanent Trinity" is intended to suggest distinctions which refer not only to God's activity but are immanent in his being. Thus, in general usage, economic Trinity is the term used to refer to the triunity of God in the revelation in Jesus Christ, i.e. the threefold self-manifestation of God in history, or the Trinity relative to man. Immanent Trinity usually designates the manifoldness of God's being or essence, the Trinity as referring to God's eternal being, apart from his relation to the world; hence this is also spoken of as an "essential" or "ontological" Trinity. Thus W. Fulton (art. "Trinity," *ERE*, XII, 461) contrasts Trinity of manifestation with Trinity (or Triunity) of essence.

This distinction, while useful, is not altogether unambiguous. Taken strictly, the notion of economic Trinity as defined above contains nothing which would exclude the possibility of a Sabellian interpretation, which would make of Father, Son and Spirit only temporary or successive manifestations of God in relation to the world (so-called after the third-century Roman, Sabellius; whether Sabellius actually taught that these aspects of God's being are temporary is open to question, but this has been the usual interpretation of his thought). Yet Tertullian's doctrine of economic Trinity certainly includes the affirmation of the eternity and essentiality of the triune distinctions (cf. *Adv. Prax.* 5, 10, though contrary passages can be found, e.g. *Adv. Hermog.* 3, 18), as well as the notion of the generation of the Son and the procession of the Spirit. On the other hand, there are those who would insist on the eternity and essential character of the distinctions, but would say nothing about the "internal relations" or processions.

Some advantage might be gained by distinguishing three sorts of notions: 1) the threefoldness of God in his revelation or historical manifestation; 2) the doctrines of *homoousios*, coeternity and coequality, and such terms as *hypostasis* and *persona* as indications of the "essential" character of the divine distinctions; and 3) the doctrines of internal relations (i.e. generation and procession) and coinherence. These three might be designated respectively as *oikonomia*, essential Trinity, and immanent Trinity. I do not believe, however, that there would be any great material advantage in offering a formal substitute for the traditional categories. They are, after all, primarily guides to the understanding of expositions of the doctrine of the Trinity—and here they have real utility when used with care. In the cases where I have made use of the customary distinction, it will be clear from the context what meaning is intended; of course, in not a few instances, the ambiguity of the distinction between economic Trinity and immanent Trinity is not simply in the terms but is inherent in the views being considered. For my own part, as should be apparent, I quite agree with Schleiermacher that there can be no doctrine worthy of the name Trinity which does not affirm the "essential" character of the distinctions—to say less than this is only to point to the event of revelation, and inadequately at that—and I should also hold that there can be no doctrine of an "essential" Trinity that does not include the doctrine of relations.

Appendix B

Leonard Hodgson's View of the Social Analogy
in the History of Trinitarian Doctrine

The majority of historians of Christian thought are agreed that the dominant pattern of interpretation of the doctrine of the Trinity, at least in the West, has been along the lines of the psychological analogy. And among the proponents of the social analogy, Charles Lowry readily accedes to this view. Leonard Hodgson, however, has made the claim not only that the social analogy has had a respectable history in trinitarian theology (e.g. in the Cappadocian Fathers), but that it can be attributed even to Augustine and Aquinas, who are commonly thought to be the arch-exponents of the psychological analogy. In Ch. VIII, we have discussed the general historical question with some care; but in view of the really startling nature of Hodgson's assertion, it will not be out of place here to look briefly at the evidence which he adduces in support of his claim.

With respect to Augustine, Hodgson is mainly concerned to refute the charge that that writer makes of the Holy Spirit a "relation" (between Father and Son) rather than a coequal Person. The Trinity of lover, loved and love, on which that charge is based, is not, Hodgson contends, the fundamental analogy which Augustine draws. It is mentioned only incidentally in the early books of *De Trinitate*, and the implied depersonalization of the Spirit is inconsistent with Book XV. The Holy Spirit is called a relation only in the same sense in which Father and Son are called relations. Thus Augustine maintains the full equality and sameness of mode of subsistence, or personality, of all three Persons.

Hodgson passes quickly over the analogies developed in Books IX to XIV, pausing to point out that in the analogy from the image of God (Bk. XIV) there is no hint of a separate and less personal status for the Spirit. He mentions Augustine's hesitancy with regard to the use of *persona* only to comment that "there is nothing to suggest that the word is to mean anything different as applied to the Father and the Son, and to the Spirit." [1] Then citing Augustine's criticism of the analogy from the self on the grounds that while the Trinity of the self is one person, the divine Trinity is three Persons (Bk. XV, 11, 42f.), Hodgson concludes that:

Whatever may be the etymological history of the words ὑπόστασις and *persona*, it is impossible to avoid the conclusion that St. Augustine regarded each Person in the Godhead as being personal in whatever sense the word is used of conscious, intelligent and purposive human being.[2]

Aquinas is dealt with more briefly, since his trinitarian theology is fundamentally a repetition of the Augustinian view. Hodgson thinks, however, that Aquinas goes a step further than Augustine when he adopts the definitions of *persona* offered by Boethius and Richard of St. Victor, since for Augustine the term "was a technical term taking whatever theological meaning it was to have from the relations which it was intended to describe." [3]

The central element of Hodgson's discussion of Aquinas consists of an attack on Hastings Rashdall's contention that for St. Thomas the Trinity meant no more than that God is Power (or Cause), Wisdom, and Will (or Love).[4] The attack consists of two parts. Hodgson admits that certain passages in St. Thomas (those which refer to the procession of the Son and Spirit by the modes of intellect and will), if taken out of context, might be used to support Rashdall's view. But, he contends, these passages must be taken in the context of the whole of the *Tractatus*, of the *Summa*, and of the entire theological tradition in which Aquinas

---

[1] Ibid., 154.   [2] Ibid., 155.
[3] Ibid., 159. The definition of Richard of St. Victor: *Divinæ naturæ incommunicabilia existentia*—the incommunicable existence of the divine nature.
[4] This is important as indicating Hodgson's assumption that there are only two possible alternatives: a Trinity of three persons in the full sense of the word, or a Trinity simply of attributes or qualities.

stands. That this tradition stands opposed to Rashdall's view is shown by reference to Calvin's declaration that it was to refute such doctrines that the term *persona* was introduced.[5] Thus either Calvin is wrong about the intentions of the Fathers, or St. Thomas is an exception to the tradition. The second consideration advanced by Hodgson against Rashdall is that the latter held "a purely exemplarist doctrine of the atonement which did not require a christology involving the exercise of personal relations between the Father and the Son."[6] But this is clearly contrary to the tradition of the real self-offering of the Son and the eternal status of Christ. Thus Hodgson concludes that the questionable passages in Aquinas are simply reminiscent of passages in Augustine's analogy from the human mind, an analogy which Augustine deliberately refrained from pressing. In his religion, St. Thomas is a "full-blooded" trinitarian, accepting the revelation of three complete persons in God. In spite of his abstract terms and the attempt to express his religion *via* an inadequate conception of unity, "St. Thomas surely never meant his theology to be used for the purpose of desiccating the revelation . . ."[7]

Hodgson prefers Calvin's exposition of the Trinity to those of St. Augustine and St. Thomas because the Reformer confines himself more rigidly to the biblical evidence and insists that the orthodox formula is intended to express nothing else than the teaching of the Bible. Calvin's definition of *persona* and his treatment of the divine distinctions as distinctions of relations are noted only as indications that he here follows the traditional pattern. Calvin's difficulties with the doctrine of the *principium* are cited as evidence of his endeavor to reconcile the revelation with the

[5] Calvin, *Inst.* I, xiii, 4. Calvin is referring to Sabellius. Hodgson's argument here is peculiarly roundabout. He cites a comment of St. Thomas' Turin editor (on the *Summa* I, xxvii, 3, where St. Thomas is discussing the processions of the Word and Love) to the effect that "so argue Tatian, Athenagoras, Irenaeus, Cyril, Tertullian, Basil, Athanasius, especially Augustine, and almost all theologians." Then he cites Calvin's comment, and concludes that "If Calvin is right, the Turin editor shows St. Thomas to have been following a tradition which expressly repudiated" Rashdall's type of theology. Hodgson, op. cit., 161f.

[6] Op. cit., 162.   [7] Ibid., 164.

notion of unity of simplicity, and therefore as supporting the contention that if we are willing to go the whole way with the evidence and think of the unity as "unifying the Three Persons of
whom none is afore or after another, we have no further need of
the doctrine of the *principium* of the Father." [8] Hodgson feels
that of the three theologians, Calvin comes closest to avoiding
the conflict between the old idea of unity and the revelation just
because he does restrict himself more to the simple exposition of
the scriptural witness.

This is, of course, only a broad outline of what Hodgson has
to say regarding these three theologians. But it is enough to give
an accurate indication of the nature of the argument. And it also
reveals what seem to me fatal flaws in the entire analysis.

To begin with Augustine, we must agree at once with Hodgson
that the Bishop of Hippo does not mean to teach any subordination of the Spirit, but that he means to describe the Spirit as a
persona in precisely the same sense that the Father and Son are
said to be *personæ*. But this having been said, the question becomes one of the meaning of *persona* as applied equally to Father,
Son and Spirit. Hodgson *assumes almost without question* that
Augustine understands the Father and Son to be persons in the
full (modern) sense of the word, but he himself cites almost all
of the evidence needed to show that this is not the case.

The only item of "positive" evidence which Hodgson brings
forth in defence of the full "personality" of the Persons is Augustine's criticism of the analogy from the self on the grounds that
in God there are three *personæ* whereas the human self is said to
be only one *persona* (Bk. XV, 11, 42f.). [9] But in spite of Augustine's
doubts about the psychological analogy, there can be no question
but that this is the only analogy which he thinks worth pursuing
at any length. Hodgson himself cites Augustine's rejection of the
analogy from the family. [10] Furthermore, he rejects the only one
of Augustine's analogies which actually involves a distinction be-

---

[8] Ibid., 173.   [9] Hodgson, op. cit., 155.
[10] Augustine, *De Trin.*, XII, 5-9: Hodgson, op. cit., 146.

tween persons and might therefore be called a social analogy—the analogy of lover, loved and love—as not fundamental to Augustine's thought. This leaves us, then, with the analogy from memory, understanding and will as alone characteristic of Augustine's analysis. That Augustine criticizes this analogy in the way in which he does, points to the fact that Augustine is not as far from the Cappadocians as some of his psychological analogies would suggest.[11] But the fact remains that he does develop the analogy from the self at great length and repudiates social analogies. Therefore when Augustine speaks of three divine *personæ*, we cannot escape the question of whether *persona* is applied univocally to God, or only in some severely qualified sense.

Hodgson passes over Augustine's doubts regarding this word (*De Trin.*, V, 10; VII, 7ff.) with only the comment that Augustine means it to apply in the same sense to all of the Persons and the assertion that "the doctrine . . . is not to be expounded by studying the etymology of technical terms." [12] Having refused to inquire after the meaning of the term, Hodgson assumes that *persona* must obviously have the same meaning as the modern term "person." Later, however, he admits that *persona* for Augustine is a purely technical term taking its meaning entirely from the relations it describes, and refers to Augustine's doctrine that the *personæ* are distinguished only relationally.

We ought to add to this evidence Augustine's contention that "our heavenly Father" refers to the Trinity as a whole—this is diametrically opposed to Hodgson's conception of adoptive sonship—and the rule *opera trinitatis ad extra indivisa sunt*, which suggests that the Trinity is a single source of activity, one subject at least in relation to the created world.[13] All this, taken in conjunction with Augustine's idea of the coinherence of the *personæ* and his emphatic repudiation of the idea that the *personæ* are parts

---

[11] Cf. esp. *De Trin.*, V–VIII, XV.   [12] Hodgson, op. cit., 154.
[13] *De Trin.*, V, 12 and I, 4, 5, 8, 9; II, 10; IV, 21; V, 14, respectively. Hodgson does not refer to the "rule" as such, but mentions the unitary activity of the Trinity in the sending of the Son and in the indwelling in Christians.

of a Godhead that is their sum total [14] cannot but raise the most
serious doubts regarding Hodgson's interpretation of Augustine.

If this is the case with reference to Augustine, it is even more
true of Aquinas, whose whole analysis of the Trinity is oriented
around the psychological analogy, and specifically the doctrine
of the processions of the Son and Spirit by the modes of intellect
and will. Hodgson's interpretation of Aquinas is vitiated by his
assumption that the only possible alternatives are Rashdall's Trinity of attributes and a Trinity of complete persons. He is correct,
we may agree, in attacking the validity of Rashdall's positive interpretation of Aquinas, but from the fact that Aquinas meant
more than simply a Trinity of Power, Wisdom and Love, it does
not follow that he meant a Trinity of persons in Hodgson's sense.
Hodgson appears to misunderstand completely the comment
which he quotes from St. Thomas' Turin editor (concerning the
Tractatus, Q.XXVII, art. 3).[15] What the Turin editor was saying
is that the whole theological tradition stands on the side of the
Thomistic view of the processions of the Word and Love, i.e.
on the side of the psychological analogy! Moreover, Hodgson
fails to see the significance of St. Thomas' (and probably also
Augustine's) view of the purely relational distinction of the *personæ*, for he assumes that we can take away the notions of *principium, generatio* and *processio*, and have left the doctrine of three
equal persons. But Aquinas specifically teaches that if there were
no relation of opposition, i.e. of origin, in God, the *personæ* would
merge into one and there would be no distinctions.[16] Finally,
while Hodgson is probably correct in understanding Boethius'
definition to imply that *persona* is one among others, to assume
that this necessarily means one person in a society of persons is
to beg the precise question at issue.

[14] Cf. *De Trin.*, VI, 3–9. Tennant interprets Augustine's idea of coinherence as formulated in such a way as precisely to *forbid* it being interpreted
to mean the interpenetration of several agents or experients cooperating, and
each with a will in harmony with other wills. See his article in *Cong. Quart.*,
op. cit., 10.

[15] Hodgson, op. cit., 161f.   [16] *S. Theol.*, I, xxxi, 2.

Hodgson's interpretation of Calvin rests on the assumption that Calvin understood the scriptures to teach what Hodgson understands them to teach. The only passage which he cites from Calvin which seems to have direct bearing on the nature of the *personæ* is Calvin's definition of the term, but this speaks only of "subsistences" distinguished by "incommunicable properties." [17]

We may add here that not only is it impossible to attribute Hodgson's view to Augustine, Aquinas and Calvin, but it is also difficult to find such an extreme view of Father, Son and Spirit as distinct personal beings even in the Cappadocian Fathers, who are commonly noted for their use of the analogy of three men.[18] In addition to the Platonic realism which underlay their use of this illustration,[19] and the use of "essence" in a concrete rather than a generic sense, they maintained the doctrine of the *perichoresis* or coinherence of the Persons—that the Persons are *in* or interpenetrate each other, and that each of the Persons contains the whole of the Godhead [20]—and they argue at length for the identity of operation of the Persons. The latter is especially important, because the Cappadocians define Godhead as activity and argue to oneness of essence from identity of operation. Thus Gregory of Nyssa writes: "If . . . we understand that the operation of the Father, the Son and the Holy Spirit is one, differing or varying in nothing, the oneness of their nature must be inferred

[17] Hodgson, op. cit., 167f. Hodgson cites a long passage (*Inst.* I, xiii, 17) in which Calvin argues for the distinctness of Father, Son and Spirit and uses "He" in speaking of each. But all that Calvin asserts here is that the Three are "in some way distinct." Cf. Hodgson, op. cit., 168f. Cf. also Calvin's express denial that *personæ* means what is commonly meant by three persons, cited by Barth, op. cit., 410: "Les anciens docteurs ont usé de ce mot de personne et ont dit, qu'en Dieu il y a trois personnes: Non point comme nous parlons en notre langage commun appelant trois hommes, trois personnes ou comme mesmes en la papauté ils prendront ceste audace de peindre trois marmousets et voilà la trinité. Mais . . . ce mot de personnes en ceste matière est pour exprimer les propriétez lesquelles sont en l'essence de Dieu (*Congregation de la divinité de Christ*, C. R. 47, 473)."

[18] Cf. esp. Gregory of Nyssa, *On Not Three Gods* (NPN, II, 5).

[19] This is again most clearly seen in Gregory of Nyssa, who asserts that technically (when speaking of nature or essence) we ought not to say three men, for there is only one manhood.

[20] Cf. Basil of Caesarea, *De Spiritu Sancto* (NPN, II, 8), c. 18.

from the identity of their operation." [21] At the least we must say that the Cappadocians were more cautious than the modern defenders of the social analogy.

[21] *On the Holy Trinity* (NPN, II, 5). Cf. Basil, epistles 8 and 189. We may note also Basil's qualifications regarding the use of number in relation to the Persons (ep. 8) and the willingness of the Cappadocians to use the term τρόποι ὑπάρξεος, modes of being. (Basil, *De Spiritu Sancto*, 43, 44, cited by F. W. Green in Rawlinson, ed., *Essays on the Trinity and the Incarnation*, 285.)

Bibliography of Works Cited

ANSELM, ST., *Monologium*. E.T. by S. Deane. LaSalle, Ill., Open Court, 1944.

ARENDZEN, JOHN P., *The Holy Trinity*. London, Sheed & Ward, 1939.

AUGUSTINE, ST., *On the Trinity*. E.T. by A. W. Haddon. (*Nicene and Post-Nicene Fathers, First Series*, Vol. III) New York, Scribners, 1900.

AULÉN, GUSTAF, *Faith of the Christian Church*. E.T. by E. Wahlstrom and G. E. Arden. Philadelphia, Muhlenberg, 1948.

BAILLIE, DONALD M., *God Was In Christ*. Scribners, Faber, 1948.

BAILLIE, JOHN, *The Place of Jesus Christ in Modern Christianity*. New York, Scribners, 1929. Edinburgh, T. & T. Clark.

BARTH, KARL, *The Doctrine of the Word of God (Kirchliche Dogmatik, Bd. I/1)*. E.T. by G. T. Thomson. Edinburgh, T. & T. Clark, 1936.

——, *The Holy Ghost and the Christian Life*. E.T. by R. B. Hoyle. London, Frederick Muller, 1938.

——, *Die Kirchliche Dogmatik*. Bd. I: *Die Lehre vom Wort Gottes*. Bd. II: *Die Lehre von Gott*. Bd. III/1: *Die Lehre von Der Schöpfung*. Zürich, Evangelischer Verlag, 1945.

BARTLETT, CHARLES N., *The Triune God*. New York, American Tract Society, 1937.

BASIL OF CAESAREA, ST., *On The Holy Spirit*. E.T. by B. Jackson. (*Nicene and Post-Nicene Fathers, Second Series*, Vol. VIII) New York, Scribners, 1895.

BECK, J. T., *Die Christliche Lehr-Wissenschaft, nach den Biblischen Urkunden*. Erster Teil: *Die Logic der Christliche Lehre*. 2te aufl., Stuttgart, 1875.

BETHUNE-BAKER, J. F., *An Introduction to .the Early History of Christian Doctrine*. 4th ed. London, Methuen, 1929.

BIEDERMANN, A. E., *Christliche Dogmatik*, Bd. II. 2te aufl., Berlin, 1885.

BRETON, VALENTIN-M., *Trinité: histoire, doctrine, piété*. Paris, Bloud et Gay, 1931.

BROWN, WILLIAM A., *Christian Theology in Outline*. New York, Scribners, 1906.

BRUNNER, H. EMIL, *Die Christliche Lehre von Gott (Dogmatik, I)*. Zürich, Zwingli-verlag, 1946. E.T. by O. Wyon: *The Christian Doctrine of God*. Philadelphia, Westminster, 1950. London, Lutterworth, 1950.

——, *The Mediator*. E.T. by O. Wyon. London, Lutterworth, 1934.

BUSHNELL, HORACE, *God in Christ*. Hartford, Brown & Parsons, 1849.

——, *Christ in Theology*. Hartford, Brown & Parsons, 1851.

——, "The Christian Trinity a Practical Truth," *The New Englander*, November, 1854.

CAIRD, EDWARD, *The Evolution of Religion*, Vol. II. New York: Macmillan, 1893.

CALVIN, JOHN, *Institutes of the Christian Religion*, Vol. I. E.T. by J. Allen. Philadelphia, Presbyterian Board of Christian Education, 1936.

CARNELL, E. J., *An Introduction to Christian Apologetics: A Philosophic Defense of the Trinitarian-Theistic Faith*. Grand Rapids, Eerdmans, 1948.

CHAMPION, JOHN B., *Personality and the Trinity*. New York, Revell, 1935.

CHANNING, WILLIAM E., *Works*. Boston, American Unitarian Press, 1877.

CLARKE, WILLIAM N., *The Christian Doctrine of God*. New York, Scribners, 1909.

COCHRANE, CHARLES N., *Christianity and Classical Culture*. Oxford, Clarendon, 1940.

CREED, JOHN M., *The Divinity of Jesus Christ*. Cambridge University, 1938.

CULLMANN, OSCAR, *Christ and Time*. London, SCM Press, 1951.

D'ARCY, CHARLES F., *Idealism and Theology*. London, Hodder & Stoughton, 1899.

——, "Trinity," *Dictionary of Christ and the Gospels*, ed. J. Hastings, Vol. II. New York, Scribners, 1908.

DORNER, I. A., *System of Christian Doctrine*, Vols. I, II. E.T. by A. Cave and J. S. Banks. Edinburgh, T. & T. Clark, 1880.

DOWNEY, RICHARD, *The Blessed Trinity*. New York, Macmillan, 1930. (Reprinted in G. D. Smith, ed., *The Teaching of the Catholic Church*, Vol. I. New York, Macmillan, 1949.)

EDWARDS, DAVID M., *Christianity and Philosophy*. Edinburgh, T. &. T. Clark, 1932.

FAIRBAIRN, ANDREW M., *The Place of Christ in Modern Theology*. New York, Scribners, 1916.

FEUERBACH, LUDWIG, *The Essence of Christianity*. E.T. by Marian Evans. London, 1881.

FORSYTH, P. T., *The Person and Place of Jesus Christ*. New York, Eaton and Mains, 1909. London, Independent Press.

FRANK, F. H. R., *System of the Christian Certainty*. E.T. by Maurice J. Evans. Edinburgh, T. & T. Clark, 1886.

——, *System der Christliche Wahrheit*, Bd. I. 3te aufl., Erlangen, Deichert, 1894.

FULTON, WILLIAM, "Trinity," *Encyclopaedia of Religion and Ethics*, ed. J. Hastings, Vol. XII. New York, Scribners, 1922.

The Fundamentals. Chicago, Testimony Publishing Co., 1912.

GARRIGOU-LAGRANGE, R., *God: His Existence and Nature*, Vol. II. E.T. by Dom Bede Rose. St. Louis, B. Herder, 1936.

GARVIE, ALFRED E., *The Christian Doctrine of the Godhead*. New York, G. Doran, 1925.

GILSON, ETIENNE, *God and Philosophy*. New Haven, Yale University Press, 1941. O.U.P., 1941.

GORDON, GEORGE A., *Ultimate Conceptions of the Faith*. Boston, Houghton, Mifflin, 1903.

GORE, CHARLES, *Belief in Christ*. New York, Scribners. London, Murray.

——, *Incarnation of the Son of God*. New York, Scribners. London, Murray.

GRAY, ALBERT F., *Christian Theology*, Vol. I. Anderson, Ind., Warner Press, 1944.

GREGORY OF NYSSA, ST., *On the Holy Trinity. On Not Three Gods.* E.T. by H. A. Wilson. (*Nicene and Post-Nicene Fathers, Second Series*, Vol. V) New York, Scribners, 1893.

HALL, F. J., *The Trinity.* New York, Longmans, Green, 1910.

HÄRING, THEODORE, *The Christian Faith*, Vol. II. E.T. by J. Dickie and G. Ferries. London, Hodder & Stoughton, 1913.

HARKNESS, GEORGIA, *Understanding the Christian Faith.* New York: Abingdon-Cokesbury, 1947.

HARNACK, ADOLPH, *What Is Christianity?* E.T. by T. B. Saunders. New York, Putnam, 1901. London, Williams and Norgate.

HARTSHORNE, CHARLES, *Man's Vision of God.* Chicago, Willett, Clark, 1941.

HEADLAM, ARTHUR C., *Christian Theology: the Doctrine of God.* Oxford, Clarendon, 1934.

HEGEL, G. W. F., *Lectures on the Philosophy of Religion*, Vols. I, III. E.T. by E. B. Speirs and J. B. Sanderson. London, Kegan Paul, 1895.

HERRMANN, WILHELM, *Systematic Theology.* E.T. by N. Micklem and K. A. Saunders. New York, Macmillan, 1927.

HODGE, CHARLES, *Systematic Theology*, Vol. I. New York, Scribner, Armstrong & Co., 1874.

HODGSON, LEONARD, *The Doctrine of the Trinity.* New York, Scribners, 1944. London, Nisbet, 1943.

——, *Towards a Christian Philosophy.* London, Nisbet, 1942.

HORTON, W. M., *God.* New York, Association Press, 1937.

ILLINGWORTH, J. R., *The Doctrine of the Trinity.* London, Macmillan, 1907.

——, *Personality, Human and Divine.* London, Macmillan, 1894.

JUSTIN MARTYR, ST., *Apology.* E.T. by M. Dods. *Dialogue With Trypho.* E.T. by G. Reith. (*Ante-Nicene Christian Library*, Vol. II) Edinburgh, T. & T. Clark, 1868.

KAFTAN, JULIUS, *Dogmatik.* 7. und 8. aufl., Tübingen, 1920.

KÄHLER, MARTIN, *Der Sogennante Historische Jesus und der Geschichtliche, Biblische Christus.* 2te aufl., Leipzig, Deichert, 1896.

——, *Die Wissenschaft der Christlichen Lehre.* 2te aufl., Leipzig, Deichert, 1893.

KAHNIS, CARL F. A., *Die Lutherische Dogmatik Historisch-Genetisch Dargestellt*, Bd. II. 2te aufl., Leipzig, 1874–5.

KLEIN, FELIX, *The Doctrine of the Trinity.* E.T. by D. J. Sullivan. New York, Kenedy, 1940.

KNUDSON, ALBERT C., *The Doctrine of God.* New York, Abingdon, 1930.

LOWRY, CHARLES W., *The Trinity and Christian Devotion.* New York, Harper, 1946.

McGIFFERT, A. C., *A History of Christian Thought*, Vol. I. New York, Scribners, 1932.

MACINTOSH, D. C., *The Reasonableness of Christianity.* New York, Scribners, 1925.

MACKINTOSH, H. R., *Doctrine of the Person of Jesus Christ*. New York, Scribners, 1912. Edinburgh, T. & T. Clark.

——, *Types of Modern Theology*. London, Nisbet, 1937, (New York, Scribners)

MARTINEAU, J., *Essays, Reviews and Addresses*, Vol. II. London, Longmans, Green, 1891.

MASCALL, E. L., *Christ, the Christian and the Church*. London, New York, Longmans, Green, 1946.

——, *He Who Is*. London, Longmans, Green, 1943.

MATTHEWS, W. R., *God in Christian Experience*. New York, Harper, 1930. London, Nisbet, 1930.

MICKLEM, NATHANIEL, *What Is the Faith?* London, Hodder & Stoughton, 1936.

MILEY, JOHN, *Systematic Theology*, Vol. I. New York, Hunt & Eaton, 1892.

MOBERLY, R. C., *Atonement and Personality*. London, Longmans, Green, 1901.

MOBERLY, W. H., "God and the Absolute," *Foundations*, ed. B. H. Streeter. London, Macmillan, 1913.

MUELLER, JOHN T., *Christian Dogmatics*. St. Louis, Concordia, 1934.

MURPHY, GARDNER, *Personality*. New York, Harper, 1947.

NIEBUHR, H. RICHARD, "The Doctrine of the Trinity and the Unity of the Church," *Theology Today*, III (October, 1946), 371–384.

——, *The Meaning of Revelation*. New York, Macmillan, 1941.

ORIGEN, *De Principiis. Contra Celsum*. E.T. by F. Crombie. (*Ante-Nicene Christian Library*, Vols. X, XXIII). Edinburgh, T. & T. Clark, 1869, 1872.

ORR, JAMES, *The Christian View of God and the World*. New York, A. Randolph, 1893. Edinburgh, A. Elliot.

OTTLEY, ROBERT L., *The Doctrine of the Incarnation*. London, Methuen, 1908.

PAUCK, WILHELM, *Karl Barth*. New York, Harper, 1931.

PENIDO, MAURILIO, T.-L., *Le Role de l'Analogie en Theologie Dogmatique*. (*Bibliotheque Thomiste*, XV). Paris, J. Vrin, 1931.

PITTENGER, W. NORMAN, *Christ and the Christian Faith*. New York, Round Table, 1941.

POHLE, JOSEPH, *The Divine Trinity*. Adapted and edited by Arthur Preuss. St. Louis, B. Herder, 1919.

POPE, W. B., *A Compendium of Christian Theology*, Vol I. 2nd. ed. New York, Phillips & Hunt, 1877. London, Epworth.

PRINGLE-PATTISON, ANDREW S., *The Idea of God in Recent Philosophy*. London, Oxford, 1917.

RALL, HARRIS FRANKLIN, *The Christian Faith and Way*. New York, Abingdon-Cokesbury, 1947.

——, *The Meaning of God*. Nashville, Cokesbury, 1925.

RASHDALL, HASTINGS, *God and Man*. Oxford, B. Blackwell, 1930.

RAWLINSON, A. E. J., ed., *Essays on the Trinity and the Incarnation*. London, Longmans, Green, 1928.

RICHMOND, WILFRED, *Essay on Personality as a Philosophical Principle*. London, Edwin Arnold, 1900.

RITSCHL, ALBRECHT B. *The Christian Doctrine of Justification and Reconciliation*. (Vol. III) E.T. edited by H. R. Mackintosh and A. B. Macaulay. Edinburgh, T. & T. Clark, 1902.

SAYERS, DOROTHY L., *The Mind of the Maker*. London, Methuen, 1942.

SCHLEIERMACHER, FRIEDRICH, *The Christian Faith*. E.T. edited by H. R. Mackintosh and J. S. Stewart. Edinburgh, T. & T. Clark, 1928.

———, "On the Discrepancy between the Sabellian and Athanasian Method of Representing the Doctrine of the Trinity." (1822) E.T. with notes, by Moses Stuart, *The Biblical Repository and Quarterly Observer*, VI (July, 1835), 1–116.

SCHWEITZER, ALBERT, *The Quest of the Historical Jesus*. E.T. by W. Montgomery. London, Black, 1910.

SEEBERG, REINHOLD, *Christliche Dogmatik*. Bd. I: *Lehren von Gott, dem Menschen und der Geschichte*. Erlangen, Deichertsche, 1924.

SHEDD, W. G. T., *Dogmatic Theology*, Vol. I. New York, Scribners, 1888.

SHEED, F. J., *Theology and Sanity*. New York, Sheed & Ward, 1946.

SMITH, G. D., ed., *The Teaching of the Catholic Church*, Vol. I., New York, Macmillan, 1949. London, Burns, Oates, 1948.

STEENSTRA, P. H., *The Being of God as Unity and Trinity*. Boston, Houghton Mifflin, 1891.

STRAUSS, DAVID F., *Die Christliche Glaubenslehre*, Bd. I. Tübingen, Osiander, 1840.

———, *Life of Jesus*. E.T. by Marian Evans. New York, Blanshard, 1855.

STRONG, A. H., *Systematic Theology*. Vol I: *The Doctrine of God*. Philadelphia, Griffith & Rowland, 1907.

STRONG, T. B., *Manual of Theology*. London, A. C. Black, 1903.

STUART, MOSES, "Notes" on F. Schleiermacher's "On the Discrepancy between the Sabellian and Athanasian Method of Representing the Doctrine of the Trinity." *The Biblical Repository and Quarterly Review*, VI (July, 1835), 80–116.

TENNANT, F. R., *Philosophical Theology*, Vol. II. Cambridge Univ., 1930.

———, "The Present Position of the Doctrine of the Trinity," *Congregational Quarterly*, January, 1925.

TERTULLIAN, *Adversus Praxean. Adversus Hermogenes*. E.T. by A. Roberts and J. Donaldson. (*Ante-Nicene Christian Library*, Vol. XV) Edinburgh, T. & T. Clark, 1870.

THOMAS AQUINAS, ST., *Summa Theologica*, Pt. I. E.T. by the English Dominican Fathers. London, Burns, Oates, 1920.

THOMAS, GEORGE F., "Central Christian Affirmations," in H. P. Van Dusen, ed., *The Christian Answer*. New York, Scribners, 1945. London, Nisbet.

THOMASIUS, G., *Christi Person und Werk*. Bd. I: *Die Voraussetzungen der Christologie*. Erlangen, Bläsing, 1853.

THORNTON, LIONEL S., *The Incarnate Lord*. London, Longmans, Green, 1928.

——, "The Christian Conception of God," in E. G. Selwyn, ed., *Essays Catholic and Critical*. London, S.P.C.K., 1926.

VILMAR, A. F. C., *Dogmatik*. Gütersloh, 1874.

WEBB, C. C. J., *God and Personality*. London, G. Allen & Unwin, 1918.

WELCH, CLAUDE, "The Holy Spirit and the Trinity." *Theology Today*, VIII, (April, 1951), 29–40.

WHALE, J. S., *Christian Doctrine*. New York, Macmillan, 1941. C.U.P., 1941.

WHITON, JAMES M., *Gloria Patri*. New York, T. Whittaker, 1892.

WILEY, H. ORTON, *Christian Theology*, Vol. I. Kansas City, Mo., Nazarene Publishing Co., 1940.

Index

OF NAMES AND SUBJECTS

In a few subject listings the most important references are indicated by italics.